UNIVERSALISM IN AMERICA

UNIVERSALISM

IN AMERICA

A Documentary History

Edited by Ernest Cassara

Beacon Press   Boston

Copyright © 1971 by Ernest Cassara

Library of Congress catalog card number: 77-136226

International Standard Book Number: 0-8070-1664-0

Beacon Press books are published under the auspices
of the Unitarian Universalist Association

Published simultaneously in Canada by Saunders of Toronto, Ltd.

Printed in the United States of America

We wish to thank the following authors and publishers for
permission to include material in this book:

Dr. Alfred S. Cole, for his "Touch Not My Lips with the White
Fire"; Dr. Robert Cummins, for an excerpt from his *Excluded: The
Story of the Council of Churches and the Universalists* (Beacon
Reference Series #3, Dept. of Publications, UUA, Boston, 1966);
The Journal of the Universalist Historical Society, for excerpts
reprinted from *Life and Trance*, by Dr. George De Benneville, and
from *Social Implications of Universalism*, by C. R. Skinner; Dr.
Kenneth L. Patton, for excerpts from his *A Religion for One World*
(Beacon Press, Boston, copyright K. L. Patton, 1964), and from his
"Art and Symbols for a Universal Religion"; Philosophical Library,
for excerpts from *Selected Writings*, of Benjamin Rush, edited by
Dagobert D. Runes; Princeton University Press, for *Letters of Benjamin
Rush*, Vol. I: 1761–1792, edited by L. H. Butterfield, Princeton
University Press, 1951 (copyright, 1951, by the American Philosophical
Society), pp. 583–84; Dr. Clinton Lee Scott, for excerpts from his
Religion Can Make Sense (Universalist Publishing House, Boston,
1949); Mrs. Clarence R. Skinner, for an excerpt from *A Religion for
Greatness*, by Clarence R. Skinner (Universalist Publishing House,
Boston, 1945); and the Unitarian Universalist Association, Boston, for
excerpts from "New Wine and Old Bottles," by Brainard R. Gibbons
(*Christian Leader*, November 1949).

To Alfred S. Cole

Contents

Preface

A few words setting forth the rationale for the format of this book may be helpful. In the first chapter I have sketched the history of the first two hundred years or so of Universalism in America. The story is not as complete as I would have liked to make it, but space limitations have made it necessary for me to stress the most significant themes without indulging in amplification and the luxury of digressions.

In succeeding chapters I have attempted to let the men and women who have made Universalist history speak for themselves. They were prolific in their pronouncements and their writings and, again, I regret that limitations of space have prevented me from including more of them and what they had to say. Except for the obvious heroes of the movement who tradition would demand be included in any documentary history, I have chosen to accent important ideas rather than the persons expressing them.

The historical sketch and the documents in the succeeding chapters are designed to complement each other. There is overlapping of some of the points made in Chapter I and the brief introductions to the documents in Chapters II through IX. This is not only inevitable but I hope desirable.

Some may object that I have broken off the history too soon. But 1961 is a convenient stopping place because of the consolidation of the Universalist and Unitarian movements in that year. Furthermore, I believe that ideally a historian must keep a certain distance between himself and the events he describes in order to allow whatever measure of perspective and objectivity is possible in this very complex world. To give in to the temptation to comment on current issues is to become a journalist—or a prophet. Both these activities are honorable but they are not within the competence of a historian as historian.

One further word should be said on the documents I have included. There is a natural tendency for an editor to choose the very best statement on each issue of the past. To an extent this practice distorts history. I no doubt have given in to this temptation more than I should have, but I have made a conscious effort at least to resist the most felicitous statements of particular arguments in favor of less felicitous ones to give a clearer idea of what most of the literature of each period was like.

In closing I would like to thank friends and acquaintances who have contributed to the inception and completion of this history. For encouraging me to undertake the project in the first place: Keith Munson, Philip R. Giles, Raymond C. Hopkins, Max Kapp, Mrs. Ellsworth Reamon, Alan Sawyer, Geoffrey P. Seth, Mrs. J. Russell Bowman, Mrs. Helen Goundry, Nicholas Greene, Mrs. Benjamin B. Hersey, Ralph W. Burhoe, and especially Richard A. Kellaway, members of the 200th Anniversary Committee on Universalism of the Unitarian Universalist Association. For advice and insights into what should be included: Alfred S. Cole, James D. Hunt, David H. MacPherson, George N. Marshall, Elmo Robinson, Clinton Lee Scott, Alan L. Seaburg, and Carl G. Seaburg. For their time and patience in helping me complete the work: Mrs. Jeanne Nieuwejaar, librarian of the Universalist Historical Society at Tufts University, who generously allowed me convenient access to the hundreds of books, pamphlets, and manuscripts I needed; Mrs. Edith Bloom, who cheerfully undertook the hazardous task of typing from my at times ambiguous handwriting; Mrs. Ethel Wilson, who was my secretary during the time of the research and writing of this book and who spared me many of the endless demands of the academic community.

For generous financial support which has facilitated publication of this book, I would like to thank the New York Universalist State Convention, the Ohio-Meadville District Association, the Pennsylvania Universalist Convention, the Spinney

Fund of the Unitarian Universalist Church of Lynn, Massachusetts, and the Universalist National Memorial Church, Washington, D.C.

A special word of thanks to those many students in my American history classes who have helped me gain insights into the complex political and cultural forces at work through the centuries of the American experience.

In observance of a long tradition, I point out that despite the help of many friends the errors of omission and commission are, of course, solely mine.

Patch Mountain   Ernest Cassara
Greenwood, Maine
30 May 1970

PART ONE

History

Chapter One

Two Centuries of Universalism, 1741-1961:
A Brief Historical Sketch

1

Universalism arose in America in a time of political and intellectual ferment. A series of misunderstandings and confrontations between Great Britain and her colonies in North America was escalating to the point where it would become impossible for trust to be reestablished. The Americans were achieving an identity of their own and were not willing to continue a relationship which they conceived of as exploitative and repressive.

The rebelliousness which was to lead to the War of Independence manifested itself in other areas of American life, not the least of which was theological thinking. In a nation addicted to formulating and reformulating theological ideas, it was inevitable that theology should come to grips with changing times. Western man's very understanding of the universe was undergoing radical change as the Ptolemaic world-view, which had provided the comfort of assurance that the earth and man were the center of the universe and, necessarily, the center of God's attention, gave way to the Copernican, with its demonstration that the earth was but one of many planets spinning in a space so vast that it was beyond comprehending. God was now the Grand Superintendent of a mechanism so huge and complex that many found it increasingly difficult to believe that the activities of man on earth were such as to demand the deity's full attention.

The views of God fostered by traditional Christianity, especially Calvinism, were to undergo intense scrutiny, as was the traditional view of man's capability. The conviction of long standing that man, because of a certain unfortunate act on the part of his first parents, was tainted with an original sin that made him incapable of achieving in the religious realm that which he was so obviously achieving in the secular realm was bound to give way before the newly gained self-confidence of those mastering a new continent.

The new understanding of the nature of the universe led to the rejection on the part of some of the traditionally accepted revelation said to be contained in the Judaeo-Christian Scriptures. The Deists, as they were labeled, could not reconcile the wonders of the Copernican view of the universe, so ably explicated by their hero Isaac Newton, with the naive conception of creation they read in the Book of Genesis in the Old Testament. The view of the tribal deity they found there could not be squared with the vast reaches of space. The Yahweh who revealed himself as a fickle, partial God, alternately losing His temper with the Jews and making up with them, could not be the ruler of an ordered, predictable world which in every one of its features displayed the work of a Master Craftsman.

The Deists put aside the Scripture with scorn and replaced it with what they considered the god-given Reason which allowed them to read God's revelation writ large in the universe about them. There they thought they could see a God who was much too grand to treat man as the erring child the Calvinists and other Christians insisted he was. The creation of such a Craftsman must be worth more than that.

Although the Deists believed man sinned, they could not accept the Calvinistic notion that man was innately depraved and that only a relative few would escape the flames of hell—and these only because God had arbitrarily elected them (without reference to performance on their part) for salvation, indeed this election having occurred before the creation. Such a view, thought the Deists, degraded both God and man and was the product of medieval minds dominated by priestcraft.

Somewhat inconsistently the Deists pointed to Jesus as

an example of what a reasonable man could be. This model of perfection, of course, was only known to them through the Christian Scriptures which they poked fun at. But like Jefferson, who with scissors and paste created his own New Testament exclusively of the sayings of Jesus (omitting what he considered corruptions of the text, e.g., the miracles), the Deists thought they could separate the wheat from the chaff. They rejected the traditional doctrines which pictured Jesus as shedding his blood to ransom man from the devil, or to satisfy a God dissatisfied by man's bungling of his original opportunities, or to glorify God's government in man's eyes—and other variations of the doctrine of atonement—and held Jesus to be the great exemplar for man, and, incidentally, the first Deist. Although they generally held fast to the idea of worship, insisted on the advantages of living a virtuous life, and believed in an afterlife of rewards and punishments, they were convinced that they knew these things because of the natural religion which was innate in mankind long before the Jewish priests and their Christian successors had overlaid this reasonable approach with all manner of superstitions and dogmas.

The Deist position found favor with some of the most thoughtful men of the Enlightenment (Jefferson being just one example). It found exponents among English authors who were widely read in America. The most forceful American exponents of Deism were the contentious backwoods agitator and revolutionary hero, Ethan Allen of Vermont, and the most effective propagandist of the American Revolution, Thomas Paine. It is difficult to determine how much circulation Allen's *Reason the Only Oracle of Man* (1784) received, since much of the edition was destroyed in a fire that swept the print shop (much to the delight of his pious Christian opponents, of whom there were many). But there is evidence that his ideas gained much currency. Paine's *Age of Reason* (1794) was much more widely read and talked about—much to the detriment of his well-earned reputation as a revolutionary hero. Both were hard-hitting works which not only set forth the positive ideas of Deism but made great fun of Christian theology. Deism went far toward mitigating the rigidity of Christian theology in the eighteenth century and made possible the reexamination which led to the rise of the new liberalism in religion which took various forms in the late eighteenth and early nineteenth centuries.

2

While our main concern here, of course, is with Universalism, its sister movement Unitarianism cannot be ignored. The two movements developed side by side, sharing many points of view but kept apart by social factors. Although Unitarianism was introduced into Pennsylvania by English immigrants, the greater part of the movement evolved over a period of several generations within the Congregational churches of New England. The older Calvinism inherited from Puritan forebears gradually gave way before the influence of liberal ideas carried from England to the American shore between the covers of widely read books by Arminian churchmen.* Also important was the exposure of New Englanders to the rest of the world. Wide-ranging merchantmen brought back to the ports of New England not only exotic goods but the news that men of moral uprightness were to be found in infidel lands which had no knowledge of Christ and certainly had not heard of the metaphysical intricacies of the trinity.

Having made good by the sheer dint of hard work on the rocky, unyielding soil, many New Englanders found it more and more difficult to believe that man was the debased creature he was reputed to be in the old theology. Growing faith in man's ability was to be the distinguishing feature of Unitarianism—despite the fact that the movement was to be tagged with a name stressing its rejection of the trinity and affirmation of the unity of the godhead. The points were not unrelated, however; if a liberal Congregationalist could believe that man did not bear the marks of an original sin supposedly perpetrated by mankind's first parents, by the same token he had no reason to accept the old formulations which insisted that the second member of the

---

* Arminianism takes its name from the Dutch theologian Jacobus Arminius (1560–1609) who denied the truth of the Calvinist doctrine of predestination and insisted that men, cooperating with divine grace, could achieve salvation.

trinity (the Son) came to earth to die in man's behalf to satisfy the first member of the trinity (the Father). The Unitarian was free to demote the Son theologically at the same time that he enhanced his meaning for man in the person of Jesus.

Unitarianism grew up in the established churches of New England among the most well-established of its citizens. They were well placed in its society financially, and included its most literate and cultured members. Their clerical leaders were sons of Harvard College and were open to the scientific and literary currents of the day. They were tolerant, reasonable men who placed great stress in their preaching and teaching on the efficacy of tolerance and reason.

3

Although many of the same ideas were to be held by those who advocated Universalism, there were decided differences. A few of the established Congregational churches evolved into Universalist societies, but the greater number of Universalist churches were made up of the lower classes of New England society. Universalists were come-outers from many denominations; an amazingly large number came from the Baptists. They were of little education compared to the Unitarians and could not boast of a well-educated clergy. Indeed, like the Baptists, many deliberately boasted of the uneducated condition of their clergy. In their view, the Holy Spirit operated freely among men and needed not the trappings of the schools.

This differential in social rank and education was an important factor in keeping Unitarians and Universalists apart in the eighteenth and through much of the nineteenth century. Although they shared certain beliefs in common, the Unitarians, with an openness to new ideas, increasingly looked to nonbiblical sources for inspiration, witness the rise of Transcendentalism in their churches in the 1830's. The Universalists, on the other hand, maintained a more pious biblical orientation until quite late in the nineteenth century.

The most obvious difference between the two groups concerned the question of salvation. The cultural and economic advantage enjoyed by the Unitarians probably had much to do with their conviction that man possessed the ability to earn salvation through his own efforts. They put much stress on man's free will.

The Universalists, while taking a more optimistic view of man's ability than the Calvinists from whom they came, put stress on God's loving concern for man and His intention that all souls be saved and united with Him in eternity.

While the Unitarian presumably could look on equably while an individual man, with his free will, chose not to be saved, to the Universalist such a thought was impossible. Whether they chose to follow an Arminian path or the path of determinism (necessity), Universalists insisted all men must be saved. It was this difference of accent in the two movements which led to the waggish formulation by Thomas Starr King of the distinction between the Universalists and the Unitarians: "The one thinks God is too good to damn them forever, the other thinks they are too good to be damned forever."

At the risk of oversimplification, it may be said that both Unitarianism and Universalism are compromises between Christianity (especially in its Calvinistic form) and Deism. The two liberal movements were heavily influenced by the world-view of the Deists, and both accepted the importance of reason in religion. They did not reject the Scriptures as did the Deists, but they insisted on subjecting them to the analysis of reason, eschewing the long-standing Christian attitude that what cannot be understood must be accepted on faith. They accepted belief in the unity of God and a radically revised view of the atonement of Jesus. Finally, like the Deists they took a vastly more optimistic view of the nature of man. However, they did not go as far as the Deists and, as often happens with people whose positions are quite close, they often vigorously opposed them.

4

Although the Universalist movement in America cannot be said to have begun before the landing of John Murray in 1770 and his subsequent missionary and organizational activity, belief in universal salvation was to be found in the most diverse places: Universalist tendencies can be observed among the Anglicans (read Episcopals after the Revolution), the Congregationalists in New England, and various German groups such as the Dunkers (Baptists) and Schwenkfelders and other mystical and pietistic immigrants to the tolerant setting of William Penn's Pennsylvania. These movements did not stress belief in universal salvation above other elements in their creeds, so are not included within the Universalist movement.

However, it was among the mystical, pietist groups that the earliest contributor to the Universalist movement did his work. Dr. George De Benneville (1703–1793) was born in London of French Huguenot parents who had taken refuge from persecution in England. In his early teens he was excluded from the church of his parents when he admitted his conviction that all souls would be restored to God's love in the afterlife. He spent his early manhood achieving a medical education and preaching to underground groups in France and to refugee groups in Germany. It was because of his close relations with the German pietists that he was attracted to Pennsylvania, where he spent over fifty years, in the environs of Philadelphia and in the Oley Valley, practicing medicine, and preaching to the Indians as well as the white men. He was instrumental in the 1753 publication of *The Everlasting Gospel* by Paul Siegvolck (alias George Klein-Nicolai of Friessdorf), a book which had great influence in spreading Universalist notions in the late colonial period.

Given the milieu in which De Benneville worked, it is not surprising that his was a Universalist conviction which displayed pronounced mystical and pietistic elements. Indicative of this was his firm conviction that he had left his human body during a serious illness and had been made privy to a view of the stages in the afterlife in which struggling souls gradually were purified by suffering and then ushered into the presence of God as the heavenly host proclaimed throughout eternity a universal restoration of souls. This blend of the Dantean excursion with the then not uncommon conviction of similar experiences of those who had suffered from fever and apparent demise reveals an emotional experience of religion which, although it was approached in a quite different context by the preaching of John Murray, was to be quite rare among Universalists. Universalism has generally been defended on grounds of reasoned scriptural exposition.

It was on these grounds that we find its outcropping in New England Congregationalism. Jonathan Mayhew and Charles Chauncy sought to establish the truth of universal salvation through a reasoned interpretation of the Scriptures. Mayhew (1720–1766), whose brilliant career as preacher and revolutionary agitator was cut short by an untimely death, attempted to persuade his congregation at the West Church in Boston that God, being an eminently reasonable being, could not act in a manner less ethical and fair than a leading citizen of Boston by condemning some men to everlasting woe. Mayhew insisted that such an action was impossible if God were, as he believed, infinitely benevolent.

It was Mayhew's great friend, Charles Chauncy (1705–1787), pastor for sixty years of the First Church in Boston, who made the larger contribution to Universalist thought within Congregationalism. Persistent champion of the role of reason in religion in opposition to Jonathan Edwards and the other defenders of emotionalism during the Great Awakening in the 1740's, Chauncy nonetheless was hesitant to share with the world his growing conviction of the truth of universal salvation. He worked on his *Mystery Hid from Ages and Generations, or, The Salvation of All Men* for many years and then held off from publication for fear that it would upset a populace unprepared for such a radical notion. Political agitation and worse preoccupied Chauncy and his friends in the days of the Boston Tea Party and other events which led up to the Revolution. It was not till the relative calm of the 1780's that he dusted off his manuscript. But since he was basically a cautious man, in 1782 he sent up a trial balloon to test public opinion in the form of a pamphlet setting forth some reasons for believing in universal salvation. The reaction being relatively mild, he published the book in 1784—anonymously.

The Salvation of All Men, as its title has been abbreviated over the years, set forth the scriptural basis for the belief in universal salvation, and drew on the writings of leading English Arminian thinkers. Chauncy, like many other proponents, attempted to demonstrate that the Greek words αἰών and αἰώνιος usually translated into English as *everlasting* and *forever*, did not carry such meanings in the original Greek and therefore their occurrence in the New Testament could not be used to support the idea of the eternity of punishment.

Particularly interesting was Chauncy's attempt to retain the idea of the omnipotence of God at the same time that he attempted to preserve free will for man. Good Arminian that he was, he could not allow God to bully the recalcitrant soul into accepting salvation. God might attempt to persuade, but He would not force. Whether Chauncy had some of his Yankee parishioners in mind I cannot say, but he speculated that there might be various stages in the afterlife. Presumably if God had little luck in luring the hardened soul to abandon its perversity in the first stage, He might have better luck in a succeeding one. An infinitely benevolent God, after all, should have the quality of patience in infinite proportion. There is something noble in this liberal thinker's attempt to uphold in his theological structure the dignity of both God and man.

It may have been his concern with dignity that led Chauncy to publish when he did. Chauncy and the friends who shared his Universalist convictions were disturbed by the recent appearance of "a stranger," as he wrote, "who has of himself assumed the character of a preacher." Chauncy and his fellow ministers of the established order had been concerned with such self-proclaimed preachers since the Great Awakening had shaken the churches to their roots and had brought into the field all manner of emotional extremists. In this particular case, Chauncy had double reason to be concerned. Not only was this interloper preaching without proper ordination and as an itinerant, but he was proclaiming what Chauncy considered a wildly improbable exposition of Universalism. This "stranger" was John Murray.

5

When John Murray (1741–1815) landed at Good Luck on Barnegat Bay in New Jersey in 1770, he was seeking to escape from the sorrows and defeats of his former life in England. He was reared in England and Ireland by Calvinistic parents, but in Ireland he was attracted to the rising Methodist movement, in which he became a devoted follower. He was acquainted with both John Wesley and George Whitefield, whose Calvinistic views he shared. It was on his move to London that Murray became acquainted with the theological views of James Relly, who was preaching universal salvation. Relly was constantly held up to opprobrium in the sermons from the pulpit of the Methodist tabernacle Murray attended. So insistent were the suggestions that anyone who believed that all men would be saved must be capable of all sorts of loose living and vileness, that Murray and his wife could not resist the temptation to attend a Relly meeting to see for themselves. Instead of loose living they found a starkly simple meetinghouse and sober congregation. Under the influence of Relly and his book *Union, or, the Consanguinity of Christ and his Church*, the Murrays accepted Universalism and became devoted adherents.

It was a series of debts, and a stay in debtors' prison, and the death of his wife and baby, that drove Murray to the New World with the full intention of forgetting his past and never preaching again.

But, as he later believed, the hand of God guided him in 1770 to Good Luck at Cranberry Inlet on Barnegat Bay and into the life of the elderly Thomas Potter. It was Potter who, sharing the faith in universal salvation because of the influence of members of the Ephrata community (German Dunkers from Pennsylvania) who had visited him in earlier years, prevailed on Murray to preach the faith.

Murray, with the fervor that had earlier stood him in good stead among the Methodists, carried the message through the colonies. He was less than candid about his theological views, however. He insisted on using "scripture language," leading his auditors up to the recognition of the truth of universal salvation—but leaving the final leap for them to make alone. The host clergy, who had good noses for heresy, soon caught on, however, and while at the beginning many pulpits were open to this zealous preacher, most were soon closed to him as the word spread concerning his true convictions. Increasingly he met opposition, some of it rabid and ugly. His meetings were disrupted. He barely escaped lynching several times. In Boston on one occasion a potentially lethal stone flew through the window at the back of the pulpit, narrowly missing his head. Murray, never at a loss for words or a moral, held up the rock to the congregation's view, weighed it in his hand, and pronounced: "This argument is *solid*, and *weighty*, but it is neither *rational*, nor *convincing*."

It was during a visit to Boston that he was invited to Gloucester by a group which had some time before read Relly's *Union* and had become convinced of its truth. Murray was to settle among these come-outers from the First Parish in Gloucester in 1774. Here he found his second wife, Judith Sargent Stevens, widowed daughter of one of his new parishioners. The Gloucesterians formed an Independent Christian Church, and, with Murray, fought through the courts to victory recognition of their right to divert religious tax money from the established Congregational church to their new organization. Murray's status as a clergyman was later confirmed in a resolution in the Massachusetts legislature. These victories went far in establishing the rights of religious dissenters in Massachusetts, and the Universalists were considered the most vigorous advocates of separation of church and state.

Murray remained full time in Gloucester until 1788 when he began to share his time equally with the Universalist Society in Boston. He moved to Boston in 1793.

During the Revolution he had served briefly as chaplain in the Rhode Island Brigade under his friend General Varnum. Even here he had to establish his ministerial rights against the objections of the army chaplains. It took the intervention of General George Washington to settle the matter: "General Orders, September 17th, 1775.—The Rev. Mr. John Murray is appointed Chaplain to the Rhode Island Regiments, and is to be respected as such."

Although Murray was technically settled over the churches in Gloucester and Boston, he spent much of his time on the road. He was a man of tireless energy. As a result of his itineracy, churches were formed in many places from New England to Pennsylvania. He was a prime mover in bringing together representatives from the churches in the first conventions of the growing Universalist movement, in Oxford, Massachusetts, in 1785, and in Philadelphia in 1790.

Murray was a man completely sure of himself. His driving personality would never allow him to give way in an argument, theological or otherwise. If his autobiography is any guide, he was convinced that the hand of the deity was constantly supporting his efforts, even at times to the point of providing him with unexpected transportation! This conviction led him into a self-righteousness and overbearing stance that was truly objectionable to those with whom he was in contention and, one must suppose, even from time to time to his friends.

His preaching displayed these tendencies. Murray once told Dr. Benjamin Rush that he seldom read anything other than the Bible and depended on his best insights to come to him while he was in the pulpit. Although this approach might stand him in good stead with those who believed in immediate revelation, to the person who believed in rational preparation of sermons it was objectionable. After hearing Murray preach on board ship in 1788 when both were en route from England, John Adams remarked in his diary that he could never come to accept extemporaneous preaching. Murray's practice of extemporaneity in the pulpit led him into farfetched biblical analogies, and at times made a jumble of his logic. It must be said, however, that use of reason and logic does not necessarily lead to success in preaching. The fervor which had made Murray a success in English and Irish Methodist circles made him eminently successful among those who were drawn to his Universalist message in America.

This enthusiasm was one of the elements particularly distasteful to the dispassionate and discreet Charles Chauncy in Boston. Chauncy had opposed the emotionalism of the Great Awakening because he was convinced that the apostles of early Christianity had appealed to reason in winning converts to the faith. He attempted to counteract Murray, however, because of his theological views. While Chauncy took an antitrinitarian and Arminian position, Murray was both a trinitarian and a Calvinist, and he presented universal salvation in terms objectionable to Chauncy.

Murray was not an original thinker, but rather the preacher of a doctrine that he had inherited in all its parts from his master James Relly. It did not question the doctrine of the trinity, but rather laid stress on the act of salvation performed by Jesus Christ in his role as Son of God. This faith was Calvinist in its presuppositions. But whereas the Calvinists insisted that the Son died to save relatively few souls predestined by God before the creation, Relly, and Murray after him, insisted that the Elect were all mankind.

We see here the eighteenth century belief in the benevolence of God clothed in Calvinistic garments in a clever synthesis. The Rellyan synthesis was quite simple, although Relly spent the many pages of *Union* in an attempt to pile up biblical justifications for his position. Many of them, like many of the analogies in Murray's sermons, were farfetched. Relly's basic proposition was that Christ was so closely identified with mankind, as man's head at creation and as head of the church, that he was equally guilty with man of the transgressions of disobedience committed by the first parents against God's law. Moreover, there is such a close union, indeed a consanguinity, between Christ and man, that when Christ died he performed an act of satisfaction for his own sins (and man's) that is efficacious through all of time and eternity. Thus, all men are saved now and forever.

It was this relatively simple message that Murray preached, at first covertly and then openly, and it was this message which brought the condemnation of the orthodox down on his head. They were sure that such a message would undercut morality, for if the threat of future retribution were removed, what was to keep men in line?

6

Although Universalist ideas were abroad in the land before Murray landed in America in 1770, it was Murray's tireless propagation of the faith and his drive toward organization that caused him to be distinguished as the founder of Universalism in America. He was greatly aided in this task, however, by a man with whom he came into contact from time to time but who operated on his own.

Elhanan Winchester (1751–1797) came to Universalism from Baptist ranks about ten years after Murray began preaching in America. Actually he went through a series of religious changes with his father, a farmer and shoemaker from Brookline, Massachusetts, who was inspired by the preaching of George Whitefield. Winchester followed his father from the Congregational church into the "New Light" Congregational movement, one of the progeny of the several schisms caused by the Great Awakening. But Winchester moved over to the Baptists, first to the open communion branch and then to the Calvinistic Baptists. It was as a Baptist that Winchester began his preaching career. As suited the unlettered Baptists well, he had little formal education. But he was bright and intelligent; these qualities allowed him to overcome this disability. He was to educate himself to the point where he could associate comfortably with some of the finest minds of his day.

After a brief period of preaching in his native state, Winchester moved south, taking a pulpit at Welch Neck on the Great Pee Dee River in South Carolina. Here he observed slavery at first hand, and he did not like what he saw. Despite threats from the owners, Winchester taught the slaves the Christian religion. In 1788 he was to publish a work against the "peculiar institution."

Winchester was one of the many who were brought to Universalism by the reading of Paul Siegvolck's *Everlasting Gos-*

pel. At first he resisted the book, but he toyed with the ideas contained in it, from time to time trying them out on his friends —quite persuasively it seems. He was in this undetermined mental state when he moved to a flourishing Baptist congregation in Philadelphia. By 1780 he was ready to believe but he was not willing to upset his auditors by expressing his new views publicly. Winchester was strengthened in his convictions by a friendship which grew up between him and Dr. George De Benneville, who was then residing in nearby Germantown.

Try as he may to keep his new faith a secret, his friends (as friends often do) allowed the news to leak out. There were those in his congregation (as there are inevitably in every congregation) who wanted to know if the rumors were true. Winchester reluctantly admitted his beliefs, and a bitter controversy ensued which split the congregation in two. This was the start of the congregation of "Universal Baptists" in Philadelphia.

Winchester was understandably upset by the schism. Added to his problems was a troublesome wife. Winchester had previously been married four times. Each of these marriages was terminated by death in an incredibly short time. Several babies of these unions were stillborn or died in infancy. Despite the advice of his friends that he eschew further attempts at married bliss, Winchester tried a fifth time. Maria Knowles Winchester suffered from periodic mental problems. This may have contributed to Winchester's desire for a change of scene. In 1787 he and Maria sailed for England. Winchester preached far and wide among the General Baptists, planting the seed of universal salvation wherever he could. While in England he published some of the expositions of Universalism, for which he is best known, and made the acquaintance of the Methodist founder John Wesley and the leading Unitarian divines Joseph Priestley, Richard Price, and Thomas Belsham. He left England hurriedly in 1794, leaving his mad wife behind. Maria made her own way home.

Back in Philadelphia Winchester shared his pulpit with Dr. Priestley, who had migrated to the relative calm of Pennsylvania after his home and meetinghouse in Birmingham were wrecked by a reactionary mob stirred up against him because of his radical political views in support of the French Revolution.

Among the supporters of Winchester was Dr. Benjamin Rush (1745–1813), signer of the Declaration of Independence, physician, professor of medicine, and reformer of many parts. Rush had come over to Universalism from Presbyterianism, and with John Murray had been one of the planners of the Universalist Convention held in Philadelphia in 1790. He served on the committee which drafted resolutions condemning slavery and war.

His support of Winchester was generous to an extreme. He paid the preacher the ultimate compliment of the eighteenth century, likening him in theology to the great Newton in science. He promoted the publications of this "theological Newton."

Winchester no doubt warranted such support. He was a popular preacher, holding his hearers fascinated. Unlike Murray, he presented the intellectual, as well as the emotional, arguments for Universalism. His writings reflect in their graceful style a supple mind and an open-hearted, affectionate person who could present his views with conviction but without fanaticism.

Like Newton, Winchester spent much effort in trying to puzzle out the meaning of the prophecies in Scripture. His formulation of Universalism was quite different from Murray's, a fact which bothered the latter, although, like many others, he found Winchester so winning a person that it was difficult to hold his theology against him.

Unlike Murray's Rellyan formulation, which in effect relieved men of the necessity to suffer for sin which Christ in their name had once for all died for, Winchester's theology looked forward to the end of the world and a period of 50,000 years during which sinful men would undergo all manner of suffering to purge them of uncleanness. At the end of this purgatorial period, they would be united again with Christ and their pure brothers who because of their purity had escaped the flames. Winchester took what was known as a restorationist position. Souls would be restored to Christ and God after a period of purification.

This tension between the two extremes of Universalism

is to be seen through much of its history. Those who have taken one extreme have insisted that Christ's salvational act is sufficient for all time and that it is not necessary to hold out the threat of future punishment in order to keep men on the straight and narrow path. The assurance of the love of a benevolent God is sufficient to the task.

The other extreme of Universalism has insisted that, whatever may be said of God's love, it is palpably demonstrable that many of the children of Adam need correction for the sins they have indulged in in this life. Furthermore, the expectation of such punishment, even if it be for a limited period, acts as a healthy corrective in everyday life.

Proponents of both sides of the issue have sought to prove their positions through reason and the Bible. Since the Bible is such a rich treasure of materials, written over a long period of time, each faction has been able to find ample justification for its position. Universalists have been united, however, in their rejection of the orthodox Christian claim that there is punishment throughout eternity awaiting the man who, whether because of God's predestination or his own volition, is living a life of sin. No loving God, said the Universalists, could be responsible for such a dread fate.

These tensions within late eighteenth century Universalism were to continue into the new century.

7

By far the greatest thinker produced by the Universalist movement, and one in whose thinking the full impact of the Enlightenment is reflected, was Hosea Ballou, who was born in 1771, the year following the landing of John Murray in America. Like Winchester, Ballou had very little formal education but he was a powerful reasoner who did not shrink from the consequences of his thought by retreat into inconsistency.

Ballou was the son of an impoverished Calvinistic Baptist farmer-preacher who moved from Rhode Island to the frontier territory of southwestern New Hampshire. In these surroundings opportunities for formal education were few. Ballou was taught the fundamentals by his father and had a few months of schooling. He was in his teens when he was first exposed to Universalist notions. Caleb Rich and some cohorts attended Baptist meetings with the intent of raising embarrassing questions. Their questions stuck in the mind of the young Ballou: How could a good God be responsible for endless suffering in hell of men, creatures of His own making? After all, St. Paul had written, "Therefore as by the offence of one, judgment came upon all men to condemnation; even so by the righteousness of one the free gift came upon all men unto justification of life." (Romans 5:18)

Ballou was to become convinced that the only logical answers to these questions inevitably led to Universalism. He embraced the faith and began to preach it in 1790. His early years as a preacher were spent as an itinerant on circuits which took him into Vermont and Massachusetts. He eventually was settled in parishes in Portsmouth, New Hampshire, and Salem, Massachusetts. In 1817 he began a ministry of thirty-five years in Boston, where he became the leading spokesman for the movement in pulpit and in print.

Ballou began his career as a preacher with Calvinistic presuppositions. He believed in the trinity and accepted the notion that Christ had died to make salvation possible for the Elect. It was a relatively simple matter to interpret passages such as Romans 5:18 in such a way that the outcome was salvation for all. Whether he was influenced by Rellyanism in his early career is difficult to say. In his old age he insisted that he was well settled in his own belief before he became acquainted with Rellyanism through John Murray. He may have gone through a Rellyan phase after his introduction to Murray, for there seem to be strong traces of the Englishman's approach in Ballou's earliest published writings.

But this modified Calvinism gave way to a drastic transformation once Ballou came under the influence of Ethan Allen's *Reason the Only Oracle of Man*. It was through this book that Ballou and Universalism were to be most heavily influenced by the Enlightenment. The Deist insistence on the use of Reason in religion, its unitarian interpretation of the godhead, and many other aspects of Allen's work are seen in Ballou's most important writing, *A Treatise on Atonement*, published in 1805. On careful comparison of these books, the scholar will see the heavy influence of Allen on Ballou in style and content. We have the added substantiation of a statement made by Ballou himself in old age to Orestes Brownson (then in his Universalist phase) that it was Allen's book that forced him to think through his stance in theology. There are still traces of fanciful Rellyan interpretation of Scripture in the first edition of *A Treatise on Atonement*. But Ballou was to remove them from later editions.

After his exposure to Allen's book, Ballou was always to have a high opinion of the Deists. He believed the challenge of Deism to Christianity most helpful in forcing Christians to confront many of the "errors" that burden Christian theology. He believed that more damage was done to the religion of Jesus by the Christians' propensity for anathematizing their opponents than by the Deists. But Ballou was not swept off his feet by Deism; he resisted many of its more extreme points. When his friend Abner Kneeland was going through one of his periodic attacks of unbelief, Ballou advised him to follow a cure he himself had found most effective: "If you are troubled with unbelief, if this plague have entered your heart, permit me to suggest a remedy. Humility is the first step, sincere piety towards God the second, let these be followed by that for which the Bereans (Acts 17:11) were commended and the deadly virus of unbelief will soon be purged. Will you say, 'Physician, heal thyself'? I reply, I think I have found relief by the use of the prescription, and am so much in favour of it, that I am determined to continue its application myself as well as recommend it to others."

Ballou was able to balance the scepticism of Deism with the piety of his religious outlook. It was this balancing act which resulted in the great synthesis found in *A Treatise on Atonement*. This book and Ballou's persuasive oratorical powers combined to break the ties of the burgeoning Universalist movement to Calvinism and to establish it on a new base grounded in the Enlightenment.

Ballou's great synthesis contained other elements. He had read Chauncy and Winchester, but he was also influenced by the determinism found in the writing of the French Swiss minister Ferdinand Olivier Petitpierre, whose book *Thoughts on the Divine Goodness* (1786) had wide circulation among the Universalists.

Another element, which cannot be traced to literary sources, but which pervades *A Treatise on Atonement* and much of the Universalist movement in these years, is Jeffersonian democracy. The advent of Jefferson provided symbolic justification for faith in the common man. It is no coincidence that Ballou's book was published during the presidency of the man of Monticello. Universalists could not accept an aristocracy of the spirit represented by the Calvinist belief in an Elect any more than they could accept an aristocracy in America. In these years the typical Universalist was a Jeffersonian democrat.

In formulating his theology it was logical that Ballou should begin with the centrality of sin and atonement. Here, after all, is where James Relly had begun, and it was necessary for Ballou to challenge the Rellyan hold on a fair proportion of Universalists. The *Treatise* is a much more broad-gauged work than Relly's *Union* and, in a sense, it provided the Universalist with a complete course in the faith. The various theological enemies, although politely unnamed, are attacked and obliterated— often impolitely. Ballou shared with Ethan Allen a bluntness and directness of expression. Unlike Allen, he was too kind to make fools of his opponents, but he made out their arguments to be foolish. To take but one example, giving the flavor of much of the theological debate current on the frontier, Ballou characterized trinitarians as believing in "infinity multiplied by three."

Ballou's greatest debt to Ethan Allen and to Deism was his conversion to the use of reason in religion. Although Ballou had a strong bent toward logic, he had been influenced (as indicated earlier) by Relly's fanciful interpretation of Scripture. Now he came to believe that as much as possible reason should be brought into play. He was convinced that if one read the Bible with reason, much that had earlier puzzled Christians could be understood with new clarity and many of the false doctrines which had corrupted Christianity could be eliminated.

Ballou was as convinced as the Deists of the efficacy of reason. He wrote that "we ought . . . to believe, that all the truth which is necessary for our belief, is not only reasonable, but reducible to our understandings."

Among the many "corruptions" that Ballou removed was the doctrine of the trinity. Belief in the trinity was not reasonable (since infinity cannot be divided by three!) and he attempted to prove that the preponderant number of relevant scriptural passages make it clear that Christ is a being subordinate to the Father.

In place of the triune God Ballou presents the benevolent God of the eighteenth century. Christianity, he thinks, has misinterpreted the Father because of the stories in the Old Testament representing Him as fickle, wrathful, and vengeful. These stories, which had their origin in man's misunderstanding of God's intent, hide the basic nature of God: eternal, unchangeable love. It is not God who changes but man. Through all eternity God is love.

The God of Hosea Ballou, like the God of the Deists, emerges as a man-centered God. He loves man and seeks, in the eighteenth century expression, to "happify" him. Indeed, unlike much of orthodox Christianity, which insisted that fallen man must suffer in order to glorify God, Ballou insisted that God glorifies himself in making man happy.

It is clear that under such a scheme there can be no such thing as infinite sin. How could finite man sin against an infinite God? Such a belief is not reasonable. If man were capable of sinning against an infinite God, he would share His infinity!

But Ballou did not make light of sin. He believed it a serious force in life. Sin was certainly real to man, blighting much of his life and making him miserable. Ballou identified sin with misery and believed it preposterous that men (including Christian divines, who often made the claim) could believe that sin could be pleasurable. This distorted view was another example of the "carnal" mind at work. Sin and misery are one.

It was to overcome this misery that God sent Christ to earth. Not, as the orthodox claimed, to die to satisfy a God made wrathful as He contemplated man's sinfulness, but to lead man away from sin. Because God is eternal love He ever seeks reconciliation or atonement. But it is not God who needs to be reconciled but man. God ever seeks to win man to Him by demonstrating His love for him. Jesus was the greatest demonstration of God's intent. He came to show man the path of love and to set an example for man. He is the embodiment of God's love. In following Jesus man can be reconciled to God.

This salvation is for all men. God plays no favorites. All men are His beloved children. And God is intent on saving everyone. Whereas Arminians like Chauncy, in order to preserve man's free will, could see man holding out against salvation, Ballou found this idea intolerable. He was logical in believing that an all-powerful, all-loving God who was in complete control of the universe could not brook such opposition.

Ballou, then, was a determinist, a "necessitarian." God, the loving Father, had determined that all His children would be saved and was intent on carrying out this plan. If Ballou, in order to be consistent, had to accept determinism he was prepared to do it. This upset his fellow liberals, who preferred to take the inconsistent position which allowed both God his omnipotence and man his free will.

But this was not the end of the liberals' disagreement with Ballou. Given Ballou's position that God is in complete control of events, and man has no free will, they pointed out that logically this would make God the author of sin. Ballou did not shy away from this conclusion. God *is* the author of sin, but this fact makes sinful man no less sinful. In man's life sin, which equals misery, is a blight. But God, in His wisdom and love, uses man's sin to good purpose. As in the biblical story of Joseph (one of Ballou's favorites) the sin of the brothers in allowing Joseph to be sold into slavery eventuated in good (because God had planned it thus), so God uses sin to bring His love to man through that man who overcame sin, Jesus Christ.

It will be seen that Ballou's was a happy determinism. He optimistically believed that with the benevolent God of the universe in complete control man need not fear, but rather should glory in His love.

It appears that Ballou had worked his way through to a unitarian theology by 1795, ten years before he published it in *A Treatise on Atonement*. By the time of its appearance in 1805 he had pretty much won the argument among Universalist preachers. Winchester, who held very different views, was now dead. But Murray, lion of the movement, was to be very active until he was stricken with paralysis in 1809 (he died in 1815). He was bound to be unhappy with Ballou, not only because temperamentally he hated to have anyone disagree with him, but because of the radically different basis on which Ballou was presenting the message of universal salvation. He tried to tolerate the younger man, and even invited Ballou to fill his pulpit in Boston on a number of occasions when he himself was on the road. A minor scandal was created on one of these occasions when, at the conclusion of Ballou's sermon, Mrs. Murray requested a member of the choir to announce that the doctrine preached that day was not the doctrine usually preached in that house. Ballou, like Murray never at a loss for words, replied simply, "The audience will please to take notice of what our brother has said," and went on to read the concluding hymn.

The divisions between the two men were bound to increase as Ballou became more set in his views and more prominent in the movement. It pained Murray in his declining years to observe what he called "a Socinian, Deistical, Sadducean Universalist" successfully propagating errors. Ballou, it should be said, had a sense of propriety that led him to fend off efforts of his friends in Boston to persuade him to become head of a second Universalist society while Murray was still alive. After Murray's death, however, the School Street Church was built, and Ballou was installed as minister of the Second Universalist Society on Christmas Day, 1817.

It was from this strategic position that Ballou was to dominate the movement for his remaining thirty-five years. Although his preaching showed many traces of his frontier upbringing, his pulpit was a magnet that drew many to him and the Universalist movement. His efforts were made doubly effective when he established the weekly *Universalist Magazine* in 1819.

This weekly newspaper became a lively vehicle for the broadcast of his ideas, and created no little stir among orthodox Christians.

Despite the fact that Ballou was now ensconced in Boston, the citadel of Unitarianism, he was not made to feel welcome by his fellow liberals. The same social factors that almost two generations before had led Chauncy to reject Murray were at work now. Hosea Ballou, with his backwoods accent and meager formal education, was no social match for Dr. William Ellery Channing and the other Harvard-educated Unitarians who dominated the leading pulpits of Boston. Ballou's congregation was made up of humble folk who, although they were to make their way up the socioeconomic ladder to relative prominence during the very period of Ballou's ministry, were not entertained in the homes of the best families who filled the pews in the Unitarian churches.

It took great fortitude on Ballou's part not to become bitter when he observed Unitarians, fellow believers in so many points of theology, doing oratorical gymnastics to keep from being identified with the Universalists. Their views, after all, were identical on God, Christ, Reason, and Scripture, but the Unitarians still eschewed belief in universal salvation—or said they did. Like the orthodox, they believed in the efficacy to morality of the threat of eternal punishment after death. And although they eventually began to give way on this point and to accept belief in a limited period of punishment after which souls would be restored to God's presence, by then Hosea Ballou and his friends had left them behind.

8

Ultra-Universalism, as it was sometimes called, was the logical result of Ballou's presuppositions concerning God's eternal, unchangeable love. Although he wavered and resisted the conclusion for years, Ballou finally gave in to the idea that there is no punishment whatsoever in the afterlife. He became convinced that, since sin is caused by the corruptions of the flesh and sin equals misery, man gets his comeuppance in this life for the sins of which he is guilty. The sinner is miserable in his sin and cannot be said to enjoy it. Thus, punishment is not postponed, but is experienced here on earth. When man dies he enters eternal bliss immediately through the power of God's love. The more crass among the Universalists, who, like the orthodox, identified sin with pleasure, refused to accept Ballou's ideas on this subject and burlesqued his position by referring to it as "death-and-glory."

Up to this point, despite the fact that there were many divergent interpretations of Universalism, there had been no schism in the movement. Now that the number of churches was growing every month and the movement was becoming a power in American society, more was at stake. The scene was set for factionalism and consequent strife: the enemy seemed to be on the run so Universalists could indulge in the luxury of fighting among themselves.

The scene was set for the controversy when Ballou and his good friend Edward Turner of Charlestown, Massachusetts, published a series of exchanges on the question in *The Gospel Visitant* in 1817–1818. Over a period of several months this series explored the various ramifications of the question. Although Ballou, for the sake of the argument, took the position that there was no punishment in the afterlife, he was not at first sure of his position. He had wavered over the years, wavering which was evident in the various editions of his *Treatise on Atonement*. In the course of this friendly controversy, however, he was systematically to work through the problems involved to his own satisfaction. By the time he moved to Boston late in 1817 he was firmly committed to ultra-Universalism. He did not make a great point of this in his preaching, however, and there is little mention of it in his *Universalist Magazine*. But the fire of controversy had been fanned by the articles of Ballou and Turner, and there were those who feared Ballou's radical position was a threat to Universalism. Coupled with this fear was a resentment of Ballou and his leadership of the movement. Much of the resentment was on purely personal grounds; there were those who disliked him and others who envied him. Thus the controversy took on personal overtones from time to time and became quite ugly. Behind the scenes Ballou's enemies were saying such things as that "nine tenths of Brother Ballou's society are infidels," and "Mr. Ballou retain[s] nothing of Christianity but the *name*."

The public part of the controversy revolved around the familiar problem of the effect of belief on behavior. If a person believed there was no punishment whatsoever in the future life would he give in to temptation on earth, as Ballou's opponents insisted? Or was it true, as Ballou's party thought, that duty is enjoyable enough to the Christian that he will do what is right in the here and now without threat of future punishment? Those who took the first position became known as Restorationists because they believed that a limited period of punishment in the future life would prepare the erring soul of man for its restoration to God. The Restorationists were convinced that they represented the true Universalist position of old, while the ultra-Universalists seemed, to themselves at least, to be on the wave of the future. Not that they saw their position as innovation. They believed that they were ridding Christianity of yet another corruption of the centuries of priestcraft. Ballou, for instance, insisted that the Bible indicated God's intention of correcting men for their transgressions in this life—not in the future. He pointed out that if God had intended a future punishment, he would have made it plain beyond a doubt in biblical revelation. In his *Examination of the Doctrine of Future Retribution,* a book which must stand with *A Treatise on Atonement* for its contribution to Universalist thought, Ballou rehearsed the long catalogue of sins set forth in the Old Testament. And yet, he insisted, nowhere did one find future retribution threatened. The Jews were punished for their sins in this life. Turning to the New Testament, Ballou attempted to show that Jesus, too, believed in retribution in his own time, not in a future state.

Arguments availed little, however. The seed of schism had been planted and was sprouting. Even the Ballou-Turner friendship of twenty-five years could not survive. When Turner was ousted from his Charlestown pulpit he was sure that Ballou was behind it. When Ballou, because of ill health, gave up editorship of the *Universalist Magazine* the new editor opened its pages to bitter controversy on the subject. When Ballou resumed his duties he and his co-editors, Thomas Whittemore and Hosea Ballou, 2nd (his grandnephew) were accused of dealing unfairly with the Restorationists.

The end result of the haggling was a schism in which fewer than a dozen churches and ministers formed a separate denomination. Among those who withdrew were Charles Hudson of the Westminster, Massachusetts, church, a clever controversialist who later put his considerable talents to use in the political sphere as a holder of various public offices in Massachusetts and as a Whig congressman; and Adin Ballou, who, like his distant relative Hosea, was a controversialist of no mean ability.

Eventually some Restorationists quietly returned to the main fold; others, like Turner, became Unitarians. Adin Ballou, inspired by the infectious utopianism abroad in the first half of the nineteenth century, put his pacifist, Christian communist principles to work in the founding of the Hopedale Community.

By the 1850's ultra-Universalism was on the wane. Apparently the Ballou approach was too subtle for the bulk of the movement. Its members felt much more comfortable with the idea that punishment lay in the future, since there was not much tangible evidence that sinners were getting their comeuppance on earth. Also destined to go by the board was Ballou's determinism. It was out of step with American optimism. No matter how philosophically clever and logical Ballou's arguments may have been, it was impossible to convince many Americans for very long that they did not have free will. Their native optimism got the better of them. Arminianism was to win the day.

Ballou in his old age gave a very different interpretation to these developments. He saw at work in them the subtle machinations of the Unitarians. He insisted that the younger Universalists were so intent on playing up to the Unitarians that they were willing to accommodate their theology. As if to shock this younger generation of preachers and laymen into keeping the faith, Ballou took delight in publishing pieces with such titles as "God the Author of Sin"!

9

Universalists could enjoy the luxury of such disputation because there was no authoritative body to call a halt. The only hierarchy in the Universalist church was one of respect. Ballou and other old-timers were given the appellation "Father" out of a sense of gratitude and love. Father Ballou, as Father Murray before him, must keep up with the times or be left behind.

The Universalist churches were congregational in polity. Each church was free to run its own affairs. So many of them were come-outers from the Baptist and Congregational churches it is understandable that Universalists assumed that such was the proper way to organize. The convention of Universalists held in Philadelphia in 1790 specifically took cognizance of the freedom of congregationalism. In the circular letter issued following the close of the convention it was written, "The plan of church government is nearly that of the Congregational Church. We conceive it to be most friendly to Christian liberty, and most agreeable to the word of God."

Beyond the local church level, the Universalists organized their churches into associations—again a borrowing of Congregational and Baptist forms. These associations met periodically for mutual spiritual and organizational sustenance but had little or no authority over the local churches. Nonetheless, there were Universalists so independent and nonconformist that they hesitated even to meet! This classic case was reported by the Boston church to the Philadelphia Convention of 1792: "Those that are at Newport [Rhode Island] join neither with the world nor with each other. They are afraid of months, of days, and of years; and, to avoid being entangled with what they deem a yoke of bondage, they keep from even the appearance of assembling at any time."

Although Universalist groups existed in most of the colonies (states), the limited New England orientation of much of the movement can be seen in the fact that the Eastern Association consisted of churches in the District of Maine; the Southern Association of churches in Connecticut and Rhode

Island, and the Northern Association of churches in New Hampshire, Vermont, and part of New York. Breaking the bonds of New England and catering to the churches on the frontier was the Western Association in New York. These associations multiplied by subdivision as the number of churches became greater.

Since church and other social organizations tend to follow political lines, it was almost inevitable that Universalists would form state conventions. Over a period of time the state conventions absorbed the various associations within their borders.

A national organization gradually emerged from the so-called General Convention, which had its origins in the meetings begun by John Murray in Oxford in 1785. This New England convention coexisted a number of years with the Philadelphia convention organized in 1790. By 1834 the New England group had become the "General Convention of Universalists in the United States." This national organization was always to compete with the state conventions for the allegiance of Universalists. But basically allegiance was to the local church. Universalists protected their local organizations from all possible encroachments—real or imagined—by the larger groups. This remained true even following the Civil War when the Universalists, like other denominations in that age of consolidation, attempted to bring together various autonomous agencies of the church into a superstructure known as the Universalist General Convention.

This amount of organization was a minimum for a movement that was booming. By the 1840's the faith was prospering in all of the states and territories of the new nation. Universalists could count about 700 societies and over 300 preachers. By the 1850's these figures were to double and, all told, 800,000 members were claimed for the movement.

Impressive as these figures may seem, it is a question whether the looseness of organization was not a handicap of serious proportions. This can best be illustrated not so much in the old settlements with their relative stability but on the frontier. The Methodists, for instance, were able to consolidate their gains on the frontier because of their episcopal form of church government. Their bishops or superintendents were able to assign riders to the various circuits to make sure that clusters of the faithful were visited on a regular basis and sustained by the word, both orally and in the books the circuit riders brought with them. Because of this mode of organization the Methodists were eminently successful in gaining and keeping adherents.

The Universalists, on the other hand, with their congregational churches and very loose "superstructures" were subject to the whims of individual preachers. The Methodist Peter Cartwright complained that wherever he went on the frontier a Universalist had already been, purveying his damnable heresy. But whereas Cartwright could assure continuity of visitations and preaching, such was not the case with the Universalists. When a Universalist circuit rider became ill, died, or simply yearned to move on to a different circuit, there was no bishop to make sure he was replaced. The result was that new, hopeful groups often withered. Under the attacks of their more orthodox neighbors they disbanded and, as individuals, gradually joined other churches or maintained their liberal faith in the privacy of their homes.

Universalists have generally been unwilling to pay the price of uniformity in matters of belief as well as organization. Given this penchant for freedom, it seems an anomaly that attempts have been made over the years to draw together in statements or professions the essentials of the faith. Each of these attempts has inevitably reflected the spirit of the times within the movement. The creed which grew out of the Philadelphia Convention in 1790 attempted to balance contending forces. Dr. Benjamin Rush was given the task of polishing it. The creed did a good job of balancing the interests of the Rellyan followers of Murray with those of the Winchesterians. And since the question of the trinity was being seriously debated in the land, with Deists affirming the unity of God, and others taking at the least an anti-trinitarian position, reference to the trinity is not made explicit, although references to Father, Son, and Holy Ghost are made.

The second attempt at an acceptable statement was

made by the General Convention of the New England States meeting at Winchester, New Hampshire, in 1803. Walter Ferriss of Vermont, who had agitated for such a statement at a few previous meetings of the convention, was made chairman of a committee to draft it. We know from a recently rediscovered manuscript of Ferriss' reminiscences that he was concerned that the General Convention agree on the essential beliefs of Universalism in order to dispel the charge of other denominations that the Universalists were "wholly divided amongst [themselves] and agreeing in nothing essential, but to vilify other sects and oppose all ecclesiastical order."

As often happens with committees, this one did not meet in the intervening year, and Ferriss went to the Winchester convention with a draft which he presented to his colleagues on very short notice. It is clear that Ferriss used the Philadelphia creed as a model. But he made this statement much more concise. He removed the trinitarian overtones of the Philadelphia statement —Ballou, after all, was a member of his committee—and included the sentiment that "holiness and happiness are inseparably connected"—another favorite Ballou approach.

It is difficult to know how seriously these creeds were taken. The church of Murray in Boston felt very free to alter the one adopted at Philadelphia to suit their own Rellyan ends. The convention itself stated that the "Winchester Profession" could be adapted to meet local needs. These creeds probably served to bring a minimum of uniformity into Universalist ranks, but it is difficult to believe that they were considered seriously binding. In this sense they have not carried the importance among Universalists that the historic creeds of the early Church have among more orthodox Christians generally.

10

Although the creedal difference between Universalists and other American denominations may appear less stark when viewed through present-day ecumenical eyes, they were considered extreme by contemporaries. Universalists were viewed with suspicion and hate by their fellow Christians, who considered them immoral and subversive. This opposition was not limited to the religious sphere. Universalists were threatened with serious civil disabilities. In Massachusetts, for example, it was argued by many that they should be barred from service on juries and not allowed to testify in court because no one who did not believe in eternal punishment could be trusted with such serious responsibilities.

This type of ostracism was reflected in all areas of life. In order to survive, Universalists found a certain amount of separatism necessary. They could not send their children to schools controlled by other religious groups for they found the pressure on them to conform so great that children would often turn against the belief of their parents. Many a family found that children returning home during school vacations would denounce their parents for their belief in universal salvation and announce their conviction that the folks would end up in hell.

Under the circumstances it was inevitable that Universalists would respond by establishing their own schools. Over a period of fifty years, starting in 1819, more than twenty were founded in New England and the Midwest. Their founders eschewed sectarianism to the point that the word Universalist did not appear in the names of any of these schools. Consistent with their resentment of the treatment of their own children at the hands of the orthodox, they did not require religious courses and did not attempt to indoctrinate the children in their care. It was inevitable, of course, that the relatively liberal atmosphere in the schools would have its effect on the beliefs and attitudes of the children.

When Horace Mann began his reform work as secretary of the newly established Board of Education in Massachusetts in 1837, the Universalists on the whole were sympathetic to his aims and lent their support. Mann—who was a Unitarian who believed in universal salvation—set out to remove sectarian religion from the public schools by insisting that the only proper religious instruction should consist of the reading of the Bible without comment. The outcry of the orthodox that the schools would become godless did not deter Mann, who always enjoyed a good battle. The argument of the orthodox that Mann was introducing his own religious belief into the school system was not without foundation, since it was a conviction of the Unitarians that if the Bible were read "straight" it would be seen to support unitarian positions.

Although Universalists might agree on the need for secondary schools, the attempt of some of the younger ministers in the 1840's to promote the establishment of theological seminaries for the education of ministers was stalwartly opposed by the old-timers. Many of them, like the venerable Father Ballou, were convinced that theological schools were the vehicles for the perpetuation of the corruptions of Christianity. Furthermore, they believed that a deadening similarity of approach would result if ministers were to be cast in the same die by one or two professors in a theological school. They wanted to perpetuate the diversity of the early movement, and raised the question whether it had suffered from the ministrations of men like Murray and Winchester who had never been exposed to a theological education.

In this position the old-timers displayed the prejudices of their background. Many of them had come from the ranks of the Baptists, who believed that education of the ministry was unnecessary. The Holy Spirit was perfectly capable of choosing His spokesmen without the intervention of theological schools.

On the other hand, the prejudices of men like Ballou did not extend to what they called "literary institutions." Ballou himself had spent a few months in an academy when in his teens and, good Jeffersonian that he was, he believed in the efficacy of education for all of the people. It is more than symbolic that the first Universalist theological school did not get under way until after Ballou's death in 1852, while the first Universalist college was chartered that year.

In establishing their own colleges the Universalists were following the example of many other denominations. The United States saw a plethora of such institutions come into being, many in the most unlikely places, as each denomination vied for a place in the higher education status race. Many of these institutions did not survive. Among the Universalist colleges which did, Tufts, St. Lawrence, Buchtel (now part of the

University of Akron), and Throop (now the California Institute of Technology) have grown into excellent institutions.

As with their secondary schools, the Universalist colleges attempted to maintain a nonsectarian stance. There were no creedal statements required. We cannot ignore the fact, however, that in a day of required attendance at chapel, non-Universalist students in these institutions would receive a good dose of Universalist truth on a continuing basis. In addition, of course, the presidents and many of the faculty members were drawn from the ministry, thus insuring a religious flavor to many of the colleges' activities.

This religious flavor was no doubt strengthened by the fact that a substantial number of the early students in these institutions were headed for ministerial careers. The standard mid-nineteenth century curriculum, which included such courses as natural theology, was expected of all students alike. Even the establishment of separate programs for the ministerial students did not relieve other students from the religious concerns of the institutions. This was only accomplished by changing curricular fashions, which relegated religion to the position of just one of many subjects in the elective system.

Universalists also sought to educate their adult members through the printed medium. The Universalist newspapers—there was a rash of them—carried the battle to the enemy. Their columns were filled with argumentation which attempted to refute the "partialists" and to establish the truth of the "universalists." Ballou's weekly newspaper, *The Universalist Magazine*, established in 1819, was just the first of many. As the movement spread, so did the number of papers multiply. The West and the South were to sponsor their full share of them.

Less successful was the attempt to establish more serious journals. *The Universalist Expositor*, established in 1830, died an early death. Its successor had difficulty in supporting itself. Ministers no doubt appreciated it, but the greater number of Universalist laymen, like most laymen, found the scholarly pretensions of such journals outside of their interest and preferred the news columns which reported the victories and defeats of an expanding faith.

11

It has generally been assumed that the Civil War so preoccupied religious groups that there was little in the way of theological speculation and controversy during this period. Whatever may be true of other denominations such was not the case with the Universalists, who became exercised over the twin challenges to Christianity posed by Higher Criticism of the Bible and the publication in America in 1860 of Charles Darwin's *Origin of Species* (1859).

Although some denominations were shaken to their roots by the battle between science and religion, the Universalists came through relatively unscathed. Instead of retreating into what became known as fundamentalism, the Universalists because of their liberal heritage of the use of reason in religion chose to confront the challenge head on and to adapt to new truth.

The new criticism of the Bible grew out of the literary scholarship of the German universities. The same literary techniques which indicated that the Homeric books were the work of many men, when applied to the Bible shattered the preconceptions of the Judaeo-Christians that the biblical books were unities and the work of the men whose names were traditionally associated with them. The challenges posed by such Deists as Ethan Allen and Thomas Paine a hundred years before were now shown to have substance. Detailed comparisons made of vocabulary of the biblical books demonstrated that they were the work of many men at different periods of time. The belief that the books of the Bible were literally inspired by the Holy Ghost was no longer tenable to those who were willing to look at the results of literary science. The infallibility of the Bible, an idea basic to Christianity, could be maintained only by the device of ignoring the mounting evidence presented by the scholars —most of them churchmen themselves.

But more was at stake than literal inspiration. If the biblical books were the work of fallible men, it was difficult to accept the authenticity of many of the more incredible events reported therein. The very miracles attributed to Jesus could be explained as the misunderstanding of his disciples or, even more disturbing, as the inevitable growth of legend and myth.

Painful as it was, the Universalists gradually came to the position that the revelation of God can take many forms and can even use as vehicles imperfect books written by fallible men. In this they were helped by one of the most notable biblical scholars in the United States. Orello Cone (1835–1905), Universalist minister, professor, scholar, and college president, interpreted the Higher Criticism to a whole generation of Americans in such books as *Gospel-Criticism and Historical Christianity* (1891) and *The Gospel and Its Earliest Interpretations* (1893).

Cone also was prominent in helping Universalists to absorb the blows struck to religious presuppositions by Darwin's exposition of evolution. Darwin's theory that life presently on earth evolved from simpler forms which had survived changing conditions by adapting through natural selection held in it the greatest challenge Christianity had faced since Copernicus and Galileo. If Darwin was right, the Bible's account of God's instantaneous creation of man and other creatures was wrong. Evolutionary theory was in direct contradiction to the creation story in Genesis.

Evolutionary theories (Darwin's was only one) were bolstered by the fact that geologists were discovering fossils of flora and fauna in deep strata of the earth. These findings also raised questions concerning the popularly accepted notions of the antiquity of the earth. Universalists, like many other Christians, had accepted the biblical chronology set forth by the seventeenth century Irish Archbishop James Ussher. By working back through the lives of patriarchs of the Old Testament Ussher had estimated that the creation had taken place in the year 4004 B.C. —on 23 October—at 9:00 A.M.! This exquisite certainty was now shattered.

Universalists took the time to debate Darwin's findings even though the Civil War was raging in the United States. The debate began shortly after the American edition of *The Origin of Species* appeared in 1860, and continued to the turn of the twentieth century.

Even though Universalism at the period was a faith

grounded in the Bible, since Ballou's day there had been a strong current of rationality running through Universalist piety. This is not to say that Universalist thinkers embraced Darwinism on its appearance. Many of them reacted with the same vigorous hostility as members of other denominations. They considered this "mere theory" degrading to man, who, they were convinced, was God's immutable creation.

The initial hostility of shock soon gave way to a willingness to entertain the idea—however cautiously. Universalist thinkers in the vanguard insisted that religion had nothing to fear from science. By the 1870's they began to display an open sympathy which allowed them to begin the task of adapting the faith to the new scientific truth. They said that, after all, the Bible is not a science textbook, that it cannot be taken literally in many of its parts. The believer must look for the spirit behind the letter. Orello Cone insisted that the spheres of science and religion do not conflict but complement each other, science speaking of the "how" of things while religion speaks of the "whence." Men of religion should realize that evolution can be interpreted either theistically or atheistically and should "meet the theories of materialism with well-chosen weapons from the armory of theistic philosophy."

Like other Christians, Universalists began to get the better of the Darwinian challenge when they attempted to absorb it within their theistic systems. Thomas B. Thayer, a leading Universalist theologian, insisted that the Darwinian conception of development was inconceivable without the presence of mind. This was the vehicle by which Universalist thinkers in the late 1870's and early 1880's transferred from one concept of God to another. God had not been responsible for an instantaneous creation but was rather working through evolution; He was continuously at work in the universe.

It was this type of argument that led to wholehearted acceptance of evolution. Evolution was not a blind force at work but, as the leading minister John Coleman Adams insisted, a process that displayed every indication of design. "The doctrines of Darwin have multiplied the evidences of intelligence, purpose, design, in creation a hundred-fold."

With the publication of Marion Shutter's *Applied Evolution* in 1900, Universalists had completed two generations of adaptation to new modes of thinking. Shutter's book, which was widely advertised and read, had been given first as a series of lectures to his church in Minneapolis. Dedicated to John Fiske, the American historian who was the major force in popularizing Darwinism, it reflected a boundless optimism concerning man's limitless possibilities on earth.

Such optimism is also reflected in the creed adopted by the Universalist General Convention in Boston in 1899. Dissatisfactions with the Winchester Profession of 1803 had been expressed at conventions for about twenty-five years. Particularly objectionable was the passage which stated that the Holy Spirit would "restore" mankind to "holiness and happiness." The implication that man had fallen from a previous state of grace and could be "restored" was out of line with the conviction born of Darwinism that man was evolving to higher and higher forms.

12

On the verge of a new century, Universalists increasingly looked beyond the borders of America to non-Christian lands. An earlier reluctance to engage in missionary work gave way to the lure of the Far East. The annexation of overseas territory at the conclusion of the Spanish-American War of 1898 was just the most dramatic example of a cultural imperialism which had swept the Western world. The desire to bring the non-Christian peoples of Japan to Universalism is an indication that Universalists still conceived of their movement within a typical Protestant framework. The Universalist mission in Japan, begun by dedicated workers in 1890, was a modest success. Convictions of the efficacy of self-help and local leadership emerged from the shambles of the Second World War and the Japan Free Religious Association formed in 1948 is one result of growing conviction on the part of Universalists that indigenous religion must be respected. Another result of this belief was the formation of the Universalist Service Committee in 1945, which made no efforts at conversion but was concerned solely with assuaging human suffering.

There were other signs that Universalism had taken its place as one of many respectable denominations in the American Protestant world. With the rise and development of the social gospel movement between the Civil War and the outbreak of World War I, denominational differences tended to be submerged in a greater concern for the application of Christian principles in social and economic spheres. In addition, the profound effect of Higher Criticism and Darwinism on American religious groups led to a liberalization the effect of which was to lessen the opposition to Universalist ideas. If mainline American denominations did not openly espouse universal salvation, they at least no longer overtly opposed it. If the end result was more comfort for Universalists in Zion, the same comfort and respectability led to a slowdown of expansion and growth. If a person could be comfortable with Universalist ideas while retaining his membership in a mainline denomination, he saw little reason to change. And with lessening of opposition (and persecution) Universalists tended to lose their fervor. The resulting slump can be measured by the decline of the number of individual members and churches. Whereas in 1888 Universalism was claimed to be the sixth largest denomination in the United States, by the second quarter of the twentieth century it was on its way to becoming one of the smallest. (Because of the various ways of counting membership in Protestant groups, caution must always be exercised in estimates of this kind.)

The distinctive message of universal salvation seemed less important, and the desire to preach and spread it less pressing. Like some other American denominations, the Universalists affirmed their attachment to Jesus in increasingly mawkish terms. He was no longer the great Savior with a transcendent mission but more a friend and companion. Universalists experienced a "rosy glow" when they thought of the friend they had in Jesus.

With this lessening of denominational fervor and drive there seemed to be fewer and fewer reasons to maintain a distinctive organization. Universalists had always maintained the superiority of congregational church government, and the liberalization of the theology of the Congregational churches seemed to lead logically to the merger of these two groups. The close proximity of the two denominational headquarters in Boston and the close relations between the staffs of the two helped facilitate such a flirtation. In 1923 serious negotiations were undertaken. That a merger never took place was probably due to the objection of the Unitarians, who accused the Universalists of a lapse from liberalism in their entertainment of such a marriage. The Unitarians themselves had been contemplating a union with the Universalists. The differences in theology, education, and social standing which had separated these two despite their great similarities in the early nineteenth century had become less great in the intervening hundred years.

Having turned away from a possible merger with the Congregationalists, the Universalists took more seriously the possibilities of bridging the remaining chasms separating them from the Unitarians. The first serious attempt, after many years of expressed good intentions, resulted in the Free Church Fellowship formed in the 1930's. Because this was an organization of individuals and churches and was open to other liberal Christians, it did not address itself to the complex problem of merging the denominational structures of the American Unitarian Association and the Universalist Church of America. Not until 1953 was this accomplished in the formation of the Council of Liberal Churches (Universalist-Unitarian). The CLC brought together the religious education, public relations, and some of the publishing activities of the two denominations. This "federal union" approach, although it proved too slow for a growing number of leaders in both denominations, served the purpose of providing the setting for Universalists and Unitarians to learn to work together and gradually to overcome the remaining differences among them. Having accomplished this, the urgings of some that a true consolidation take place soon seemed less traumatic. A merger commission was established in 1956 under the chairmanship of William B. Rice. It is significant that Rice was a Unitarian minister educated in a Universalist college and seminary. Like many other denominational leaders, he had learned by experience that the differences separating the two denominations were matters of style and procedure, not of substance. Under his patient, skillful leadership, the merger of the two groups into the Unitarian Universalist Association was voted in 1961.

13

The challenge of humanism was to preoccupy Universalists in the generation from the mid-1930's to the mid-1950's. Despite the depression in America and the rise of totalitarianism in Europe—or possibly because of them—a small band of liberal thinkers published "The Humanist Manifesto" in 1933. It was an affirmation of man's faith in himself, a faith that through the use of disciplined thought man could reorder society in such a way as to assure a world of peace and plenty. The humanists asserted that man must do it on his own, not expecting intervention by divine power. They denied the very basis of the faith of the theists in the liberal churches.

Although Clinton Lee Scott, then minister of the Universalist church in Peoria, Illinois, was the only Universalist to sign the manifesto, the Universalist churches were swept up in the controversy, which also raged in the Unitarian churches. This fact demonstrates the common concerns of the two denominations. The denominational journals inevitably devoted much attention to the argument, and ministerial candidates were scrutinized with keen eyes—and ears—by churches too liberal to openly question a man's creed in a supposedly creedless church. Inevitably as the heat of passion cooled the more irenically inclined announced confidently that, after all, humanists and theists thought pretty much alike and the argument had been exaggerated.

Although there was more poetry than truth in such statements, the controversy had served the useful purpose of allowing the Universalists and Unitarians to discover that they, indeed, no longer expected divine intervention in man's life. Although the concept of God served still as an inspiration to some, the bulk of Universalists and Unitarians had become the most basic of humanists. They believed, like Confucius, that although there may be a divine power somewhere in the universe, if man's problems are to be solved he must solve them himself. The rise of neo-orthodoxy among other Protestant denominations only confirmed the liberals in their humanist faith. Even the Bond of Faith, proposed in 1933 and adopted by the Universalists in 1935, while certainly not intended to give aid and comfort to the humanists, and while avowing "faith in God as Eternal and All-Conquering Love," puts the responsibility for life on earth on man's shoulders when it speaks of "the power of men of good-will and sacrificial spirit to overcome all evil and progressively [to] establish the Kingdom of God."

In the resolution of the humanist controversy Universalists and Unitarians took a step which carried them beyond Christianity. Probably because of their aversion to Christian creeds they had always been sympathetic to the claims of other religions, even while affirming their allegiance to Jesus. As early as 1805 Hosea Ballou in A Treatise on Atonement stated his belief that "the divine grace of reconciliation may be communicated to those who have never been privileged with the volume of divine revelation, and who have never heard the name of a Mediator proclaimed, as the only way of life and salvation." In 1882–1883 James Freeman Clarke, a Unitarian, published his sympathetic treatment of Ten Great Religions. Both denominations were active in sponsoring the World Parliament of Religions, held in conjunction with the Columbian Exposition in Chicago in 1893. In secular affairs, they were among the most staunch supporters of the idea of the League of Nations and then the United Nations, and in their Service Committees sought to meet the needs of men in many parts of the world without regard to their religious beliefs.

Paradoxically, the rise of humanism in the 1930's, with its denial of the existence of any deity, caused the liberals to look with a more tolerant eye on the claims of non-Christian religions. The Scriptures of Buddhism, Hinduism, and Taoism (among others) were introduced into services on an equal footing with those of Christianity. Universalists and Unitarians seemed to be saying that man possesses within him a basic religious need which has to be met and which has been expressed in various formulations in different cultures.

Within the leadership of the Universalist Church of America, this more inclusive view of Universalism gained sympathy from a series of General Superintendents. Robert Cummins, who served in that executive office from 1938 to 1953, lent his support, as did Brainard F. Gibbons, who served from 1953 to 1956, and Philip R. Giles, who served from 1957 to the time of consolidation with the Unitarians in 1961.

A measure of the grassroots support for such a stance is difficult to determine. But Gibbons' outspoken address on the subject delivered at the General Assembly in Rochester, New York, in October, 1949, did not stand in the way of his election to the presidency of the Universalist Church of America in 1951 —nor to his appointment later as General Superintendent.

That some were not prepared for such a giant step is indicated by the controversy which arose in 1949 over the extension of fellowship to the Charles Street Meeting House in Boston. The Meeting House had been acquired by the Massachusetts Universalist Convention under its Superintendent, Dr. Clinton Lee Scott. At issue were the views of the minister of the church, Kenneth L. Patton, an avowed humanist.

Under Patton the Charles Street Meeting House had adopted a deliberate policy of syncretism. The building was radically altered to incorporate the symbols of the religions of the world. Worship materials were compiled by the minister and members of the congregation with the same end in mind.

Patton and the congregation of the Meeting House were self-consciously experimental in their approach. They were convinced that man can successfully create a new, world religion that can bridge the cultural differences which perpetuate a superficial division among the nations and tribes of the earth.

14

As the Universalists faced the question of consolidation with the Unitarians in the 1950's they were filled with questionings and uncertainties. The greater wealth of the American Unitarian Association and the renewed vigor the Unitarians were displaying with the establishment of new fellowships and churches, especially in the West, raised fears that the Universalists would be swallowed up in a merger of the two. Efforts to initiate new programs among the Universalists tended to be thwarted by a wait-and-see attitude.

In numbers and wealth, the Universalists, indeed, were at a disadvantage when the consolidation was finally achieved in 1961. Whether the new-found message Universalism brought to the merger would compensate for these deficiencies only time would tell. But there was no turning back. If there were inevitable doubts, a measure of reassurance could be had from the words of L. B. Fisher, written forty years before in a similar period of uncertainty: "Universalists are often asked to tell where they stand. The only true answer to give to this question is that we do not stand at all, we move."

PART TWO

Documents

Chapter Two

Forerunners and Founders

A belief in God's universal love to all his creatures, and that he will finally restore all those of them that are miserable to happiness, is a polar truth.

Dr. Benjamin Rush

A Universalist strain ran through much of American religious thinking in the eighteenth century. Many of the propagators of the belief that all men would be saved had no intention of furthering the development of a new religious denomination. They simply spoke the truth as they understood it. Although Charles Chauncy cannot be considered a denominational founder, for instance, omission of his widely read work would distort the early history of the movement. Thus this chapter will include selections not only from men like John Murray and Elhanan Winchester, but from those who were influential in the development of Universalism even though they were not later reckoned as founders.

The mystical frame of mind of Dr. George De Benneville (1703–1793) is best conveyed in his own words. His *Life and Trance*, translated from the French of the original, was published in 1800 through the efforts of Elhanan Winchester. Winchester, who knew some would consider the account of De Benneville's adventures absurd, apparently believed it himself and wanted to share with the world the experiences of "such an humble, pious, loving man. . . ."

De Benneville writes first of his early life in England, where his Huguenot family lived in refuge from persecution by the Catholic majority in France.

‘ ‘ \ ‘ ‘

As it was designed that I should learn navigation, I was
sent to sea in a vessel of war belonging to a little fleet bound to
the coast of Barbary with presents, and to renew the peace with
Algiers, Tunis, and Tripolis. Being arrived at Algiers, as I walked
upon deck I saw some Moors who brought some refreshments to
sell. One of them slipped down and tore a piece out of one of
his legs. Two of his companions, having lain him on the deck,
each of them kissed the wound, shedding tears upon it, then
turned towards the rising of the sun, they cried in such a manner
that I was much moved with anger at their making such a noise
and ordered my waiter to bring them before me. Upon demanding the reason of their noise, they perceived that I was angry,
asked my pardon, and told me the cause was owing to one of
their brothers having hurt his leg by a fall and that they kissed
the wound in order to sympathize with him, and likewise shed
tears upon it and took part with him; and as tears were saltish,
they [were] a good remedy to heal the same; and the reason of
their turning towards the sun's rising was to invoke him who created the sun to have compassion upon their poor brother, and
prayed he would please to heal him. Upon that I was so
convinced, and moved within, that I thought my heart would
break, and that my life was about to leave me. My eyes were
filled with tears, and I felt such an internal condemnation, that
I was obliged to cry out and say, "Are these Heathens? No; I
confess before God they are Christians, and I myself am a
Heathen!" Behold the first conviction that the grace of our Sovereign Good employed: he was pleased to convince a white person by blacks! One who carried the name of a Christian by a
pagan, and who was obliged to confess himself but a heathen.
But that was soon overcome and forgot. But God who always
seeks to convince and save his poor creatures, did not leave his
poor wandering sheep. For some time after my return home,
being present by invitation at a ball, and having over-heated
myself, I ordered my servant to prepare linen for me to change.
And as I was putting it on, I fell into a fainting fit, and had a vision of myself burning as a firebrand in hell. And coming to my-

self—again I cried out, "I am damned!" Prayers were desired in the French Churches for one who had lost his senses and was melancholy. The ministers often visited me, and would fain have made me believe that I had not committed any very great sins, and that I had behaved according to my rank and station. Then I was obliged to answer them that if they had no other things than those to tell me, they could answer no purpose but as fig leaves to cover my shame, and my damnable estate; that it was in vain to come and visit me with such comfort, for that I felt myself condemned. Then they answered me in another manner than before, saying, since I would not receive their remonstrances it might be looked upon as a mark that peradventure I was destined from the beginning to condemnation.

Then they gave me up and came no more to visit me. After that, I continued in the state of condemnation during the space of fifteen months, believing that all the world but myself might be saved, and that I never could be saved because my sins, as I thought, were too many and too great to be forgiven. At length, after the fifteen months were expired, after having passed through many temptations, it happened to me one day, having laid myself down to repose, that I was awakened out of my sleep, and heard a voice within me, which pronounced the sentence of my condemnation, and left me no room to hope. I then discovered the root of all my sins and iniquities within my heart. That discovery brought me into an extreme agony, and despair entered into my soul which was now pressed on all sides with misery, caused especially by such great unbelief and hardness of heart, which was the most insupportable of all my troubles. I could discover no remedy for my disease but thought that my sentence of damnation was going to be executed. The sorrow of my soul was even to death. I desired to die but death fled from me. I could find no remedy but to leave myself to the justice of my judge for a condemned criminal as I was. I knew that his judgments were just and that I had merited much more than I felt.

Thus abandoning myself to justice, and waiting for its accomplishment in me, I discovered between justice and me the criminal, one of a most majestic appearance, whose beauty, brightness and grandeur, can never be described. He cast such a look of grace and mercy upon me, and such a look of love as penetrated through me, the fire of which so embraced my soul that I loved him again with the same love. He persuaded me in my heart that he was my savior, mediator and reconciliator. And while I thought thereon, he began to intercede for me in this manner, saying, "My father, behold me with thy paternal regard. I have made expiation for this sinner, who has received in himself the sentence of condemnation. I have taken human nature for him. I have suffered all kind of ignominy for him. I have shed my blood even to the last drop for him. I have suffered the shameful death of the cross for him. I have descended into the abyss of hell for him, that I might deliver him. I have been put to death for his offences, and raised again for his justification, and where his sins abound, our grace abounds much more. Oh! my heavenly father, pardon this poor sinner, and cause thy mercy to come to him." The judge or justice had nothing more to say. The sentence disappeared. Then I heard his eternal universal voice, which penetrated through me with divine power, saying, "Take courage, my son, thy sins are forgiven thee." Immediately all the burden of my sins and iniquities was gone, all the stings and reproaches ceased in a moment; a living faith came in their stead, and the tears of sorrow were all wiped from my eyes. I cast myself at the feet of my mediator, reconciler, savior and intercessor, and embraced him with an enlivening faith, melting into tears of love, humility and nothingness.

.   .   .

. . . I received a voice of grace inwardly to go and preach the gospel in France. I resisted it more than once or twice, fearing persecution. But I was struck with a sickness and had pain like the agony of death, was ready to die; and knowing it was because I had not harkened to that voice that had called me to bear witness to the truth in France, I humbled myself before my God through Jesus Christ my Lord, asked pardon for my offences, and promising to submit myself to follow his voice, upon which I was immediately healed; and grew more robust than I had even been before. Then I heard his voice once more, calling me to go to France to preach the gospel, and I found myself obliged in my soul to follow the voice, though with fear and trembling.

I took passage at Dover for Calais, and immediately upon my arrival I began to preach and proclaim the good news in the market, even the eternal salvation by Jesus Christ within us; and that each one of us might be saved by pure grace, and that whosoever knowing himself, feeling the burden of his iniquities, having recourse to Jesus Christ, resigning himself without reserve, with all his sins, even had he found himself in his damnable estate, should be delivered and obtain the pardon of all his sins.

As soon as I had done, I was taken before a magistrate, who made me to know that my conduct was contrary to the statute of the king. I was then conducted to prison where I was no sooner arrived than all the fear of persecution vanished. My soul was strengthened in the Lord Jesus. I felt the love of my divine savior very near, accompanied with his divine light. After some days had past, I was brought before the justice, and examined by what order I preached. I told him who I was, and that I was drawn by the special grace of my God in Jesus Christ, by the power of his holy spirit, to teach the nations, and that for refusing to obey the voice of my God I was taken very sick. While they were examining me, there came in an old man with a white beard. All the justices saluted him. He said to them: "Have nothing to do with this person, for I have suffered much this night past on his account," and retired immediately.

I was then condemned to eight days imprisonment, as it was the first time, and to be conducted by the servant of the magistrate out of the bounds of the city, letting me know that if I was found employed in the same manner a second time my life would be in danger.

I was about 17 years of age when I began to preach in France. In this manner I employed two years in that kingdom, preaching the gospel in high and low Normandy, the country of my father, for he was born in the city of Rouen.

There were many ministers of us together: Messieurs Durant, de la Chevrette, Dumoulin, L'Achar, etc. We met together in mountains and woods, to the number of 400, where God very often wrought great wonders by the power of the gospel, among men and women, even boys and girls of the age of twelve or fifteen years, that did not even know how to read or write. They were convinced by the power of grace and began to proclaim the gospel with a most marvelous strength of spirit, without any fear, being embraced by love divine.

We were many times taken prisoners during the two years, sometimes by means of our own brothers, who would go and inform the soldiers in the Marshalsea where we were met together.

Many of us were hanged, others whipped by the hands of the hangman and branded with a hot iron; all their goods [were] confiscated, and they sent on board the galleys. But all that did not weaken us, but on the contrary, the grace of our divine love strengthened us in a wonderful manner.

At last we were surrounded by a party of soldiers one day when we were assembled by the side of Dieppe, where many of us were taken prisoners, among whom was myself, and a M. Durant, a young man about 24 years of age, of Geneva.

After a month imprisonment we were condemned to die, he to be hanged, and I to have my head cut off.* We were conducted together to the place of execution; he sang the 126th psalm when on the ladder, and died joyfully.

I was then conducted to the scaffold. My eyes were ordered to be bound to prevent my seeing, but on my earnest request that was omitted.

I then fell upon my knees, and praying the Lord that he would not require my blood at their hands, as they knew not what they did, my soul was filled with exceeding joy. The executioner bound my hands, and while he was employed in so doing, a courier arrived from the King, which was Louis XV, with a reprieve for the criminal. Immediately the joy of my heart was gone and darkness entered into my soul. I was then reconducted to prison at Paris where I was confined some time before I was liberated through the intercession of the Queen.

* The two forms of capital punishment distinguish De Benneville as a member of the nobility from Durant, a commoner.

Many things happened to me during my exile in France and the time of my confinement. One may easily discover here that the grace of our God never leaves those who trust in him and are faithful until death.

. . .

After I had passed about 18 years in Germany and Holland, I became sickly of a consumptive disorder occasioned by being greatly concerned for the salvation of souls and much disquieted because the greatest part by far walked in the ways of perverseness and neglected their conversion, which caused me great trouble. And I took it so to heart that I believed my happiness would be incomplete while one creature remained miserable. Sometimes I was a little comforted within by grace in some manner, but that did not last long.

I dwelt at that time in the country with the brethren near the city of Mons in Hainaut, near the borders of France, in the emperor's dominions.

My fever increased in such a manner as reduced me almost to a skeleton so that they were obliged to feed me as an infant. While I lay in this weak situation, I was favored through grace with many visions. In one it appeared to me that I was conducted into a fine plain filled with all kinds of fruit trees agreeable both to the sight and smell, loaded with all kinds of the most delicious fruits which came to my mouth and satisfied me as with a river of pleasure. [At the] same time I beheld the inhabitants. They were beautiful beyond expression, clothed in garments as white as snow. They were filled with humility, and their friendship and love was towards all beings. They saluted me with the most profound reverence and most lovely air, saying to me with the voice of love which penetrated through me: "Dear soul, take courage, be comforted, for in a little time you shall see the wonders of God in the restoration of all the human species without exception."

The weakness of my body so increased that I was certain of dying. I exhorted my brethren to be faithful unto death, to be steadfast, immovable, and to be always turning inward with an enlivening faith to behold with a fixed attention the Lamb of

God, with believing eyes, and to harken to his eternal word within them, and that they should receive of the fulness of Christ's grace upon grace, by which they should be strengthened to abide steadfast unto the end.

As I had communion with many assemblies of brethren, but in particular with that connected with my dear brother Marsey, the brethren there had a vision of my death and sent brother Marsey to see me.

When he arrived he found me in the agonies of death. He embraced me with a kiss of peace and love and saluted me in the name of the brethren, who recommended themselves to me, and desired that I would remember them before the throne of God and the Lamb.

He then took leave of me and I felt myself die by degrees, and exactly at midnight I was separated from my body* and saw the people occupied in watching it according to the custom of the country. I had a great desire to be freed from the sight of my body, and immediately I was drawn up as in a cloud and beheld great wonders where I passed, impossible to be written or expressed. I quickly came to a place which appeared to my eyes as a level plain, so extensive that my sight was not able to reach its limits, filled with all sorts of delightful fruit trees, agreeable to behold, and which sent forth such fragrant odors that all the air was filled as with incense. In this place I found that I had two guardians, one at my right hand and the other at my left, exceeding beautiful beyond expression, whose boundless friendship and love seemed to penetrate through all my inward parts. They had wings and resembled angels, having shining bodies and white garments.

, ,

De Benneville, using imagery reminiscent of the Book of Revelation and Dante's *Divine Comedy*, recounts in detail

* De Benneville's experience apparently was not unique. Dr. Benjamin Rush discusses cases of apparent death in his lectures "On Natural and Medical Sciences." See *The Selected Writings of Benjamin Rush*, ed. Dagobert D. Runes (New York, Philosophical Library, 1947), 160–164. (E. C.)

his visit to the realms of being beyond earthly life. He is conducted through the realms where souls are tormented for earthly sins into heaven where he witnesses the Son interceding for men with the Father and hears universal restoration of souls proclaimed.

‹ ‹

Then my guardian took me up and reconducted me to the house from whence I came, where I perceived the people assembled. And discovering my body in the coffin, I was re-united with the same and found myself lodged within my earthly tabernacle. And coming to myself, I knew my dear brother Marsey and many others who gave me an account of my being 25 hours in the coffin, and 17 hours before they put me in the coffin, which altogether made 42 hours. To me they seemed as many years. Beginning then to preach the universal gospel, I was presently put in prison but soon set at liberty again. I visited all my brethren, preaching the gospel and taking leave of them all, because that my God and Sovereign Good called me to go into America and preach the gospel there. I took my departure for the same in the 38th year of my age, and it is 41 years since I first arrived here. The 28th of July next, 1782, I shall be 79 years of age. Blessed be the name of the Lord forever.[1]

, ,

De Benneville founded no churches but his influence in behalf of Universalism was notable. He sponsored the publication of an American edition of Siegvolck's *The Everlasting Gospel*, referred to many times in testimonials of the spread of the faith. Elhanan Winchester is one example of a person profoundly influenced by it. De Benneville's mystical pietism, however, limited his influence on the whole to the pietistic groups among whom he worked and labored.

It is John Murray who figures as the first great organizer of Universalism as a distinct movement. His autobiography recounts in a colorful manner his conversion to Universalism in England, his migration to America in 1770, and his ultimate decision to preach. His strong personality comes through without doubt in the passages below. It is interesting that such a willful, self-assured man can write with a certain humor concerning his own failings.

Murray had heard many denunciations of James Relly in the Whitefieldian circles in which he travelled in London, denunciations all the more bitter because Relly had himself been a follower of George Whitefield but had broken with him on the subject of universal salvation. Whitefield considered Relly's particular formulation antinomian, an approach that could lead only to sin and corruption.

' '

. . . I had heard much of Mr. Relly; he was a conscientious, and zealous preacher, in the city of London. He had, through many revolving years, continued faithful to the ministry committed to him, and he was the theme of every religious sect. He appeared, as he was represented to me, highly erroneous; and my indignation against him . . . was very strong. I had frequently been solicited to hear him, merely that I might be an ear witness of what was termed his *blasphemies*; but, I arrogantly said, I would not be a *murderer of time*. Thus I passed on for a number of years, hearing all manner of evil said of Mr. Relly, and *believing all I heard*, while every day augmented the inveterate hatred, which I bore the man, and his adherents. When a worshipping brother, or sister, belonging to the communion, which I considered as honoured by the approbation of Deity, was, by this deceiver, drawn from the paths of rectitude, the anguish of my spirit was indescribable; and I was ready to say, the secular arm ought to interpose to prevent the perdition of souls. I recollect one instance in particular, which pierced me to the soul. A young lady, of irreproachable life, remarkable for piety, and highly respected by the Tabernacle congregation and church, of which I was a devout member, had been ensnared; to my great astonishment, she had been induced to hear, and having heard, she had embraced the pernicious errors of this detestable babbler; she was become a believer, a firm, and unwavering believer of universal redemption! Horrible! most horrible! So high an opinion was entertained of my talents, having myself been a teacher among the Methodists, and such was my standing in Mr. Whitefield's church, that I was deemed adequate to reclaiming this wanderer, and I was strongly urged to the pursuit. The poor, deluded young woman was abundantly worthy our most arduous efforts. *He, that coverteth the sinner from the error of his way, shall save a soul from death, and shall hide a multitude of sins.* Thus I thought, thus I said, and, swelled with a high idea of my own importance, I went, accompanied by two or three of my Christian brethren, to see, to converse with, and, if need were, to admonish this simple, weak, but, as we heretofore believed, meritorious female. Fully persuaded, that I could easily convince her of her errors, I entertained no doubt respecting the result of my undertaking. The young lady received us with much kindness and condescension, while, as I glanced my eye upon her fine countenance, beaming with intelligence, mingling pity and contempt grew in my bosom. After the first ceremonies, we sat for some time silent; at length I drew up a heavy sigh, and uttered a pathetic sentiment, relative to the deplorable condition of those, who live, and die in unbelief; and I concluded a violent declamation, by pronouncing, with great earnestness, *He, that believeth not, shall be damned.*

"And pray, sir," said the young lady, with great sweetness, "Pray, sir, what is the unbeliever damned for not believing?"

What is he damned for not believing? Why, *he is damned for not believing.*

"But, my dear sir, I asked what was that, which he did not believe, for which he was damned?"

Why, for not believing in Jesus Christ, to be sure.

"Do you mean to say, that unbelievers are damned, for not believing there was such a person as Jesus Christ?"

No, I do not; a man may believe there was such a person, and yet be damned.

"What then, sir, must he believe, in order to avoid damnation?"

Why he must believe, that Jesus Christ is a complete Saviour.

"Well, suppose he were to believe, that Jesus Christ was the complete Saviour of others, would this belief save him?"

No, he must believe, that Christ Jesus is his complete Saviour; every individual must believe for *himself, that Jesus Christ is his complete Saviour.*

"Why, sir, is Jesus Christ the Saviour of any *unbelievers?*"

No, madam.

"Why, then, should any *unbeliever* believe, that Jesus Christ is his Saviour, *if he be not his Saviour?*"

I say, he is not the Saviour of any one, until he believes.

"Then, if Jesus be not the Saviour of the *unbeliever,* until he *believes,* the *unbeliever* is called upon to believe a lie. It appears to me, sir, that Jesus is the complete Saviour of *unbelievers;* and that unbelievers are called upon to believe the truth; and that, *by believing, they are saved, in their own apprehension, saved from all those dreadful fears,* which are consequent upon a state of conscious condemnation."

No, madam; you are dreadfully, I trust not fatally, misled. Jesus never was, nor never will be, the Saviour of any unbeliever.

"Do you think Jesus is your Saviour, sir?"

I hope he is.

"Were you *always* a believer, sir?"

No, madam.

"Then you were once an unbeliever; that is, you once believed, that Jesus Christ was not your Saviour. Now, as you say, he never *was,* nor never *will be,* the Saviour of any *unbeliever;* as you were once an unbeliever, he never can be your Saviour."

He never was my Saviour, till I believed.

"Did he never die for you, till you believed, sir?"

Here I was extremely embarrassed, and most devoutly wished myself out of her habitation; I sighed bitterly, expressed deep commiseration for those deluded souls, who had nothing but head-knowledge; drew out my watch, *discovered it was late;*

and, recollecting an engagement, observed it was time to take leave.

I was extremely mortified; the young lady observed my confusion, but was too generous to pursue her triumph. I arose to depart; the company arose; she urged us to tarry; addressed each of us in the language of kindness. Her countenance seemed to wear a resemblance of the heaven, which she contemplated; it was stamped by benignity, and when we bade her adieu, she enriched us by her good wishes.

I suspected, that my religious brethren saw she had the advantage of me; and I *felt*, that her remarks were indeed *unanswerable*. My pride was hurt, and I determined to ascertain the exact sentiments of my associates, respecting this interview. Poor soul, said I, she is far gone in error. True, said they; but she is, notwithstanding, a very sensible woman. Ay, ay, thought I, they have assuredly discovered, that she has proved too mighty for me. Yes, said I, she has a great deal of *head* knowledge; but yet she may be a lost, damned soul. I hope not, returned one of my friends; she is a very good young woman. I saw, and it was with extreme chagrin, that the result of this visit had depreciated me in the opinion of my companions. But I could only censure and condemn, solemnly observing: It was better not to converse with any of those apostates, and it would be judicious never to associate with them upon any occasion. From this period, I myself carefully avoided every Universalist, and *most cordially did I hate* them. My ear was open to the public calumniator, to the secret whisperer, and I yielded credence to every scandalous report, however improbable. My informers were *good people*; I had no doubt of their veracity; and I believed it would be difficult to paint Relly, and his connexions, in colours too black.

.   .   .

. . . There was a religious society established in Cannon-street, in an independent meeting-house, for the purpose of elucidating difficult passages of scripture. This society chose for their president a Mr. Mason, who, although not a clerical gentleman, was, nevertheless, of high standing in the religious world: frequent applications were made to him, in the character of a physician to the sinking, sorrowing, sin-sick soul. His figure was commanding, and well calculated to fill the minds of young converts with religious awe. When this company of serious inquirers were assembled, the president addressed the throne of grace, in a solemn, and appropriate prayer, and the subject for the evening was next proposed. Every member of the society was indulged with the privilege of expressing his sentiments, for the space of five minutes; a glass was upon the table, which ran accurately the given term. The president held in his hand a small ivory hammer: when the speaker's time had expired, he had a right to give him notice by a stroke on the table, round which the assembled members were seated. But, if he approved of what was delivered, it was optional with him to extend the limits of his term. When the question had gone round the table, the president summed up the evidences, gave his own judgment, and, having proposed the question for the next evening, concluded with prayer.

Upon this society I was a constant attendant, and I was frequently gratified by the indulgence of the president and the implied approbation of the society. It was on the close of one of those evenings, which were to me very precious opportunities, that the president took me by the hand, and requested me to accompany him into the vestry. "Sit down, my good sir: you cannot but have seen, that I have long distinguished you in this society; that I have been pleased with your observations; and I have given indisputable evidence, that both my reason, and my judgment, approved your remarks." I bowed respectfully, and endeavoured to express my gratitude, in a manner becoming an occasion so truly flattering.

"My object," said he, "in seeking to engage you in private, is to request you would take home with you a pamphlet I have written against Relly's Union. I have long wondered, that some able servant of our Master has not taken up this subject. But, as my superiors are silent, I have been urged by a sense of duty to make a stand, and I have done all in my power to prevent the pernicious tendency of this soul-destroying book."

Although, at this period, I had never seen Relly's Union, yet my heart rejoiced, that Mason, this great and good man, had undertaken to write against it, and, from the abundance of my heart, my mouth overflowed with thankfulness.

"All that I request of you," said Mr. Mason, "is to take this manuscript home with you, and keep it till our next meeting. Meet me in this vestry, a little before the usual time. Read it, I entreat you, carefully, and favour me with your unbiassed sentiments." I was elated by the honour done me, and I evinced much astonishment at the confidence reposed in me. But he was pleased to express a high opinion of my judgment, abilities, and goodness of heart, and he begged leave to avail himself of those qualities, with which his fancy had invested me.

I took the manuscript home, perused it carefully, and with much pleasure, until I came to a passage at which I was constrained to pause, *painfully to pause.* Mr. Relly had said, speaking of the record, which God gave of his Son: *This life is in his Son, and he, that believeth not this record, maketh God a liar;* from whence, inferred Mr. Relly, it is plain, that God hath given this eternal life *in the Son* to unbelievers, as fully as to believers, *else the unbeliever could not, by his unbelief, make God a liar.* This, said Mr. Mason, *punning upon the author's name,* is just as clear, as that this writer is an *Irish Bishop.* I was grieved to observe, that Mr. Mason could say no more upon a subject so momentous; nor could I forbear allowing more, than I wished to allow, to the reasoning of Mr. Relly. Most devoutly did I lament, that the advantage in argument did not rest with my admired friend, Mason; and I was especially desirous, that this last argument should have been completely confuted. I was positive, *that God never gave eternal life to any unbeliever;* and yet I was perplexed to decide how, *if God had not given life to unbelievers,* they could possibly *make God a liar, by believing that he had not.* My mind was incessantly exercised, and greatly embarrassed upon this question. What is it to make any one a liar, but to deny the truth of what he has said? But, if God had no where said, he had given life to unbelievers, how could the *unbeliever make God a liar?* The stronger this argument seemed in favour of the grace and love of God, the more distressed and unhappy I became; and most earnestly did I wish, that Mr. Mason's pamphlet might contain something, that was more rational, more scriptural, than a *mere pun;* that he might be able to adduce proof positive, that the *gift* of God, which is everlasting life, was never *given to any, but believers.* I was indisputably assured, that I myself was a believer; and right precious did I hold my *exclusive* property in the Son of God.

At the appointed time, I met Mr. Mason in the vestry. "Well, sir, I presume you have read my manuscript?" I have, sir, and I have read it repeatedly. "Well, sir, speak freely, is there any thing in the manuscript which you dislike?" Why, sir, as you are so good as to indulge me with the liberty of speaking, I will venture to point out one passage, which appears to me not sufficiently clear. Pardon me, sir, but surely *argument, especially upon religious subjects, is preferable to ridicule, to punning upon the name of an author.* "And where, pray, is the objectionable paragraph, to which you advert?" I pointed it out; but, on looking in his face, I observed his countenance fallen, it was no longer toward me. Mr. Mason questioned my judgment, and never afterward honoured me by his attention. However, I still believed *Mason right, and Relly wrong;* for if Relly were right, the conclusion was unavoidable, *all men must finally be saved.* But this was out of the question, utterly impossible; all religious denominations agreed to condemn this heresy, to consider it as a damnable doctrine, and what every religious denomination united to condemn, must be false.

, ,

In his flight from personal misfortunes to the shores of a new world in 1770, Murray had—he thought—resolutely left behind his religious connections. Old Thomas Potter, his host at Good Luck, on Cranberry Inlet, Barnegat Bay, New Jersey, where Murray's ship was becalmed, had other ideas. Potter attempted to persuade Murray to preach in the meetinghouse he had built years before with the full assurance that God would send him a preacher who would bring the message of universal salvation.

‹ ‹

My mind continued subjected to the most torturing reflections. I could not bring myself to yield to the entreaties of Mr. Potter, and still I urged the necessity of departing, the moment the wind would answer. Mr. Potter was positive the wind would not change, until I had spoken to the people. Most ardently did I desire to escape the importunities of this good man. The idea of a crowd, of making a public exhibition of myself, was, to my desolate, woe-worn mind, intolerable; and the suspense, in which I was held, was perfectly agonizing. I could not forbear acknowledging an uncommon coincidence of circumstances. The hopes and fears of this honest man, so long in operation, yet he evinced great warmth of disposition, and was evidently tinctured with enthusiasm; but, after making every allowance for these propensities, it could not be denied, that an over-ruling Power seemed to operate, in an unusual, and remarkable manner. I could not forbear looking back upon the mistakes, made during our passage, even to the coming in to this particular inlet, where no vessel, of the size of the brig "Hand-in-Hand," had ever before entered; every circumstance contributed to bring me to this house. Mr. Potter's address on seeing me; his assurance, that he knew I was on board the vessel, when he saw her at a distance: all these considerations pressed with powerful conviction on my mind, and I was ready to say, If God Almighty has, in his providence, so ordered events, as to bring me into this country for the purpose of making manifest the savour of his name, and of bringing many to the knowledge of the truth; though I would infinitely prefer death, to entering into a character, which will subject me to what is infinitely worse than death; yet, as the issues of life and death are not under my direction, am I not bound to submit to the dispensations of providence? I wished, however, to be convinced, that it was the will of God, that I should step forth in a character, which would be considered as obnoxious, as truly detestable. I was fully convinced, it was not by the will of the flesh, nor by the will of the world, nor by the will of the god of this world; all these were strongly opposed thereto. One moment, I felt my resolution give way; the path, pointed out, seemed to brighten upon me: but the next, the difficulties, from within and without, obscured the prospect, and I relapsed into a firm resolution to shelter myself, in solitude, from the hopes, and fears, and the various contentions of men.

While I thus balanced, the Sabbath advanced. I had ventured to implore the God, who had sometimes condescended to indulge individuals with tokens of his approbation, graciously to indulge me, upon this important occasion; and that, if it were his will, that I should obtain the desire of my soul, by passing through life in a private character. If it were *not* his will, that I should engage as a preacher of the ministry of reconciliation, he would vouchsafe to grant me such a wind, as might bear me from this shore, before the return of another Sabbath. I determined to take the changing of the wind for an answer; and, had the wind changed, it would have borne on its wings full conviction, because it would have corresponded with my wishes. But the wind changed not, and Saturday morning arrived. "Well," said my anxious friend, "now let me give notice to my neighbours." No, sir, not yet; should the wind change by the middle of the afternoon, I must depart. No tongue can tell, nor heart conceive, how much I suffered this afternoon; but the evening came on, and it was necessary I should determine; and at last, with much fear and trembling, I yielded a reluctant consent. Mr. Potter then immediately dispatched his servants, on horseback, to spread the intelligence far and wide, and they were to continue their information, until ten in the evening.

I had no rest through the night. What should I say, or how address the people? Yet I recollected the admonition of our Lord: "*Take no thought, what you shall say; it shall be given you, in that same hour, what you shall say.*" Ay, but this promise was made to his disciples. Well, by this, I shall know if I am a disciple. If God, in his providence, is committing to me a dispensation of the Gospel, He will furnish me with matter, without my thought, or care. If this thing be not of God, He will desert me, and this shall be another sign; on this, then, I rested. Sunday morning succeeded; my host was in transports. I was—I cannot describe how I was. I entered the house; it was neat and convenient, expressive of the character of the builder. There were no pews; the pulpit was rather in the Quaker mode; the seats were constructed with backs roomy, and even elegant. I said there were no pews; there was one large square pew, just before the pulpit; in this sat the venerable man and his family, particular friends, and visiting strangers. In this pew sat, upon this occasion, this happy man, and, surely, no man, upon this side heaven, was ever more completely happy. He looked up to the pulpit with eyes sparkling with pleasure; it appeared to him, as the fulfilment of a promise long deferred; and he reflected, with abundant consolation, on the strong faith, which he had cherished, while his associates would tauntingly question, "Well, Potter, where is this minister, who is to be sent to you?" "He is coming along, in God's own good time." "And do you still believe any such preacher will visit you?" "O yes, assuredly." He reflected upon all this, and tears of transport filled his eyes; he looked round upon the people, and every feature seemed to say, "There, what think you now?" When I returned to his house, he caught me in his arms, "Now, now, I am willing to depart; Oh, my God! I will praise thee; thou hast granted me my desire. After this truth I have been seeking, but I have never found it, until now; I knew, that God, who put it into my heart to build a house for his worship, would send a servant of his own to proclaim his own gospel. I knew, he would; I knew the time was come, when I saw the vessel grounded; I knew, you were the man, when I saw you approach my door, and my heart leaped for joy." Visitors poured into the house; he took each by the hand. "This is the happiest day of my life," said the transported man: "There, neighbours, there is the minister God promised to send me; how do you like God's minister?" I ran from the company, and prostrating myself before the throne of grace, besought my God to take me, and do with me, whatever he pleased. I am, said I, I am, O Lord God, in thine hand, as clay in the hand of the potter. If thou, in thy providence, hast brought me into this new world to make known, unto this people, the grace and the blessings of the new covenant; if thou hast thought proper, by making choice of so weak an instrument, to confound the wise; if thou hast been pleased to show to a babe, possessing neither wisdom nor prudence, what thou hast hid from the wise and prudent,—be it so, O Father, for so it seemeth good in thy sight. But, O my merciful God! leave me not, I beseech thee, for a single moment; for without thee, I can do nothing. O, make thy strength perfect in my weakness, that the world may see that thine is the power, and that, therefore, thine ought to be the glory. Thus my heart prayed, while supplicating tears bedewed my face.

I felt, however, relieved and tranquillized, for I had power given me to trust in the name of the Lord; to stay upon the God of my salvation. Immediately upon my return to the company, my boatmen entered the house: "The wind is fair, sir." Well, then, we will depart. It is late in the afternoon, but no matter, I will embark directly; I have been determined to embrace the first opportunity, well knowing the suspense the captain must be in, and the pain attendant thereon. Accordingly, as soon as matters could be adjusted, I set off; but not till my old friend, taking me by the hand, said: "You are now going to New-York; I am afraid you will, when there, forget the man, to whom your Master sent you. But I do beseech you, come back to me again as soon, as possible." The tears gushed into his eyes, and, regarding me with a look, indicative of the strongest affection, he threw his arms around me, repeating his importunities, that I would not unnecessarily delay my return. I was greatly affected, reiterating the strongest assurances, that I would conform to his wishes. Why should I not? said I; what is there to prevent me? I do not know an individual in New-York; no one knows me; what should induce me to tarry there? "Ah, my friend," said he, "you will find many in New-York, who will love and admire you, and they will wish to detain you in that city. But you have promised you will return, and I am sure you will perform your promise; and in the mean time, may the God of heaven be with you." Unable to reply, I hurried from his door; and, on entering the vessel, I found the good old man had generously attended, to what had made no part of my care, by making ample provision, both for me and the boatmen, during our little voyage.

I retired to the cabin; I had leisure for serious reflections, and serious reflections crowded upon me. I was astonished, I was lost in wonder, in love, and in praise; I saw, as evidently as I could see any object, visibly exhibited before me, that the good hand of God was in all these things. It is, I spontaneously exclaimed, it is the Lord's doings! and it is marvellous in my eyes.

.   .   .

The combined efforts of the clergy in Philadelphia barred against me the door of every house of public worship in the city. Bachelor's-Hall was in Kensington. But at Bachelor's-Hall the people attended, and a few were enabled to believe the good word of their God. There was in the city, a minister of the Seventh-day Baptist persuasion; for a season he appeared attached to me, but soon became very virulent in his opposition. He told me, he passed on foot nine miles, upon the return of every Saturday, to preach. I asked him, how many his congregation contained? "About an hundred." How many of this hundred do you suppose are elected to everlasting life? "I cannot tell." Do you believe fifty are elected? "Oh no, nor twenty." Ten perhaps? "There may be ten." Do you think the non-elect can take any step to extricate themselves from the tremendous situation, in which the decrees of heaven have placed them? "Oh no, they might as well attempt to pull the stars from the firmament of heaven." And do you think your preaching can assist them? "Certainly not; every sermon they hear will sink them deeper, and deeper in damnation." And so, then, you walk nine miles every Saturday, to sink ninety persons out of a hundred deeper and deeper in never-ending misery!

Reports, injurious to my peace, were now very generally circulated; and although I expected all manner of evil would be said of me falsely, for his sake, whose servant I was, yet did the shafts of slander possess a deadly power, by which I was sorely wounded. Had the poisoned weapon been aimed by characters, wicked in the common acceptation of the word, it would have fallen harmless; nay, the fire of their indignation would have acted as a purifier of my name; but reports, originating from those, who were deemed holy and reverend—alas! their bite was mortal. Again I sighed for retirement, again I hastened to the bosom of my patron, and again my reception was most cordial. Yet, although so much evil was said of me, many, glancing at the source, made candid deductions, and were careful to proportion their acts of kindness to the magnitude of my wrongs. Invitations met me upon the road, and, wafted upon the wings of fame, I could enter no town, or village, which my name had not reached; in which I did not receive good, and evil treatment. The clergy and their connexions were generally inveterate enemies; while those, who had will and power to act for themselves, and chanced to be favourably impressed, were very warm in their attachments. Thus my friends were very *cordial*, and my enemies very malignant; and, as my enemies were generally at a distance, and my friends at my elbow, but for officious individuals, who brought me intelligence of all they heard, I might have gone on my way with abundant satisfaction. At Brunswick, which I had been earnestly solicited to visit, I was received into a most worthy family. The Rev. Mr. Dunham was of the Seventh-day Baptist persuasion; a man of real integrity, who, although he could not see, as I saw, threw open the doors of his meeting-house; conducted me into his pulpit; and discharged toward me, in every particular, the duty of a Christian. His neighbour, a clergyman, who was a First-day Baptist, exhibited a complete contrast to Mr. Dunham. He invited me, it is true, to his house; asked me to lodge there; we conversed together, prayed together, he appeared very kind, and much pleased, and I believed him my confirmed friend, until, leaving Brunswick, I called upon some, whose deportment to me was the reverse of what it had heretofore been. I demanded a reason; when they frankly informed me, that the Rev. Mr. ———— had made such representations, as had destroyed all the pleasure, they had been accustomed to derive from my presence. This affected me beyond expression, a stranger as I was; and, suffering in the dread of what I had to expect, I turned from the door of those deceived persons, without uttering a word. I quitted their habitations forever; invidious remarks were made upon my silence; but of these I was careless; on other occasions I might have been affected, but treachery from a man, who had entertained me so hospitably, and who stood so high in the ranks of piety, shocked me beyond the power of utterance.

Upon the afternoon of this day, on which I had been so deeply hurt, I was engaged to deliver my peaceful message in the pulpit of Mr. Dunham, in the vicinity of this perfidious man. Some time had elapsed since I had seen him, and I then met him upon the road; he advanced toward me with an extended hand, and a countenance expressive of Christian affection: "You are a great stranger, sir." Yes, sir, I am a stranger, and sojourner, in every place, as all my fathers were before me. "Well, how have you been, since I saw you?" Thanks be to God, I have been preserved, and owned, and blessed, notwithstanding the slanders of the adversary, and his agents. He saw he was detected, and he determined immediately to drop the mask. "Well, I will do all in my power to obstruct your progress, in every place." Had you, sir, made this declaration at an earlier period, I should at least have believed you an honest man. But to pass yourself upon me as my friend, my sincere friend, while you were aiming at me a vital stab! Oh sir, I am astonished at you. "And I am more astonished at you; do you not tremble, when you think, that God must have a quarrel with you? and that all His ministers in America hate you?" Sir, I do not believe my Creator is a quarrelsome Being, neither do I credit the information, that all God's ministers hate me; a minister of God is incapable of hating any human being. "But are you not confounded, when you consider, that you must be right, and we wrong; or you wrong, and all God's ministers right? Surely, it is more probable we should be all right, and you wrong, than you right, and we all wrong." I have no apprehensions upon this head; some one might have questioned, in the days of Elijah, when he was opposed by eight hundred and fifty prophets: "Do you not tremble to see all these holy, and reverend priests on one side, and you alone on the other? either they must be wrong, and you right, or you wrong, and they right." So in Jerusalem, our divine Master might have been asked: "Are you not appalled at beholding all the ministers of God, all the rulers of the people, in opposition? Either they must be wrong, and you right, or you wrong, and they right; and which, pray, is the most probable?" And the people might have been asked: "Have any of our rulers believed on him? He is a Devil, and mad, why hear ye him?" "I am astonished at your dar-

ing blasphemy, in comparing yourself either to Elijah, or
Christ." Why, was not Elijah a man of like passions with us? and
are we not taught to put on the Lord Jesus Christ? Who is it
that asks, If they have called the Master of the house Beelzebub?
what ought the servants of his household to expect? Elijah is a
member in the same body with me; but the Redeemer is still
nearer; He is my head, the head of every man; He indulges me
with the privilege of denying myself, my sinful self, and he allows me to acknowledge no other than his blessed self; that, thus
standing in his name, I may stand in the presence of the Father,
the *Divinity*, with exceeding joy; that, asking in the name of his
immaculate humanity, I may be sure to receive, that my joy may
be full. Nor can all that you, nor any one else can say, be able to
shake me from this my strong hold. "Ay, perhaps you may be
mistaken—you may be deceived." If I am deceived, I am deceived; but I will venture. "You know this is not the privilege of
all, and therefore it may not be yours." I do not know, that this
is not the privilege of all; but, if it be of any, it is of the believer;
and, as I believe, it must be mine. They shall, said my divine
Master, say all manner of evil of you, *falsely*. You, sir, have been
in Brunswick, fulfilling this scripture; and I rejoice, that I have
made the discovery. You can never deceive me again; but, as I
am not naturally suspicious, others may obtain a lease of my
good opinion, from which they will never, but upon the strongest conviction, be ejected. I left this good man beyond measure
enraged; and, no doubt, believing he should really render God
service, by doing me the most essential injury. I immediately re-
paired to the pulpit of my friend Dunham, where, preaching
peace, I recovered my lost serenity; and it gladdened my heart to
believe, that the inveterate enemy, with whom I had parted
upon the road, was included in the redemption it was my business to proclaim.[2]

, ,

The message which so enraged Murray's opposition was
Relly's peculiar exposition of universal salvation. Relly's book
Union maintained that Christ and man were so closely iden-

tified—Christ being the "head" of mankind—that Adam's sin was Christ's sin (as well as man's) and Christ's death atoned once and for all for man's sin.

ɩ ɩ

Union between *Christ* and the *Church*, is a matter universally acknowledged; where that deference, which is justly due to the scriptures, is paid: though, it is a subject very rarely treated of: Which silence concerning it, implies, either a general ignorance of the nature thereof, or, that it is respected as a matter, neither conducive to the glory of God, nor the happiness of mankind: and therefore not necessary to be taught. And where the nature thereof is in some measure known amongst men, and the utility of the doctrine allowed, they are much divided about its antiquity; before our believing, or faith in Christ, say some: Whilst others with as much strenuousness assert the contrary. But, if what I have already offered to the consideration of the public, shall be allowed to have any weight, or argumentative force; it will appear, that our *union* with *Christ* is not only antecedent to our faith, and believing, but also to all that *he* did, and suffered, for us men and for our salvation. The matter proposed in the gospel to be believed is true: and relates to the person of Christ and his benefits. That he was the Son of God, the Christ, the true *Messiah*, the *I am*, is a matter proposed to be believed, upon the credit of the divine testimony: Because this is a truth, therefore it is to be believed, and as it is a truth before believing; it is evident that it is not made a truth by believing; but is in itself a truth, perfect, and permanent, whether believed or not.

So also with relation unto his benefits, that the Father is well pleased in the beloved Son, is a truth; to be believed: and not to be made a truth, by believing. "I have blotted out as a thick cloud thy transgressions, and as a cloud thy sins, return unto me, for I have redeemed thee." Isa. xliv. 22. This positive testimony of redemption, and the forgiveness of sins, is declared unto them who believed not; upon the credit of which truth, they are called upon to return unto their God. "Cry unto her

that her warfare is accomplished, that her iniquity is pardoned."
Isa. xl. 2. This was a truth concerning those who knew it not,
and was to be declared unto them as such, that they believing it,
might be comforted. That he hath "put away sin by the sacrifice
of himself," was delivered for our offences, and raised again for
our justification, is true; and therefore recorded to be credited,
and rejoiced in. And, if it appear that the gospel is true before
our believing, then *union* with *Christ* before *faith* is true; The
latter being necessary to the truth of the former; as I have sufficiently shewn under the first proposition in this treatise; where
the *necessity* of union with him, not only as previous unto our
faith in him, but also unto his suffering for our sins, I think appears pretty obvious. That God loved mankind before Jesus died
for them, the scriptures affirm: where they made the latter, a
fruit of the former; and if God loved them before, he certainly
saw them in a sinless state; for it is contrary to the holiness of
his nature, to love the *unclean*, being of purer eyes than to behold iniquity: But in themselves, as related unto the earthy
Adam, they were unclean: Therefore he must have beheld them
in Christ, loved them in *him:* which if true, then were they in
him: And, as being in him in this sense, doth not suppose their
knowledge of his person, through the belief of the gospel, but a
passivity with respect to them; as branches hidden in the stock,
or the woman in the man; it implies the closest union, and the
necessity thereof (before their believing) to render and preserve
them objects worthy of the divine love and favour.

Jesus in his appeal unto the Father, says, "thou hast
loved them, as thou hast loved me." And again; "thou lovedst
me before the foundation of the world." In those words, the
love of the Father unto the Son, is represented as the grand Ar-
chetype of his love unto the people: The Father loved the Son
before the foundation of the world; but saith the Son, thou hast
loved *them*, as thou hast loved *me*. The Father loved the Son, as
the brightness of his glory, and his own express image: But saith
the Son, thou hast loved *them*, as thou hast loved *me*. The Father loved the Son, and preferred him before angels, having not
said unto any of them, thou art my Son, this day have I begotten thee: But saith the Son, of the children of men, thou hast

loved *them* as thou hast loved *me*. The Father loves the Son
with everlasting, unchangeable delight and pleasure: But saith
the Son, thou hast loved *them* as thou hast loved *me*. The Father loveth the Son, and hath revealed it unto him, yea, hath
given him the knowledge of it above measure: But, saith the
Son, "that the world may know that thou hast sent me, and hast
loved them as thou hast loved me." From all which it appears,
that *Christ* and the *Church*, are one object of the Father's love;
of his choice, good-will, delight, and pleasure. *He* the head, and
they the body, constituting the elect precious, the Man beloved
of God and accepted. But the head being the *medium*, between
God, and the body, hath the pre-eminence in all things. And, as
the head was never without the body, nor the body without the
head in the Lord, the body hath always been by *union* with the
head, entitled unto all the blessings, honours, and glories
thereof.[3]

, ,

Since Murray indulged in extempore preaching, his sermons as published are reconstructions after the fact and do not
display in pure form the sudden flights of allegorical fancy for
which he was famous. The following extract, therefore, is probably a pale example of his exposition of the union of Christ and
men.

‹ ‹

The motto of the Christian is, not unto us, not unto us;
but unto thy name, O Lord, be all the glory. Offences against
the Majesty of heaven are committed, and for those offences the
Lamb of God is, by the Father of angels and of men, delivered
up!!

But for whom was this Lamb of God delivered up? This
is a most important question. If God delivered him up for me, I
cannot be delivered up and cast into prison for myself. If God
raised him up for my justification, then I am justified; and if I
am justified, who is he that condemneth? But if he were not delivered up to death for my offences, I must be delivered up for

myself: for God is true and he hath said, *the soul that sinneth shall die*. If he were not raised for my justification, then I am not justified by his resurrection; but if not by his resurrection, I cannot be justified in any other way, for we are informed, Acts iv. 12, "Neither is there salvation in any other: for there is none other name under heaven given among men, whereby we must be saved."

Either therefore Jesus Christ was delivered up for my offences, and raised again for my justification, or he was not. If he were, I am to all intents and purposes saved in Jesus Christ with an everlasting salvation. If he were not, I am to all intents and purposes, doomed to everlasting misery. For he were not delivered up for my offences, then he never can be; for having died once, he dieth no more, and without shedding of blood there can be no remission of sins.

It is then of the last importance for us to determine whether he was delivered up for us or not. But how are we to determine this momentous question? It is a generally received opinion that Jesus Christ was not delivered up for all. Well, if I could determine who those were for whom he was not delivered up, I should say nothing to them, because it would be to no effect. But you will say, we do not know who they are; then certainly we do not know who the others are, and therefore we cannot with propriety preach to any individual. We cannot exhort any one in particular to glorify God in their body or spirit, because we cannot decisively say, "ye are bought with a price." If it be said Jesus was delivered up for the elect, still we are at a loss to distinguish the elect; the scriptures do not call them by name, neither are they designated from the rest of mankind by any peculiar excellency. On the contrary, there are writers who assure us that God, to show the greatness of his mercy, has made choice of the greatest offenders among the human race! But could not God have shown the greatness of his mercy by the *quantity*, as well as the *quality*? and does not God in a redemption so partial, appear a respecter of persons? nay, is it not a reflection upon his justice to suppose that he chooses his elect for the greatness of their offences?

But again; How am I to determine that I am one of the

Forerunners and Founders 75

elect? Why, I must look into my own heart: but looking into my own heart I must be forever at a loss, since if I trust my own heart, I am a fool. My heart is deceitful above all things. If I take the word of another, still I am in an error, for man in his best estate is vanity: and as I cannot know the reprobate until his death, so neither can I, until that period, discern the elect; for in this state all things change, marks and evidences may fail, and he who is to-day eminent, may to-morrow be cast down, while the hard heart may be softened, and the transgressor may apparently turn from that thorny path which is indeed hard.

Yet we are exhorted to make our calling and our election *sure*; but in doing this we must have recourse to the *sure* word of prophecy, to which we do well to give heed, as to a light shining in a dark place. Here indeed we shall be able to render it *certain* and to our never failing satisfaction, that we are truly the called and elected of God; that we are called and elected in him, who was the called, and the elect precious; that we are *members* of his *body*, of his *flesh*, and of *his bone*.

We are told that the scriptures of the Old and New Testament are the only rule given to direct us, how we may glorify God. Surely the way to glorify God, is to give credit to his word. Thus Abraham was strong in faith, giving glory to God. The only *certain* rule by which we can determine who they are, for whom God delivered up Jesus Christ to death, or for whose offences he was delivered up, and for whose justification he was raised again, is the unerring word of God. This sacred word will assure us, that the righteous God, who without respect of persons, denounced in his righteous law, an irrevocable curse, upon every one who continued not in all things written in the book thereof, to do them, by his grace delivered up Christ Jesus, once for *all*, gave him to be a ransom for *all*, and that he is therefore the Saviour of *all*. But we are told *all*, does not mean *all*, and therefore we should have no dependance on such testimonies. Well, should this be the case, which, blessed be God, it is not, yet we are not left without witnesses; for the sacred oracles assure us, that Jesus Christ, by the grace of God, tasted death for every man, and thus became the propitiation for our sins, and not for ours only, but for the sins of the whole world.

Such is the magnitude of that mercy exhibited by him who is the just God and the Saviour, that when manifested in the character *Son*, the Son born unto us, it was not to condemn the world, but that the world *through him might be saved*. Believing these glad tidings of good things, we say to every sinner, "*By grace ye are saved*," and as many as accept our report, enter into rest, and are saved from the condemnation of their own consciences; their hearts condemn them not. Why? Because they have the answer of a good conscience, by the resurrection of Jesus Christ from the dead." They are not under the "spirit of bondage again to fear." They know the *just God is the Saviour*, that they lost their lives according to that law, which proclaimeth, *the soul that sinneth shall assuredly die*, and that therefore their faith cannot make void the law. Did the justice of God demand the death of the sinner? Then the justice of God has received its demand, and hence the love of Christ constrained the apostles, when they thus judged, "that if one died for all, then were all dead." It is from the records of truth we learn, that the death of the Redeemer of men, is the death of all men, "for it pleased the Father that in him all fulness should dwell," it was therefore that he must needs suffer, and then enter into his glory. Did it please the Lord to bruise him, when his soul was made an offering for sin, it was, that mercy and truth should meet together, that righteousness and peace should embrace each other, and that God who had said he would by no means clear the guilty, and that he would bruise the hairy scalp of them who went on in iniquity, with all the other threatenings of his law, might still be the just God and the Saviour. If the death of Jesus Christ was the death of every man, then this was really the case, and the law was not against the promises, nor does our faith in them make void the law. If it were not the case, then, consistent with truth and justice, no sinner can be saved, nor would it have been necessary for the Saviour to have suffered; nay, consistent with truth and justice, he could not have suffered. The justice in condemning and punishing the Redeemer, and exempting the offender, is based on that mysterious union, subsisting between the head and members, Christ being *absolutely* the head of every man; thus the one is the many, the many gathered into one; and thus, looking with a single eye, we behold the death of the head, the death of the members, *all the members. One member may die and the rest live, but if the head die, all the members die with it.*

Hence the death of Christ was the death of all men, and he, now living, to die no more, emphatically, and most affectingly says, "Because I live ye shall live also:" and it is therefore he is called the life of the world, that the world may live through him. . . .

It is in this divinely glorious, consistent plan, that all the scriptures harmonize. In this view they are all *yea* and *amen* to the glory of the Father. This is the gospel, the everlasting gospel, which by the grace of God is now preached unto you.

Blessed are the people who know the joyful sound, they walk in the light of God's countenance, they shall never come into condemnation, nor shall they ever be ashamed, world without end.[4]

, ,

Jonathan Mayhew of the West Church in Boston was one of the first in the Congregational churches to question the proposition that God had predestined a large portion of mankind to everlasting misery. He could not reconcile this proposition with his idea of the benevolence of God. The fact that Mayhew and others questioned the propriety of such a belief is a measure of the intellectual and moral chasm that had developed between Calvin in the sixteenth century and some of his spiritual descendents in the American Congregational churches of 1763.

‹ ‹

What shall we say to the doctrine of God's having reprobated a great proportion of mankind; or, from eternity devoted them in his absolute decree and purpose to eternal torments, without any respect or regard to any sins of theirs as the procuring and meritorious cause of their perdition? And this, at the same time, to make manifest and glorify his JUSTICE! What can be said of this; and how shall it be reconciled with the supposition that God's tender mercies are over all his works?

I will tell you, in a very few words, what I have to say to it at present. And that is, first, that if any persons really hold such a doctrine, neither any man on earth nor angel in heaven can reconcile it with the goodness of God. And secondly, that I have not the least inclination to attempt a reconciliation of these doctrines; being persuaded that they are just as contrary as light and darkness, Christ and Belial; that one of them is most true and scriptural, joyful to man, and honorable to God; and the other most false and unscriptural, horrible to the last degree to all men of an undepraved judgment, and blasphemous against the God of heaven and earth. Neither is it possible for any man who really believes what the Scriptures teach concerning the goodness of God even to think of this other doctrine but with great indignation." . . .

The consideration of God's goodness and mercy, particularly as manifested in the Scriptures, in the redemption of the world by Christ, naturally suggests very pleasing hopes, and a glorious prospect, with reference to the conclusion, or final result of that most wonderful interposition of grace. It cannot be denied that ever since the apostasy of our first parents there have been, and still are, some things of a dark and gloomy appearance, when considered by themselves. So much folly, superstition, and wickedness there is "in this present evil world." But when we consider the declared end of Christ's manifestation in the flesh, to give his life a ransom for all, and to destroy the works of the devil; when we consider the numerous prophecies concerning the destruction of sin and death, and the future glory of Christ's kingdom ON EARTH; when we consider that he must reign till he hath put *all* enemies under his feet, the last of which is death—and until he hath subdued *all* things to himself; when we reflect, that according to the apostle Paul, where sin has abounded grace does much more abound, and that the same creature (or creation) which was originally made subject to vanity is to be delivered from the bondage of corruption into the glorious liberty of the children of God; when we consider the parallel which is instituted and carried on by the same apostle betwixt the first and second Adam, in his epistle to the Romans, and his express assertion in another that, "as in Adam *all die,* even so in Christ shall *all* be made alive, *but every man in his own order;"* in a word, when we duly consider that there is a certain restitution of *all things,* spoken by the mouth of all the holy prophets since the world began; when we duly consider these things, I say, light and comfort rise out of darkness and sorrow.

And we may, without the least presumption, conclude in general that, in the revolution of ages, something far more grand, important, and glorious than any thing which is vulgarly imagined, shall actually be the result of Christ's coming down from heaven to die on a cross, of his resurrection from the dead, and of his being crowned with glory and honor, as Lord both of the *dead* and the *living.* The word of God, and his mercy, endure forever; nor will he leave any thing which is truly his work unfinished.[5]

, ,

Mayhew is a good example of those who had become more ethical than the Calvinistic God. They sought to interpret Christianity in such a way as to rid it of the unpalatable doctrines which represented God as a vengeful being and to adapt it to the world-view of the eighteenth century Enlightenment.

Charles Chauncy, pastor of the First Church in Boston, proved to be the most effective of the liberal Congregational churchmen. Although he hesitated for years for reasons of prudence to publish his belief in universalism, his *Salvation of All Men* (1784) was to have great impact for years to come.

Chauncy was probably the first of a long line of universalists whose exegesis of αἰών and αἰώνιος attempted to demonstrate that these Greek words never should have been translated as "forever" or "everlasting."

' '

It is obvious to remark, that the substantive αιων, and its derivative αιωνιος, commonly translated in the Bible eternity, eter-

nal, or *everlasting*, MAY signify *a limited duration*. None acquainted with Greek will deny this, because they know, or easily may know whenever they please, that they are in fact often used in this sense, in the sacred writings. . . .

Now, from this remark only, had we nothing further to say, it follows, that the preceding evidence, in favour of *universal salvation*, remains strong and valid, notwithstanding the *scripture* has joined the word αιωνιος, translated *everlasting*, with the *punishment* of wicked men, in the future world; because this same word is often used, in the *scripture itself*, to signify a *limited* duration only. Though therefore it is true, not only that the wicked shall be bid, at the great day, to *depart* away, εις το πυρ το αιωνιον, *into everlasting fire*; but that they shall likewise, in consequence of this doom, actually go away, εις κολασιν αιωνιον, *into everlasting punishment:* Yet it MAY notwithstanding be as true, that they shall, in the final issue of things, be made *happy*; because the scriptures have informed us, in numerous places, that the word αιωνιος MAY mean nothing more than a *limited period of duration*. All I insist upon, in consequence of the present remark, is only this, that the word αιωνιος, translated *everlasting*, MAY signify a *period of time only*; and if it MAY be construed in this sense, there is not the shadow of an interference between its connection with the *punishment* of wicked men, and their being *finally saved*. In order to destroy the above evidence, in a way of strict and conclusive reasoning from this word, it must be shown, that it not only means an *endless duration*, but that it cannot be understood in any other sense; which every one, that knows any thing of Greek, knows to be beside the truth of fact.

These words, αιων and αιωνιος, are evidently more *loose* and *general* in their meaning, than the English words *eternity*, *everlasting*, by which they are commonly rendered in our Bibles. If it were not so, how comes it to pass, that αιων and αιωνιος will not always bear being translated *eternity*, *everlasting*? It would many times sound quite harsh to call that, in English, *eternal* or *everlasting*, which yet, with great propriety, might have the word αιωνιος joined with it. A few examples will bring this down to the lowest understanding. *Before the eternal times* is an impropriety in English; but προχρονων αιωνιων is a beautiful Greek phrase, put-

ting us upon looking back beyond *former ages:* The translators
of the New Testament have accordingly rendered it, Tit. i. 2,
Before the world began. So when our Saviour says to his apostles,
and to their successors, for their encouragement in their work,
"Lo, I am with you alway," εως της συντελειας του αιωνος; the words
are a promise very easily and naturally assuring them of his
presence, *through the whole time of the gospel-dispensation.* It is
accordingly rendered, in our Bibles, "even to the end of the
world:" But the natural force of the English word *eternal* would
not allow of its being translated, *to the end of eternity.* In like
manner, when the evangelist Luke speaks of *holy prophets which
have been* απ' αιωνος, it is translated, *since the world began:* But
the rendering would have been uncouth, *from eternity;* nor would
such a translation have conveyed a right meaning. In fine, for
I would not needlessly multiply instances, when the apostle
Paul speaks of *the mystery which hath been hid,* απο των αιωνων, it
is very justly translated, *from ages that are passed:* But it would
have been a solecism in English to have said, *from past eter-
nities.* . . .

The plain truth is, these Greek words have a different
natural force from the English ones, by which they are mostly
rendered in the Bible; being more *loose* in their meaning, and
not so certainly signifying *duration without bounds or limits:*
Otherwise they might, without impropriety in sense, or indeed
any harshness in sound, be always translated by them, or used
with like additions to them; which we have seen they cannot.

Now, from this remark, it is obvious, that the *sacred
writers* ought not to be looked upon as having in their minds the
same idea, when they apply the words αιων and αιωνιος to the *future torments,* pointing out their continuance, which we are naturally led to have, when we connect with them the words *eternity, everlasting.* Those acquainted with the English language
only, having used, from their childhood, to join the idea of
endless duration with the words *eternity, everlasting,* are apt at
once to put this sense upon them, whenever they see them, in
the scriptures, applied to the *hereafter punishment* of the
wicked. But it is far from being certain, or indeed so much as
probable, that the *sacred penmen* were, in the same manner,

ready, when they used the *original* words, to which these *translated* ones are made to answer, to understand them in the same
sense. We have seen they have a *different* force; and consequently the idea *they* applied to them must be *proportionably
different*, that is, not so determinately significative of *continuance beyond all bounds or limits*.

The word αιων, and its derivative αιωνιος, are so far from
being confined in their meaning to *endless* duration, that they
really signify nothing more than an *age, dispensation, period of
continuance*, either longer or shorter. It is certain, this is the sense
in which they are commonly, if not always, used in the sacred
pages. The texts in proof of this are almost numberless.

.   .   .

It does not appear to me, that it would be honourable
to the infinitely righteous and benevolent Governor of the
world, to make wicked men *everlastingly miserable*. For, in what
point of light soever we take a view of *sin*, it is certainly, in its
nature, a *finite* evil. It is the fault of a *finite* creature, and the effect
of *finite* principles, passions, and appetites. To say, therefore, that
the sinner is doomed to *infinite* misery for the *finite* faults of a
finite life, looks like a reflection on the *infinite* justice, as well as
goodness, of God. I know it has been often urged, that *sin* is an *infinite* evil, because committed against an *infinite object*; for
which reason, an *infinite punishment* is no more than its *due
desert*. But this *metaphysical nicety* proves a great deal too much,
if it proves any thing at all. For, according to this way of argu-
ing, all sinners must suffer *to the utmost* in degree, as well as *duration*; otherwise, they will not suffer *so much* as they *might* do,
and as they *ought* to do: Which is plainly inconsistent with that
difference the scripture often declares there shall be in the
punishment of wicked men, according to the *difference* there
has been in the *nature* and *number* of their evil deeds.

The *smallness* of the *difference* between those, in this
world, to whom the character of *wicked* belongs in the *lowest*
sense, and those to whom the character of *good* is applicable in
the *like* sense, renders it incredible, that such an *amazingly great
difference* should be made between them in the *future* world,

The *former differ* from the latter, by a difference, as to us, so *imperceptible*, that it is, perhaps, impossible we should be able so much as to distinguish the one from the *other*, with any manner of certainty: And yet, the *difference* between them, in the other world, according to the common opinion, will be *doubly infinite*; for the *good* are screened from *infinite misery*, and rewarded with *infinite happiness*; whereas the *wicked* are excluded from *infinite happiness*, and doomed to *infinite misery*. For the *reward* and *punishment*, being both eternal, however small they may be supposed to be in each finite portion of time, they must at last become infinite in magnitude. How to reconcile this with the absolutely accurate *impartiality* of God, is, I confess, beyond me.

A very great part of those, who will be miserable in the *other world*, were not, that we know of, INCURABLY sinful in *this*. Multitudes are taken off before they have had opportunity to make themselves *hardened abandoned* sinners: And, so far as we are able to judge, had they been continued in life, they might have been formed to a *virtuous temper* of mind by a suitable mixture of *correction, instruction,* and the like. And can it be supposed, with respect to such, that an infinitely benevolent God, without any *other trial,* in order to effect their *reformation,* will consign them over to *endless* and *irreversible torment*? Would this be to conduct himself towards them like a *Father*? Let the heart of a *father on earth* speak upon this occasion. Nay, it does not appear, that any *sinners* are so INCORRIGIBLE in wickedness, as to be *beyond recovery* by still further methods within the reach of *infinite wisdom*: And if the infinitely wise God can, in any wise methods, recover them, even in any *other state of trial,* may we not argue, from his *infinite benevolence,* that he will? And is it not far more reasonable to suppose, that the *miseries of the other world* are a *proper discipline* in order to accomplish this *end*, than that they should be *final* and *vindictive* only? [6]

, ,

Elhanan Winchester also attempted to refute the accuracy of the translation of those significant words. Along with

Chauncy's book, his *Universal Restoration exhibited in Four Di-alogues* (1792) was used to good effect by Universalists in their struggle with the orthodox. In the following extract Winchester deals with the claim that pressed on Universalists from all sides that belief in universal salvation led to licentiousness and sin.

‘ , ‘ ‘ ‘

The universal benevolence of the Deity, or the love of God to his creatures, is one of the first principles from which the general Restoration is deduced; and who can say that this leads to licentiousness? If those who believe that God loves them, in particular, find *that* consideration the strongest obligation on them to love him again, and to obey his will; by the same rule, if all the individuals of the whole human race, were to believe that God loved each one of them, would not the same cause produce the same effect? And if so, can this be charged as a licentious doctrine, which is expressly grounded upon a cause which power-fully operates to produce holiness? Is there anything like argu-ment in this reasoning? I know that God loves me, and seeks to do me good; therefore, I must hate him. What should we think of a woman who should leave her husband; and do all in her power against him, and should be able to give no better reasons for it than the following: "My husband loves me, and I know it, and he has always loved me, and always will; and therefore I am determined to hate, ridicule, despise, and contemn him, and have left him for this cause, and am determined never to love or obey him more." Bad as human nature is, I question whether such instances often occur. We commonly say, that love begets love. "We love him because he first loved us;" says the apostle, I John iv. 19. Therefore, the doctrine of God's universal benevo-lence, cannot lead to licentiousness, in any light in which it can be viewed: for if he really loves us, he will do all in his power to bring us to love him again, and to be like him; and I am sure the consideration of his love to us, goes as far as moral persuasion can go, to induce us to love him again; nay, the belief of it is ac-knowledged to be one of the strongest motives to obedience; and the love of God, shed abroad in the heart, produces the best effects, and is the most powerful principle, and spring, of good and virtuous actions, that we are acquainted with. This being a first principle, from which the Universal Restoration is concluded, we are happy to find, that "God is love:" and that he "so loved the world, as to give his only begotten Son, that whosoever believeth in him, should not perish, but have everlasting life: For, God sent not his Son into the world to condemn the world; but that the world through him might be saved." See 1 John iv. 16. St. John iii. 16, 17. But it is not so much my business now to shew, that the sentiment is scriptural, as to shew that it is not of a dangerous tendency. The following words, however, are so beautiful, that I take the liberty to mention them:—"but thou hast mercy upon all; for thou canst do all things, and winkest at the sins of men, because they should amend. For thou lovest all the things that are, and abhorrest nothing which thou hast made; for never wouldst thou have made any thing, if thou hadst hated it. And how could any thing have endured, if it had not been thy will; or been preserved, if not called by thee? But thou sparest all; for they are thine, O Lord, thou lover of souls. For thine incorruptible Spirit is in all things: therefore chasteneth thou them, by little and little, that offend, and warnest them, by putting them in remembrance wherein they have offended, that leaving their wickedness, they may believe on thee, O Lord. For thy power is the beginning of righteousness; and because thou art the Lord of all, it maketh thee to be gracious unto all. But thou, O God, art gracious and true; long suffering, and in mercy ordering all things. For if we sin, we are thine, knowing thy power; but we will not sin, knowing that we are counted thine." Wisdom of Solomon xi. 23, 26; xii. 1, 2, 16; xv. 1, 2. "Jehovah is gracious and full of compassion, slow to anger and of great mercy. Jehovah is good to all; and his tender mercies are over all his works. All thy works shall praise thee, O Jehovah; and thy saints shall bless thee." Psal. cxlv. 8–10.

·   ·   ·

But it is not only from reasoning, but from facts, that I am able to prove that the belief of the doctrine of the Universal

Restoration, does not lead men to sin. The Tunkers, or German Baptists, in Pennsylvania, and the states adjacent, who take the Scriptures as their only guide, in matters both of faith and practice, have always (as far as I know) received, and universally, at present, hold these sentiments: but such Christians, I have never seen as they are; so averse are they to all sin, and to many things that other Christians esteem lawful, that they not only refuse to swear, to go to war, &c., but are so afraid of doing any thing contrary to the commands of Christ, that no temptation would prevail upon them even to sue any person at law, for either name, character, estate, or any debt, be it ever so just. They are industrious, sober, temperate, kind, charitable people; envying not the great, nor despising the mean: They read much, they sing and pray much, they are constant attendants upon the worship of God; their dwelling houses are all houses of prayer; they walk in the commandments and ordinances of the Lord blameless, both in public and private. They bring up their children in the nurture and admonition of the Lord. No noise of rudeness, shameless mirth, loud, vain laughter, is heard within their doors. The law of kindness is in their mouths; no sourness or moroseness, disgraces their religion; and whatsoever they believe their Saviour commands, they practice, without inquiring or regarding what others do.

I remember the Rev. Morgan Edwards, formerly minister of the Baptist church in Philadelphia, once said to me, "GOD always will have a visible people on earth; and these are his people at present, above any other in the world." And in his history of the Baptists in Pennsylvania, speaking of these people, he says: "General redemption they certainly held, and, withal, general salvation; which tenets (though wrong) are consistent. In a word, they are meek and pious Christians; and have justly acquired the character of *the harmless Tunkers*."

Thus have I proved that this doctrine is not licentious; both from the first principles on which it is founded, from the nature of experimental and practical religion, and from facts.[7]

, ,

When the radical English Unitarian theologian and scientist Joseph Priestley sought refuge from persecution for his left-wing political views in favor of the French Revolution, he sought out the company of fellow emigrés in Pennsylvania. At the conclusion of a series of lectures delivered in the winter of 1796 at the Philadelphia Universalist church of his friend Elhanan Winchester* he expressed his views on universal salvation. The warmth and breadth of the human concern of this Christian friend of the Enlightenment is well displayed in these words, which link his belief in the Fatherhood of God with his belief in the potential of man.

‘ ‘

. . . I shall take the liberty (especially as I have been indulged with an opportunity of pleading what I believe to be the cause of truth in this place) to express my concurrence with the minister and the congregation worshipping here, in their opinion concerning the final happiness of all the human race,—a doctrine eminently calculated to promote a like gratitude to God and benevolence to man, and consequently every other virtue; and since this doctrine is perfectly consistent with the belief of the adequate punishment of all sin, it is far from giving any encouragement to sinners.

The doctrine of *eternal torments* is altogether indefensible on any principles of justice or equity; for all the crimes of finite creatures being of course finite, cannot in equity deserve infinite punishment. The Judge of all the earth, who appeals to men that *all his ways are equal*, we may rest assured will do that which is *right*. Nay, *in the midst of judgment he ever remembers mercy*, and he has declared that *he retaineth not anger forever*.

But I do not lay much stress on particular texts of Scripture in this case, because it does not appear to me to have been the proper object of the mission of Christ or of any other

* The difference in the appeal of Unitarianism and Universalism can be gauged from the observation of Dr. Rush that the Priestley series in the morning attracted the upper classes while Winchester's preaching in the evening appealed to the lower classes.

prophet, to announce this doctrine; nor does it appear that any of them considered the subject in its full extent. But it may be inferred from the general maxims of God's moral government, and from the spirit and tendency of the whole system of revelation. Since all the dead are to be raised, the wicked as well as the righteous, it is highly improbable that this will be merely for the sake of their being punished and then consigned to annihilation, as if they were incapable of improvement.

No human beings can be so depraved as that it shall not be in the power of proper discipline to reclaim them, so as to make them valuable characters. What great things have the excellent regulations of the public prison in this city effected in this respect! They are regulations worthy to be imitated in all the United States and through the whole world. How often do vices arise from false views of things, occasioned by the circumstances in which men are unavoidably placed, which, therefore, a more favorable situation and better information would easily cure! The natural operation of all punishment here is the reformation of the offender; and if human nature will continue to be the same thing that it now is, it must have the same operation hereafter, and the *time* that is often the only thing wanting to produce its proper effect at present, will not be wanting then.

Many vicious persons, and especially unbelievers, are men of great natural talents and powers, capable of the happiest exertions if only well directed; and is their Maker incapable of giving them that due direction? After having made use of them for the wise and benevolent purposes of his providence here in promoting, as they indirectly do, the virtue and happiness of others, will he cast them away as of no further use? For, as I have observed, moral as well as natural evils are necessary in this state of trial and discipline. Would not any man be justly censured for destroying any animal that might be rendered useful merely because he was vicious? Or would any parent abandon a child for any fault that he could be guilty of? It would be said that judicious treatment would cure those vices, whatever they were. And is the Divine Being less skilful or less benevolent than man?

Consider, further, how is it possible for good men to

whom the happiness of heaven is promised, to have any enjoyment of that happiness themselves, if those for whom they cannot but have the strongest affection, especially their children and other near relations and friends, be, I do not say consigned to everlasting torments, but even annihilated, or in any other way only excluded from all possibility of attaining such a state as will make their existence a blessing to them? If David lamented as he did the death of his rebellious son Absalom, what would he have felt in the idea of his utter destruction? A parent myself, allow me to speak to the feelings of others who are also parents. But is not God the true parent of us all? Are not our children as much his as they are ours? And is an earthly parent who is deserving of the name incapable of wholly abandoning any of his children? and will God, whose *tender mercies are over all his works* (Psalm cxlv. 9), and whose love and compassion far exceed ours, abandon any of his? Like a true parent, he will ever correct in *measure* and with *mercy*.[8]

, ,

One of the most notable of the early converts to Universalism, Dr. Benjamin Rush of Philadelphia, made it a point to relate his faith to the political and social issues of the day. The first excerpt is from a letter 2 June 1787 to Dr. Price, an old associate of Dr. Joseph Priestley and leading nonconformist English clergyman.

‘ ‘

Accept of my thanks for the copy of your Sermons by Dr. White. I have read them with great pleasure. I have even done more. I have transcribed part of one of them for the benefit of a pious and accomplished female correspondent in a neighbouring State. I am pleased with the moderation with which you have discussed the controverted doctrines in the first five discourses. I confess I have not and cannot admit your opinions, having long before I met with the Arian or Socinian controversies, embraced the doctrines of universal salvation and final restitution. My belief in these doctrines is founded wholly upon the Calvinistical account (and which I believe to be agreeable to the tenor of Scripture) of the person, power, goodness, mercy, and other divine attributes of the Saviour of the World. These principles, my dear friend, have bound me to the whole human race; these are the principles which animate me in all my labors for the interests of my fellow creatures. No particle of benevolence, no wish for the liberty of a slave or the reformation of a criminal will be lost. They must all be finally made effectual, for they all flow from the great author of goodness who implants no principles of action in man in vain. I acknowledge I was surprised to find you express yourself so cautiously and sceptically upon this point. Had you examined your own heart, you would have found in it the strongest proof of the truth of the doctrine. It is this light which shineth in darkness, and which the darkness as yet comprehendeth not, that has rendered you so useful to your country and to the world.

I beg pardon for this digression from the ordinary subjects of our correspondence. I submit my opinions with humility to that being who will not, as you happily express it, punish involuntary errors, if such have been embraced by me. I seldom distress myself with speculative inquiries in religion, being fully satisfied that our business is to be *good* here, that we may be *wise* hereafter.[9]

, ,

To Elhanan Winchester

Dear Sir,   Philadelphia, May 11, 1791

I sit down with great pleasure to thank you for the instruction I have derived from reading your *Lectures on the Prophecies.*

You have made the Old and New Testaments intelligible books and added greatly to our obligations to love and admire them.

To pry into the meaning of the prophecies is certainly a duty. Our Saviour condemns his disciples for being slow of heart in believing all that the Scriptures say concerning him, and commends Abraham for beholding his day afar off and rejoicing in the great events which were to follow it.

Perhaps a great part of the errors in principle and luke-warmness in practice of all sects of Christians arise chiefly from their ignorance of the literal meaning and extent of the prophecies which relate to the kingdom of our Lord and Saviour Jesus Christ.

Go on, my dear sir, in your researches. As the best natural philosophers are those who examine the works of nature most minutely, so they are the best divines who search and compare the Scriptures most carefully. Your works are beyond the present state of knowledge in our world, but the time must come when they will rise into universal estimation and bear down all the modern systems of our schools. They are founded on a rock, and the more reason and religion prevail in the world, the more their beauty, symmetry, and sublimacy will be seen and admired. He is not a Jew who is one outwardly; we are all alike prone to Jewish infidelity. We condemn the Jews for looking for a temporary deliverer when our Saviour came into the world. We act their folly over again in looking for a (mere) spiritual instead of a temporal kingdom in the Millennium.

The Universal doctrine prevails more and more in our country, particularly among persons eminent for their piety, in whom it is not a mere speculation but a new principle of action in the heart prompting to practical godliness.

Your native country is rising daily in industry, order, and in everything else that can constitute national happiness. The present wise and just administration of our government refutes all that can be said in Europe in favor of the necessity or advantages of monarchy or aristocracy.

Your account of the *Restoration of Sacrifices* after the coming of our Saviour is the only part of your *Lectures* that I object to. I suspect they ought to have been placed a short time before the commencement of his personal government. Perhaps you may reconsider this subject in the next edition of them.

Adieu, from, dear sir, yours sincerely,

Benjamin Rush[10]

‘ ‘

Dr. Rush's sentiments regarding universal salvation are expressed in this letter of 6 June 1791 to the Reverend Jeremy Belknap, leading New England Congregational minister. Belknap, friend of Charles Chauncy, had been privy to Dr. Chauncy's intent to publish *The Salvation of All Men* (1784).

, ,

Have you read Paine's and Priestley's answers to Burke's pamphlet? They are both masterly performances, although they possess different species of merit. Paine destroys error by successive flashes of lightning. Priestley wears it away by successive strokes of electricity. The government both civil and ecclesiastical of England must undergo a change. Corruption there boils over. It would have been difficult for that country to have escaped the influence of *the example* of the United States upon their affairs, but France is too near them not to awaken them. Mankind have hitherto treated republican forms of government as divines now treat the doctrine of final restitution. Both have been condemned before an appeal had been made to experiments, for both have been accused of leading to disorder and licentiousness. Both charges I believe are equally destitute of foundation. The charges might with more reason be made against monarchy and the present doctrines of all the Protestant churches. What disorders have not existed under kingly governments? And what crime can be named against God, against man, or against society, which has not been perpetrated by men who believe in endless punishment?

A belief in God's universal love to all his creatures, and that he will finally restore all those of them that are miserable to happiness, is a *polar* truth. It leads to truths upon all subjects, more especially upon the subject of government. It establishes the *equality* of mankind—it abolishes the punishment of death for any crime—and converts jails into houses of repentance and reformation.

All truths are related, or rather there is but one truth. Republicanism is a part of the truth of Christianity. It derives power from its true source. It teaches us to view our rulers in their true light. It abolishes the false glare which surrounds kingly government, and tends to promote the true happiness of all its members as well as of the whole world, for peace with everybody is the true interest of all republics.[11]

, ,

When the Universalists gathered in convention in Philadelphia in 1790, it was natural that they should draw on the considerable literary talents of Dr. Rush. Despite the fact that he had advocated a convention open to all Christian sects and had been overruled, he agreed to revise the Articles of Faith, Plan of Church Government, and Recommendations* for presentation to the gathering.

‘ ‘ ‘ ‘ ‘ ‘ ‘ ‘ ‘ ‘ ‘ ‘ ‘ ‘ ‘ ‘ ‘₁ ‘ ‘ ‘ ‘ ‘ ‘

ARTICLES OF FAITH.

Sect. I. Of the Holy Scriptures.

We believe the scriptures of the Old and New Testament to contain a revelation of the perfections and will of God and the rule of faith and practice.

Sect. II. Of the Supreme Being.

We believe in one God, infinite in all his perfections; and that these perfections are all modifications of infinite, adorable, incomprehensible and unchangeable love.

Sect. III. Of the Mediator.

man, the man, Christ Jesus, in whom dwelleth all the fulness of
We believe that there is one Mediator between God and
the Godhead bodily; who, by giving himself a ransom for all, hath redeemed them to God by his blood; and who, by the merit

* See Chapter VI.

of his death and the efficacy of his spirit, will finally restore the whole human race to happiness.

Sect. IV. Of the Holy Ghost.

We believe in the *Holy Ghost*, whose office it is to make known to sinners the truth of their salvation, through the medium of the holy scriptures, and to reconcile the hearts of the children of men to God, and thereby to dispose them to genuine holiness.

Sect. V. Of Good Works.

We believe in the obligation of the moral law, as the rule of life; and we hold, that the love of God, manifested to man in a Redeemer, is the best means of producing obedience to that law, and promoting a holy, active and useful life.[12]

, ,

Chapter Three

Universalism of the Enlightenment

> *If we admit that our Creator made us reasonable beings,*
> *we ought, of course, to believe that all the truth which is*
> *necessary for our belief is not only reasonable, but reduci-*
> *ble to our understandings.*
>
> Hosea Ballou

It is in the preaching and writing of Hosea Ballou that the full impact of the world-view of the eighteenth century Enlightenment makes its appearance in the budding Universalist denomination. His unitarian views of God and the atonement of Christ and his insistence that the Bible must be interpreted by the light of reason won the day against the Rellyan views of Murray and the apocalyptic views of Winchester.

Ballou's *Treatise on Atonement* was published in 1805, about ten years after he had worked through from the Calvinistic Universalism of his earliest career to his Enlightenment position. The book was written while Ballou was still riding circuit among several Vermont churches, using Barnard as his home base. While succeeding editions reflect the changes Ballou went through, both in ridding himself of the last traces of Rellyan allegorical interpretation and in the urbanization of his use of English, the first edition (from which the following excerpts are taken) best displays the informal argumentative tone of back country preaching.

‘ ‘

. . . If sin be infinite in its nature, there can be no one sin greater than another. The smallest offence against the good of society is equal to blasphemy against the Holy Ghost. If what we call a small crime be not infinite, the greatest cannot be, providing there is any proportion between the great and the small. Are not the words of Christ (Matt. xii. 31), where he speaks of sins and blasphemies that should be forgiven unto men, and of blasphemies that should not be forgiven men, a sufficient evidence that some sins are more heinous than others? Again (1 Epistle of John v. 16), where some sins are said to be not unto death, and some unto death, etc.

Now, admitting the matter proved, that sin is not infinite, it follows, of course, that it is proved to be finite. However, we will now attend to the direct evidences of the finite nature of sin.

The law which takes cognizance of sin is not infinite, it being produced by the legislature which I have before noticed, viz., a capacity to understand, connected with the causes and means of knowledge. In order for a law to be infinite, the legislature must be so; but man's ability to understand is finite, and all the means which are in his power for the acquisition of knowledge are finite; all his knowledge is circumscribed, and the law produced by such causes must be like them, not infinite but finite. An infinite law would be far above the capacity of a finite being, and it would be unreasonable to suppose man amenable to a law above his capacity. All our knowledge of good and evil is obtained by comparison. We call an action evil by comparing it with one which we call good. Were it in our power to embrace all the consequences that are connected with our actions in our intentions, our meanings would seldom be what they now are. Had it been so with the brethren of Joseph, when they sold him to the Ishmaelites, that they then knew all the consequences which would attend the event, they would not have meant it, as they did, for evil, but seeing with perfectly unbeclouded eyes their own salvation, and that of the whole family of promise, they would have meant it for good, as did the Almighty who superintended the affair. Now the act of selling Joseph was sin, in the meaning of those who sold him; but it was finite, considered as sin, for it was bounded by the narrowness of their understandings, limited by their ignorance, and circumscribed by the wisdom and goodness of him who meant it for good. If this sin had been infinite, nothing we can justly call good, could have been the consequence; but who ever read the event without seeing that the best of consequences were connected with it?

.   .   .

. . . God saw fit, in his plan of divine wisdom, to make the creature subject to vanity; to give him a mortal constitution; to fix in his nature those faculties which would, in their operation, oppose the spirit of the heavenly nature. It is, therefore, said that God put enmity between the seed of the woman and that of the serpent. And it was by the passions which arose from the fleshy nature that the whole mind became carnal, and man was captivated thereby. But perhaps the objector will say this denies the liberty of the will, and makes God the author of sin. To which I reply, desiring the reader to recollect what I have said of sin in showing its nature; by which, it is discovered, that God may be the innocent and holy cause of that, which, in a limited sense, is sin; but as it respects the meaning of God, it is intended for good. It is not casting any disagreeable reflections on the Almighty to say he determined all things for good; and to believe he supersedes all the affairs of the universe, not excepting sin, is a million times more to the honor of God than to believe he cannot, or that he does not when he can. The reader will then ask, if God must be considered as the first, the holy, and the innocent cause of sin, is there any unholy or impure cause? I answer, there is, but in a limited sense. There is no divine holiness in any fleshly or carnal exercise; there is no holiness nor purity in all the deceptions ever experienced by imperfect beings; and these are the immediate causes of sin; and as such, they make the best of men on earth groan, and cry out, "Who shall deliver me from the body of this death?"

If it should be granted that sin will finally terminate for good, in the moral system, it will then be necessary to admit that God is its first cause, or we cannot say that God is the author of all good.

.   .   .

Man's main object, in all he does, is happiness; and were it not for that, he never could have any other particular object. What would induce men to form societies; to be at the expense of supporting government; to acquire knowledge; to learn the sciences, or till the earth, if they believed they could be as happy without as with? The fact is, man would not be the being that he now is, as there would not be any stimulus to action; he must become inert, therefore cease to be. As men are never without this grand object, so they are never without their wants, which render such an object desirable. But their minor objects vary, according as their understandings vary, and their passions differ. Then, says the objector, there is no such thing as disinterested benevolence. I answer, words are used to communicate ideas; there is that often in our experience, which is meant by disinterested benevolence. An American is travelling in Europe; he meets in the street a young and beautiful fair, bathed in tears, her breast swollen with grief, and her countenance perfectly sad. His heart, fraught with the keenest sensibility, is moved compassionately to inquire the cause of her grief; he is informed that her father, in a late sickness, became indebted to his physician twenty guineas, for which he was that hour committed to gaol, when he had but partially recovered his health. Our traveller no sooner hears the story than he advances the twenty guineas to discharge the debt, and gives her fifty more as a reward for her generous concern. As our traveller did not expect any pecuniary reward, either directly or indirectly, his charity is called disinterested benevolence. But, strictly speaking, he was greatly interested; he was interested in the afflictions of father and child; their relief was his object, and charity his passion. Now did he not act for his own happiness? Yes, as much as ever a man did in life. What must have been his misery, possessing the same disposition, without the means to relieve? And what a sublime satisfaction he enjoyed by the bestowment of his favor!

Sacred truth informs us, "It is more blessed to give than to receive."

We find some men honest and industrious who think, and think justly, that happiness is not to be found in any other way. Others are indolent and knavish, and they expect to obtain happiness in so being. But they are deceived in their objects, and will finally learn that they must be, what conscience has often told them they ought to be, honest and just, in order to be happy.

The objector will say, to admit that our happiness is the grand object of all we do, destroys the purity of religion, and reduces the whole to nothing but selfishness. To which, I reply, a man acting for his own happiness, if he seek it in the heavenly system of universal benevolence, knowing that his own happiness is connected with the happiness of his fellow-men, which induces him to do justly and to deal mercifully with all men, he is no more selfish than he ought to be. But a man acting for his own happiness, if he seek it in the narrow circle of partiality and covetousness, his selfishness is irreligious and wicked.

I know it is frequently contended that we ought to love God for what he is, and not for what we receive from him; that we ought to love holiness for holiness' sake, and not for any advantage such a principle is to us. This is what I have often been told, but what I never could see any reason for, or propriety in. I am asked if I love an orange; I answer I never tasted of one; but I am told I must love the orange for what it is! Now I ask, is it possible for me either to like or dislike the orange, in reality, until I taste it? Well, I taste of it, and like it. Do you like it? says my friend. Yes, I reply, its flavor is exquisitely agreeable. But that will not do, says my friend; you must not like it because its taste is agreeable, but you must like it because it is an orange. If there be any propriety in what my friend says, it is out of my sight. A man is travelling on the sands of Arabia, he finds no water for a number of days; the sun scorches and he is exceedingly dry; at last he finds water and drinks to his satisfaction; never did water taste half so agreeably before. To say that this man loves the water because it is water, and not because of the advantage which he receives from it, betrays a large share of inconsistency. Would not this thirsty traveller have loved the burning sand as well as he did the water if it had tasted as agreeably and quenched his thirst as well? The sweet Psalmist of Israel said, "O taste and see that the Lord is good." And an apostle says, "We love him because he first loved us." What attribute do we ascribe to God that we do not esteem on account of its advantage to us? Justice would have been no more likely to be attributed to the Almighty than injustice if it had not first been discovered that justice was of greater advantage to mankind than injustice. And so of power, were it of no more advantage to human society than weakness, the latter would have been as likely to have been esteemed an attribute of God as the former. If wisdom were of no greater service to man than folly, it would not have been adored in the Almighty any more than folly. If love were no more happifying to man than hatred, hatred would as soon have been esteemed an attribute of God as love.

.   .   .

A mistaken idea has been entertained of sin even by professors. I have often heard sincere ministers preach, in their reproofs to their hearers, that it was the greatest folly in the world for people to forego salvation in a future state for the comforts and pleasures of sin in this. Such exhortations really defeat their intentions. The wish of the honest preacher is that the wicked should repent of their sins and do better; but, at the same time, he indicates that sin, at present, is more productive of happiness than righteousness; but that the bad will come in another world; that, although doing well is a hard way, yet its advantages will be great in another state. Just as much as any person thinks sin to be more happifying than righteousness, he is sinful; his heart esteems it, though in some possible cases, for fear of the loss of salvation in the world to come, he may abstain from some outward enormities; yet his heart is full of the desire of doing them. A thief passes a merchant's shop, wishes to steal some of his goods, but durst not for fear of apprehension and punishment. Is this man less a thief at heart for not actually taking the goods? I have been told, by persons of high professions in Christianity, that if they were certain of salvation in the world to come they would commit every sin to which their unbridled passions might lead them; even from the lips of some who profess to preach the righteousness of Christ have I heard such-like expressions! I do not mention these things to cast reflections on any person or denomination in the world; for I have a favorable hope that there are some in all denominations who are not to be deceived; but I mention them in order to show how deceiving sin is to the mind. It is as much the nature of sin to torment the mind as it is the nature of fire to burn our flesh. Sin deprives us of every rational enjoyment, so far as it captivates the mind; it was never able to furnish one drop of cordial for the soul; her tender mercies are cruelty, and her breasts of consolation are gall and wormwood. Sin is a false mirror, by which the sinner is deceived in everything on which his mind contemplates. If he think of his Maker, who is his best friend, it strikes him with awe, fills his mind with fearful apprehensions, and he wishes there was no such being. If he think of any duty which he owes his Maker, he says, in a moment, God is a hard master, why should he require of me what is so contrary to my happiness? Religion is only calculated to make men miserable; righteousness blunts my passions, and deprives me of pleasures for which I long. But it represents stolen waters to be sweet, and bread eaten in secret to be pleasant. In a word, sin is of a torment-giving nature to every faculty of the soul, and is the moral death of the mind.

Well, says the reader, can sin have all those evil effects and not be infinite? Undoubtedly; as all those evil effects are experienced in this finite state. Thousands, who, I hope, are gone to greater degrees of rest than the most upright enjoy here, were once tormented with sin, were once under the dominion of the carnal mind. The effects of sin as sin are not endless, but limited to the state in which it is committed.

.   .   .

. . . I wish to inquire into the propriety of an innocent person's suffering for one who is guilty. It is Scripture, reason, and good law never to condemn the innocent in order to exculpate the delinquent. Supposing a foreign court sends a person who is old in conspiracies and blood, to America, to lay a deep concerted plan to murder the President of the Union, and a number of the first officers in the Federal government, for purposes mischievous to our political existence; and he should so far succeed as to engage a number in this wicked design, and finally makes the attempt: his plans are discovered by government and detected, but not until numbers have fallen a sacrifice to his mischievous endeavors. The leader of these seditious murders is taken and condemned to be executed; and the voice of every friend of justice and equity is against the criminal. But what would be the consternation of the good people of the United States on being informed that the good president of the Union, the man whom the people delighted to honor, was executed in the room of this seditious person, and the wicked murderer set at liberty? Is it possible to conceive that there is a single person in the world who would call this a just execution? If it be said that the president freely offered himself in the room of the criminal, it alters not the case in the eye of justice. If an innocent man can justly be put to death because he consents to it willingly, a guilty one may be acquitted because he prefers it. But it is further argued that the authority had power to raise the president from the dead, which done, renders the work just and glorious. I say, in answer, that if the authority had this power, it might as well have executed the real criminal, and raised him from the dead, as to perform this work on one who was not guilty. What is the most shocking of anything in this system of atonement, is the partiality represented in the Almighty; for admitting the plan rational, as it respects those circumstances in which I have shown its absurdity, what can we find in Scripture or reason that justifies such infinite partiality in our Creator? or what can, in the least, serve as evidence to prove him possessed of it? Have we not reason to believe our Creator possessed of as much goodness as he has communicated to us? Can we rationally believe that he is wanting in those principles of goodness which he has placed in our understanding? When he saw the whole progeny of Adam in the same situation by reason of sin, one no more guilty than another, why should he propose a plan of mercy for some few of them, and disregard the awful circumstances of the rest? The sacred oracle declares God to be no respecter of persons; if this be true, he is not a partial being. Jesus taught the character of God to his disciples by turning their attention to nature, observing the equal distribution of rain and sunshine, on the evil and on the good, on the just and on the unjust. Supposing Joseph had dealt out bread plentifully to two of his brethren in Egypt, and had starved the rest to death, would it have looked like impartiality? It is argued that none of them deserved a crumb from Joseph, whom they had sold; and if he pleased to give to one and not to another, he had a right so to do. Then, I say, he had a right to be partial. I am travelling through a large and extensive wood, and many miles from any inhabitants; I find ten persons who are lost; they have been out of provisions for several days; and having fatigued themselves in wandering from hill to hill, from stream to stream, striving, to the utmost of their abilities to find inhabitants; having given up all hopes of ever seeing their homes again, and having, in their minds, bid their wives and children a long farewell, they are waiting for hunger to do its last work! The moment I discover myself to them, with large supplies of wholesome and rich provisions, every eye glistens with unexpected joy; the current of life starts afresh in their veins, and they all advance to meet me on their enfeebled hands and knees, with eagerness to receive the staff of life! I hasten to improve the opportunity of showing my sovereignty and goodness; I feed five of them to the full, the other five I neglect. They beg for the smallest crust, which I do not want, but to no effect. Those whom I feed solicit me, every mouthful they eat, to bestow some on their fellow-sufferers, but I refuse. I tell them, however, not to construe my conduct into partiality, but to learn my power and sovereignty by it. The five whom I have fed I assist out of the wood, and leave the rest to their wants. My conduct in the above affair appears so much blacker than my paper is white, I choose rather to leave the reader to make his comments than to write my own.

I inquire still further, did the Almighty know, before he made man that he would become a sinner? Did he know that he would deserve an endless punishment? If the answer be in the negative, it supposes God to be wanting in knowledge, and that he created beings at an infinite risk, as he did not know what would be the consequences. If the question be answered in the positive, it proves that an infinite cruelty existed in God; for unless that was the case he would never have created beings who he knew would be infinitely the losers by their existence.

Those who believe in the system which I am examining, believe in the existence of the devil, whose existence I have refuted in this work. I am willing, however, for the sake of the argument, to admit the existence of their God and devil likewise. But I wish to inquire, which of them is, in reality, the worst being. God, when he created mankind, perfectly knew that some of them would suffer endless torment for their sins; he must, therefore, have intended them for that purpose. For, it is inconsistent to suppose that the Almighty would create without a purpose; and his purpose could not be contrary to his knowledge. The matter then stands thus, God created millions of beings for endless misery, which they could not escape; the devil is desirous of having them miserable, and does all in his power to effect it. Now, reader, judge between these two beings. Had this devil been consulted by the Almighty when he laid the plan of man's final destiny, I cannot conceive him capable of inventing one more eligible to his infernal disposition than this which I am now disputing.

.   .   .

. . . It is . . . man that needs reconciliation. Men, while dictated by a carnal mind, are dissatisfied with God; they accuse him of being a hard master, reaping where he has not sown, and gathering where he has not strewed. They think on the Almighty, but desire not the knowledge of his ways. They behold no beauty in him; he appears as a tyrant, regardless of his creatures. A consciousness of sin, without the knowledge of God, represents Deity as angry, and full of vengeance; in which sense, many Scriptures are written, as I have before observed. How often do we find that God has been provoked to wrath and jealousy, and his fury raised to a flame against the sinner? And how often do the Scriptures represent him repenting of his anger, and growing calm! All these Scriptures are written according to the circumstance of the creature, and the apprehensions which the unreconciled entertain of God. Viewing man in this state of unreconciliation to God and holiness, it appears evidently necessary that he should receive an atonement productive of a renewal of love to his Maker. Without atonement, God could never be seen as he is, "altogether lovely, and the chiefest among ten thousand;" nor could he be loved with the whole heart, mind, might and strength. How often are men grumbling at Providence, that things should be governed as they are? How often are men displeased at the Supreme Being himself? What an infinite number of hard speeches have sinners spoken against God? All which argue the necessity of atonement, whereby those maladies may be healed.

What an infinite difference there is between the All-gracious and Merciful, and his lost and bewildered creatures? He, all glorious, without a spot in the whole infinitude of his nature; all lovely, without exception, and loving, without partiality. Who can tell the thousandth part of his love to his offspring? And this invariably the same through every dispensation, without the smallest abatement. But what can we say of man? Lost in the wilderness of sin, wandering in the by-paths of iniquity, lost to the knowledge of his heavenly Benefactor, and dissatisfied with his God; he goes on grumbling and complaining, attributing the worst of characters to the most merciful, and entertaining no regard for the fountain of all his comforts. God never called for a sacrifice to reconcile himself to man; but loved man so infinitely, that he was pleased to bruise his Son for our good, to give him to die, in attestation of love to sinners.[1]

, ,

It has been estimated that the greater number of Universalist ministers had been converted to Ballou's unitarian views by the time his *Treatise on Atonement* appeared in 1805. The book, however, went through many editions in succeeding years, spreading his influence far and wide.

Ballou's unitarianism was reflected in the Profession of

Faith adopted by the New England Convention at Winchester, New Hampshire, in 1803. Although he served on the committee commissioned to compose the statement, it did not meet until the convention gathered. The Profession meanwhile had been drafted by the committee chairman, Walter Ferriss, of Charlotte, Vermont, whose work was apparently accepted with little change. Ferriss' journal gives us a picture of the colorful contention between the advocates of a creed, who believed that it would help distinguish the Universalists from the Congregationalists and thus help their claims to their share of religious tax money and to the legitimacy of their ministry, and those who feared that a creed, like creeds of the past, would be used to enforce conformity.

‘   ‘

In September [1803] I went to the annual convention at Winchester, N. Hampshire. On my way thither I preached on Sunday at Shrewsbury[.]

I arrived at Winchester on the 20th. I had not, before my arrival at Winchester, been favored with an opportunity to consult with all the brethren of the committee appointed with me at the preceding Convention to draw up a plan of fellowship. I had drawn one however, and brought it with me. It was not so particular in some respects, both with regard to doctrine and ecclesiastical regulations as I could have wished. It was however, as full as I had reason to hope the brethren of the Convention at large would agree to accept. And I thought it would be much better than none, especially as I had so drawn it as to leave liberty to the several churches or to smaller associations of churches, if such should be formed within the limits of the general association, to adopt any more full or particular plan as they should see best, provided it was not contradictory to the general plan. When I proposed this plan which I had drawn to the rest of the committee, they agreed to it with very little amendment, and laid it before the Convention, which was the most numerous I had ever attended. When it was laid before the Convention I had the pleasure of seeing it instantly assented to by the brethren who had opposed me the year before at Strafford.

They saw nothing in it of the tendency to divide the association, which they had been afraid of, but were convinced that it would rather tend to strengthen our union. But the Rev. Noah Murray, from the north part of Pennsylvania, who had never before attended one of our Conventions, though he had long been a preacher of our order, objected in a new and singular manner against having any written form at all. He said much on the subject, and enlivened his pleas by quaint similitudes, drawn from calves, bulls, half bushels, etc., in which I thought he displayed more wit than solid sense, and more pathos than sound reasoning. But as he was a venerable old preacher, a man of real natural abilities, and possessed in some degree of a winning address, he was followed immediately by a number of other brethren who had not attended at Strafford the year before, amongst whom was the Rev. Mr. Glover, of Newtown in Connecticut. These brethren all seemed to approve of the plan which we had produced, as to its substance both with regard to doctrine and external regulations, but argued that it would be of no utility, if not of dangerous tendency, to commit, that or any other form to writing as an act of the association. I have seen good honest men, before these, who, because they could not write themselves, thought that writing was of but little use in the world.

On the other side it was powerfully urged by brothers Richards, Young, H. Ballou and others, that not only the reputation of the universalists already suffered much for want of an evidence to the world that they were, as a christian people, actually agreed in something essential both as to faith and practice, but also that individuals suffered considerably for want of some document to evince that they belonged to a denomination of christians distinct from the standing order of congregationalists. Amongst other cases, that of brother C. Erskine was dwelt upon, and with propriety, as the convention had already made some public efforts for his relief, without the desired effect. He had been obliged to pay heavy taxes to the support of a congregational minister, and large costs of suit for want of being able to prove that the universalists were not the same denomination as the congregationalists.

The discussion was carried on with decency and with

great ingenuity on both sides. At length the opposition rather seemed to flag. Brothers Murray and Glover with their companion Deacon Peck of Newtown expressed a desire to withdraw, as the time grew late, and as they had far to go. They assured us that they did not withdraw of disgust or coldness towards us, and took their leave very affectionately. After they had retired the discussion still went on. Several brethren of the opposition made a handsome retraction confessing themselves convinced; and when the question was put for adopting the platform all the brethren present voted in the affirmative.[2]

, ,

Nathaniel Stacy, looking back over many years, provided in his autobiography (1850) his recollection of the debate at Winchester.

‘ ‘

There was a measure called for, at this time, which, in its adoption by the council, produced considerable argument in the discussion, and no little sensation among the brethren; which was, the adoption of a written creed or confession of faith. It became absolutely necessary, to save Universalists in New England, and particularly in New Hampshire, from clerical oppression. In those days, the Presbyterians and Congregationalists were denominated the *Standing Order*; and they had a legal right to tax every individual in the parish, for the support of the clergy; and the only remedy the individual had to avoid paying such tax to them, was to join some other sect, and bring a certificate from them to the Standing Order, that he had joined that society, and actually paid taxes to them. This had been done in one or more cases, in the State of New Hampshire; but, nevertheless, the Standing Order proceeded to collect the tax. Resistance was made, and the case was finally carried up to the Supreme Court, which decided that there was no such order known as Universalists, for they had no creed or profession of faith to distinguish them from the Standing Order; and they were, consequently, compelled to pay taxes to them. Our brethren felt afraid of creeds. They had read, seen, and experienced, as they supposed, the distracting, illiberal, and persecuting effects of human creeds; and they wished to avoid the vortex of that whirlpool into which they had seen so many drawn to inevitable destruction. The Bible was a sufficient creed—it was all the creed they wanted—all they needed—it was sufficiently definite—and each one had an equal right to construe it for himself, while he did not deny its inspiration and authority. They felt no inclination to take upon themselves a "yoke, which neither they nor their fathers had been able to bear." They had so far lived without a creed; and they had lived in perfect union. Now, they very much feared, should they go to making creeds, they would become divided, and, like others who had gone before them, begin to cherish an exclusive and persecuting spirit. But what should be done? They sympathized deeply with the persecuted brethren in New Hampshire; and wished, if possible, to relieve them. A committee was appointed the previous year to prepare a confession of faith, and a platform, or constitution; of which Mr. Walter Ferris was a member; and he now presented one so unobjectionable, that it was difficult to find where the most fastidious could object to it, or how it could lead to division. A motion was made to adopt it; and probably the longest and warmest debate ensued, that had ever been known in that deliberative body. It was, however, conducted throughout with the kindest feelings, but with much earnestness and considerable sensibility; tears and smiles by the attentive auditors, alternately followed the pathetic appeals of the speakers on each side. Among its warmest advocates were George Richards, Hosea Ballou, Walter Ferris, and Zephaniah Lathe; and among its opposers, Edward Turner and Noah Murray. I distinctly recollect a metaphor in one of Mr. Murray's arguments, and Mr. Lathe's reply. Mr. Murray said, in allusion to the confession of faith, "It is harmless now—it is a calf, and its horns have not yet made their appearance; but it will soon grow older—its horns will grow, and then it will begin to hook." Mr. Lathe arose, and replied, "All that Br. Murray has said would be correct, had he not made a mistake in the animal. It is not a calf; it is a dove; and who ever heard of a dove having horns, at any age?" But the confession was adopted

without alteration, I believe, as reported by the committee, through Mr. Ferris. The opposition yielding, it passed, (if my memory well serves me,) by the unanimous voice of the council, with a *ever be made, hereafter, to the confession of faith.*[3]
resolution appended to it to this effect, that *no alteration should*

, ,

The Winchester Profession served the Universalists until 1899, when it was superseded by a statement reflecting changes of belief over a ninety-six-year period.

Ferriss, apparently using the Philadelphia Articles of Faith as a guide, produced a statement unitarian in tone. An explicit attempt is made in Article III to counter the charge that Universalism inevitably led to sin.

' '

Article I. We believe that the Holy Scriptures of the Old and New Testament contain a revelation of the character of God, and of the duty, interest and final destination of mankind.

Article II. We believe that there is one God, whose nature is Love, revealed in one Lord Jesus Christ, by one Holy Spirit of Grace, who will finally restore the whole family of mankind to holiness and happiness.

Article III. We believe that holiness and true happiness are inseparably connected, and that believers ought to be careful to maintain order and practise good works; for these things are good and profitable unto men.[4]

, ,

Chapter Four

Universalism on the Frontier

The present is the age of controversy; and the motto of the people is, "Give us facts."

E. E. Guild

Universalists, like other American religious groups, carried their message to the frontier. At the beginning of the nineteenth century the frontier meant the greater part of the American landscape. Transportation in these early years of the new nation was provided by horseback, carriage, and stage coach. The Universalist circuit rider lived a rigorous life. Walter Ferriss, Nathaniel Stacy, and S. R. Smith, whose writings are presented below for the picture they give of this era, all suffered from poor health—yet they seem to have taken their demanding routines for granted.

Walter Ferriss, a native of Quakerhill in Dutchess County, New York, came from a family of Friends. His father staked him to a farm in Charlotte in frontier Vermont (about 200 miles from his home). It was here that, through his own thinking and through the influence of William Farwell of the Universalist Society at Barre, who rode through on his circuit, Ferriss became a Universalist and eventually decided to preach as well as to farm.

‛ ‛

In the next month which was January, 1799, Mr. Farwell again came into our quarter and spent two days at my house. I informed him a little of the state of my mind. He told me that from his first conversation with me he had gathered some intimations that it was my duty to preach. What I told him now seemed to make him almost certain that it was my duty. Indeed I had become so convinced of it myself that I thought I could not feel a clear conscience 'till I made an attempt that way.

Mr. Farwell preached several sermons in our quarter at this time. After he went home a few of us agreed to hold meetings for public worship as universalists. The place we agreed upon for this purpose was in the border(s) of Hinesburgh nearly two miles from my house. No place any nearer to my house would have been convenient for those that would be likely to meet, as my near neighbours were all quakers, and the rest of the people of Charlotte mostly congregationalists.

Accordingly on Sunday the 3d of February 1799, a number of us met at the house of brother Israel Lockwood in the part of Hinesburgh before mentioned. This was the first time I ever attempted to preach. My text was Rom. 11. 32. I preached without notes. My sermon was short and so were the other parts of the exercise. After our public service was over we agreed to meet for a while once a fortnight for public worship as universalists and on the intermediate Sundays to attend severally with other denominations as might appear most convenient. This method we thought it best to adopt in the beginning considering our smallness and weakness, and this method we followed for several months.

The next time I preached was of course on the 17th of the same month. I then preached at another house in the same neighbourhood. That day I preached two sermons having the heads thereof & some passages of scripture noted on paper for the assistance of my memory. This is the method of preaching which I have most frequently followed since. However I have much oftener preached entirely without notes than I have had any whole discourse or even the greater part of it written.

During the first two or three months of my preaching I, and the few brethren who believed with me in the neighbouring towns were but very little informed respecting the general state of the universalists in New England. There had been no regular societies of that kind formed in our part of the State. We knew not what modes of discipline had been adopted where there were regular churches. We were unacquainted with most particulars concerning our brethren in distant parts, which we conceived might be for our edification to know. In order to obtain information of this kind I took a journey in the month of May 1799 to the eastern part of Vermont. On my way I tarried two or three days with Mr. Farwell and his brethren at Barre and preached to them once. From thence I proceeded to Strafford where the rev. Joab Young was settled. With him I also tarried two or three days, and preached to his congregation on Sunday. I had great satisfaction in those visits. The conversation of those experienced brethren in the ministry served to enlighten[,] comfort and encourage me. The object of my journey was completely accomplished. I arrived at home on the 22d of the month having brought with me a copy of the ecclesiastical platform which had been agreed upon by the convention of universalists at Philadelphia AD. 1790, together with several pamphlets, circular epistles, and other documents for the edification of my brethren.

In those early days of my preaching my hearers were generally very few. Sometimes so few attended meeting that I omitted preaching, and had only prayer[,] singing and religious conversation. Some of my brethren wondered that I was not discouraged, and, as they have since told me, thought I never could succeed at all as a preacher. But I was never discouraged. The sense of duty superseded every obstructing consideration. I had been too fully convinced of my call before I laid my hand to the plough to think of looking back afterwards.

In the course of the summer some ministers of other denominations publicly opposed me with great violence. This opposition aroused me to defensive exertion. People began to have a more favorable opinion of my doctrine and abilities. Opposition served to promote the very cause which Satan intended it should retard.

In the latter part of summer Mr. Farwell again visited us. I and my wife went home with him. From his house we proceeded with him to the annual convention of universalian ministers and delegates which was holden in September at Woodstock in the county of Windsor. I was received as a member of the convention and chosen as clerk for the time. I drew the circular epistle which was published by the order and in the name of that convention. At no period of my life have I enjoyed more solid pleasure than during this journey.

This convention gave me a license or letter of fellowship as a preacher, a copy of which I here insert as follows.

This may certify whom it may concern that the Association of Universalists met in Convention at Woodstock in Vermont, 4th Septr 1799, being satisfied with brother Walter Ferriss as a believer in the Gospel of Christ, and endowed with suitable qualifications to administer the Word in public; and being also certified of his moral Character as good, have given him fellowship to preach the Word wheresoever God by his Providence may open a Door.

> Signed in behalf of the Association
> Wm. *Farwell*
> David *Ballou*
> Hosea *Ballou*   Committee of Ministers.[1]

, ,

Nathaniel Stacy, despite his fragile health, was one of the most vigorous of the early Universalist circuit riders. He opened much of New York State to the faith and was active also in Pennsylvania. His various circuits carried him as far west as Ann Arbor, Michigan, which he used as a home base for five years.

Through much of his early career Stacy "kept school." It was in this manner, supplemented by subsistence farming, that many a preacher eked out a sufficient living to keep himself clothed in homespun, to support his horse, and, if he had one, his family.

When in his early twenties, Stacy met Hosea Ballou in Dana, Massachusetts, which the latter used as a base for his itineracy. Ballou, with an eye ever open for preaching talent, offered to help Stacy achieve a theological education. Ballou's philosophy of education becomes immediately apparent in this passage from Stacy's autobiography.

‘ ‘

I remained with Mr. Ballou but a short period; and, when at home, my time was devoted to the careful study of the Scriptures, hearing Mr. Ballou's comments on them, (for he was always ready to assist me, and answer any question I proposed to him,) to arranging discourses on particular subjects, and writing sketches of sermons. I also traveled with him to his appointments, very generally, that I might enjoy the benefit of his private conversation, as well as his public discourses; for he had now done riding to Vermont and Cape Ann; and his circuit, if I mistake not, was wholly confined to the county of Worcester, the towns of Dana, Brookfield, Charlton, Oxford, Sturbridge, &c.

It was in the month of October, 1802, if I rightly recollect, in the 24th year of my age, that I entered the study of Mr. Ballou. I had been with him not to exceed one month, when, one Sunday morning, being his appointment in Dana, after we had reached the village, and called at the house of our friend Amsden, Mr. Ballou was seized with a violent pain in the head, and came to me with his hand on his forehead, saying, very mournfully, "Brother Stacy, you must preach to-day; for I am in such violent pain, I can not." It was a dark, lowery morning; very few had assembled, and, in all probability, the congregation would be composed wholly of our particular friends. I looked at him to see if he was really in earnest; and seeing that he looked quite serious, I replied. "Why, I guess you can preach, well enough; and, besides, you know I can not make an attempt at beginning here, among my familiar acquaintances,—I should be confounded, and break down at once. Moreover, if you had any idea of setting me to preach to-day, you should have informed me before we left home. I have some manuscripts which I could have taken for assistance; but I have now not a scroll of writing with me. I cannot attempt to go into the desk to-day." "I am glad," he said, "you have no writing with you; it would only be a trouble to you. You must learn to preach extemporaneously; and the better way is to begin in the first place." "But," I answered, "I cannot attempt it to-day; and I never can begin here. I must go among strangers in the first place; I shall feel less embarrassment there, I'm sure. Here every body knows me, and I shall certainly break down under their suspicious gaze." "No," he said, "this is the very place; and this is the time for you to begin. There will be but a small congregation, to-day, and these, all our special friends. They know you are designing to preach, and they all want to hear you; and they will be ready to overlook your diffidence, make every allowance, and pardon every blunder; and when once you have made your *debut*, the way will be broken, and you will begin to feel a freedom. And, besides, you may say just what you please, and I'll get up and prove it all true, by Scripture;" and with that he turned away, leaving me confounded, and almost stupefied. In a few moments he returned, with some half-dozen of our friends, who surrounded me with, "Brother Stacy! come, preach to-day;—this is your time to begin —the very best time you ever can have; and when once you have made a beginning, the worst will be over; and the sooner you begin the better." By their united importunity, I was at length led, "like an ox to the slaughter," into the desk! But Belshazzar's knees could never smite together more violently, when he saw the hand-writing upon the wall, than did mine when I arose to address the congregation! They were all my intimate acquaintances, and they gazed at me with astonishment. They had, indeed, been made acquainted with my determination to try to preach; but they did not expect it that day, nor, probably, ever expect that I should attempt to make my debut in that place. I was not, however, afraid of their censure; I knew they were friends to the cause, and friends to me. But I felt my own insufficiency, my own nothingness; and the absolute preposterousness of attempting to teach those whose experience was so much greater than mine, and whose knowledge must, consequently, far exceed that of mine. But notwithstanding that, I felt no regret that I had resolved to enter the ministry; no inclination to give up exertions to become a useful laborer in the vineyard, but rather a renewed resolution to persevere; and I devoutly prayed for strength, and boldness in the good cause. The congregation took their seats, and I arose, and with a trembling voice read a hymn, or rather a psalm, for we used Watts'

psalms and hymns. And here I made a blunder in the outset—I
read a psalm and called it a hymn; and the choir would not have
found it had not Mr. Ballou corrected the mistake. This added
to my embarrassment, and I began to fear that I should not be
able to tell where my text might be found, nor read it right, if I
could find it myself. However, they sung, and I arose, made a
short prayer, and put out another hymn correctly. After the choir
had concluded singing, I again arose, and it was well that I had a
desk to lay my bible on, and to lean against, otherwise I felt sure
I could not have seen a letter, and it is very questionable
whether I should have been able to stand up. But I opened the
bible and read, I guess, intelligibly, the 8th verse of the 40th
chapter of Isaiah: "The grass withereth, and the flower fadeth;
but the word of our God shall stand forever." I spoke probably
twenty or twenty-five minutes; but I attended to every proposition of my text, and finished my discourse. Mr. Ballou then
arose and closed the service; and it appeared to me, that I never
heard so fervent and pathetic a prayer uttered by mortal man before. I heard no more of Mr. Ballou's headache—he was well
enough, as far as I could discover, when he got me into the desk;
for he made no complaint in the afternoon, but preached like an
Apostle. I told him afterwards, and I always believed it, that his
headache was feigned; though I could never make him own, or
deny it. After we had left the meeting-house, I asked Mr. Ballou
how I got along with my discourse? For, said I, it is nearly impossible for me to recollect any thing I said. O, he replied, you
did very well—I thought you sometimes made rather long pauses
between your sentences; but you preached a better sermon than
Mr. Babbit did the other day. This I set down for what it was
worth; for I supposed it was said merely to encourage me. Mr.
Babbit had been preaching about two years; and the discourse
he alluded to, was called a very good discourse. But Mr. Ballou
used every possible means he could devise to inspire me with
confidence, encourage, and help me along.

, ,

The Universalists found the Methodists to be their most
keen competitors on the frontier. With a well-organized adminis-

tration of circuits because of their episcopal government, and with a democratic gospel which stressed the possibility of man's perfectibility (but shunned universal salvation), Methodists appealed to the frontiersmen, who looked forward to the future with hope. The Methodist circuit riders tried their best to link the Universalists with immorality.

Stacy, like other Universalists, delighted in reporting an encounter with a Methodist.

‘ ‘

My school was large, and a majority of the district were Methodists. I boarded around among them, united in their family worship, and soon cultivated a social and friendly intercourse, and received numerous expressions of Christian charity, although they considered me in great error in doctrine. There was a society, or class, as they called it, organized in the place, and they had regular circuit preaching on Wednesday, each week, at four o'clock, P.M.; and I uniformly so arranged my school as to dismiss it early enough to attend; and was generally introduced to the preacher, and in most cases treated with civility. There were several different preachers on the circuit, during my residence there, and among them one who was an exception to the gentle-ell; and he was as coarse-featured, thin-faced, and raw-boned, as manly character they generally manifested. His name was Mitch-one of Pharaoh's lean kine; rather below the medium stature, a little round-shouldered, and wore a very short and narrow calico loose-gown. He appeared as though he had almost hallooed and hooted his life away. I did not reach the place of his meeting until services had commenced. They uniformly held their meetings in a room of a private house. As I entered the room, a Methodist friend arose and placed a chair for me in front of the speaker, and within six or eight feet of him. He was reading a hymn when I entered. After they had sung, he kneeled down and delivered something which I suppose he would have called a prayer; but it was rather a tissue of execrations upon the heads of such as had the temerity to think and believe differently from his divinityship. He arose and sang again, and then named, for a text, 1 Pet. 4: 18. "And if the righteous scarcely be saved, where shall the ungodly and the sinner appear?" He remarked, that he should, in the first place, show who the righteous were, and how difficult it would be for even them to be saved; secondly, describe the sinner, and the ungodly, and show where they would appear. He proceeded; and, to be brief, undertook to prove that none were righteous but those who believed and acted like himself; in a word, that none were righteous but Methodists; and it would be with the utmost difficulty that any, even of them, could get to heaven. During his discourse, he paid great attention to me. I had not been introduced to him; but it was evident he knew who I was—some of his friends, no doubt, had described me to him; for, repeatedly, when he had quoted a passage of Scripture, he would look earnestly at me, and even point at me, and say, "Don't you remember it?" I was on the point of answering him vocally; but I very well knew, although his impudence deserved it, that if I did so, it would be represented that I went there to make disturbance in their meetings, notwithstanding I uniformly attended, and had had no occasion to behave disorderly before. For I felt interested in all religious meetings, and wished to hear different opinions advanced with all the force of argument they could claim; for I had no fears that truth would suffer by investigation. Truth was what I wanted; and, to obtain it, I felt a desire to "Prove all things, and hold fast that which is good." And I felt no more inclination to disturb the meetings of others, nor infringe on their privileges, than those of my own order. But he would, without turning his eyes from me, repeat the question, "Don't you remember it?" and continued to repeat it, until I gave him a token, either by an inclination, or a shake of the head, that I did, or did not, as the case might be. After he had finally settled the destiny of *his* righteous, he began with sinners and the ungodly. Sinners, meant the ordinary sinners among mankind; but the ungodly were false teachers— those who were propagating false doctrines, and leading souls blindfold down to hell! And then, leaning forward so as to almost thrust his finger in my face, and raising his voice almost to a scream, he exclaimed, "If the righteous are scarcely saved, where do you expect to appear?" I now had to exert my patience and fortitude to the utmost, to keep my seat. I could not answer this question by a motion of the head, as before; but I resolved still to give no occasion for censure by disturbing the meeting, and therefore kept my seat. But to show him my perfect contempt of such unchristian, ungentlemanly, and insolent treatment, I smiled, disdainfully, in his face. His face instantly reddened with passion—his eyes seemed to flash fire! he leaped, it appeared to me, three feet from the floor, and smiting his fist on the Bible, his eyes steadfastly fixed on me, and mine on him with the same contemptuous smile—he exclaimed, with a voice like thunder, "I'll tell you where you'll appear—you'll appear in *hell*, with the liquid streams of fire and brimstone pouring down your throat, to all eternity!" Although I kept my seat, yet I said within myself, You and I, sir, will have a reconsideration and review of this matter, after meeting. When he closed, however, he made no pause between Amen and ordering all to leave the room without delay, but Methodists, in order to hold a class-meeting. I have often had the opportunity of witnessing the advantage which illiterate, low, vulgar, and abusive Methodist preachers take of their class-meeting arrangement, to escape rebuke for their insolent conduct. But although I implicitly obeyed the order of his ghostly highness, I resolved to wait the close of class-meeting, for an introduction to him; and did wait until long after dark; but fearing, if I did not go home, he would keep the poor Methodists all night, I concluded to retire.

.   .   .

The sixth session of our Association, (1811,) was holden in Bainbridge, Chenango county [New York]. As no meeting-house could be obtained, our friends fitted up a newly-built barn meeting-houses as that, we often had to occupy; and we felt ourselves highly accommodated when we obtained a clean one; nor 'n as convenient a manner as possible, for the occasion. Such did we think it a disgrace for Christians to worship God in a barn, inasmuch as a stable was the birth-place of the Captain of our salvation. Mr. [Paul] Dean then resided within the territorial limits of the Association, and was consequently with us; and five others, heretofore named, who were members of this ecclesiastical body, were present, and a single individual, Nathaniel

Smith, bearing credentials of appointment from the General Convention, with two other preachers of the Great Salvation, who had never before appeared among us; and singular as the circumstance may appear, one was a female.

Maria Cook, then about thirty years of age, was escorted to that place by two gentlemen of the first respectability, from the town of Sheshequin, Bradford county, Pennsylvania, where she had been visiting for several weeks, and holding meetings. They introduced her to the council as a person of irreproachable morals, and with high encomiums upon her public labors. Some of our brethren and friends were a little fastidious about allowing a woman to preach, supposing St. Paul forbade it, where he says, *he suffered not a woman to teach, nor to usurp authority*, &c., while others thought differently, believing he would not have applauded the labors of so many female *helpers in the Lord*, if he did not, under suitable circumstances, approve of their public ministration. But as the phenomenon of a female preacher appearing among us was so *extraordinary*, and curiosity was on tiptoe among the mass of the congregation, to hear a woman preach, our opposing brethren finally withdrew their objections, and she very cheerfully obliged us with a discourse. And there was not a sermon delivered with more eloquence, with more correctness of diction, or pathos, or one listened to with more devout attention; nor was there another delivered during the session so highly applauded by the whole congregation, as the one she delivered. And so excited and animated were many of the brethren by the novelty, and so highly pleased and edified with her public discourse, that a letter of fellowship for her, as a preacher of the Gospel, was almost peremptorily demanded. She, herself, appeared quite indifferent about it. But as she came well recommended, both as to her religious and moral character, and as she certainly exhibited sound faith and a becoming zeal for the promotion of the cause, was well educated and possessed more than ordinary speaking talents, an informal letter was presented to her, which she modestly accepted. This letter of fellowship, however, she destroyed in a few weeks afterwards, because she thought some of the preachers, especially Mr. Dean, did not treat her with that kindness which the letter betokened; and she conscientiously destroyed, (so she told me,) what she considered an insincere token of fellowship.

She there received numerous and earnest requests from the delegates from all the societies, and from nearly every visiting brother, to come to their respective societies and towns and hold meetings; and she readily complied with as many of these calls as her time and health would permit. She possessed no means of conveyance of her own, nor did she desire it; some friends always accompanied her, and helped her from place to place. Her meetings, for a season, were the most numerously attended of any preacher of any denomination, who had ever traveled through the country, and were certainly quite advantageous to the cause of truth, as they called out many who, had it not been for the novelty of the circumstance, could not have been induced to attend a Universalist meeting; and who, after obtaining some ideas of the doctrine from her discourses, were inclined to hear others; and her remuneration by contributions was far more liberal than any preacher of our order received, or perhaps any itinerant preacher of any denomination. But Miss Cook had numerous opposers to the course she pursued, irrespective of the doctrine she inculcated, and especially among her own sex, who thought it very improper, and even indecent for a woman to preach, and especially to itinerate as she did. She was quite sensitive; and the vituperations and uncharitable remarks which were constantly falling upon her ears considerably discomposed her, and soon began to give quite a tone to her public discourses, by leading her into long arguments in vindication of her right to preach; which would not unfrequently constitute the whole burden of her discourse. This rendered them rather stale and uninteresting; the novelty of the circumstance subsiding, invitations became less frequent, and her congregations vastly decreased in numbers. She however remained in the counties of Chenango, Madison, Oneida, Otsego, and Herkimer, something like a year. She then made a visit to the region of Troy; and quite a lengthy stay, (several months I believe,) among the Shakers; and then returned to her friends; for she had a mother, brothers, and sisters in Geneva and vicinity. After the lapse of a year or more, she made our part of the country another visit; but her reception was not so cordial and flattering as on her first tour; still she had many warm friends in different parts of the country. She preached but little; and, in the fall of the year, took up her residence among some friends in that part of the town of Otsego called Pierstown, with a design to spend the winter. But some malignant spirit, who wanted to spit his venom against Universalism in some form, and no doubt thinking that, by disturbing her, he should injure the feelings of some of her friends, and thereby ingratiate himself into the favor of the Orthodox aristocracy, entered a complaint to the proper authorities, stating that such a vagrant person was in town, and liable to become a town-charge. Nothing could have been more untrue. It was generally known that she had a sufficient income to maintain her, secured to her by the will of her deceased father—to amply provide her a support under any circumstances. Her brother, on whom I once called by her request, when traveling in Western New York, told me that, at any time when she wished to return home, he would send for her; and, at any time when she needed money, let him know it, and he would send it to her; notwithstanding, he and all her relatives were very much opposed to the course she was pursuing, and considered her under a mental derangement.

But a precept was issued by Esquire F., of Cooperstown, and put into the hands of a constable, who immediately went in pursuit of her. Her friends remonstrated with the officer—told him there was no possible necessity for disturbing her, that they would become responsible that she should not be chargeable upon the town—but all to no purpose; he had received his "letter of authority," and "haul her to prison" he would. He went where she had taken up her abode, and a ludicrous scene ensued. He was with a wagon; and he informed her, that the law required him to take her to Cooperstown, before Esq. F. She told him, he must do it then. "Well," said he, "will you take a seat in the wagon?" She replied, "No." "Well, how will you go?" She answered, "I will not go at all." "But the law requires me to carry you there." "Well, I have nothing to do with the law; and, if you have, you must do your duty." But how he should carry her, was the question, if she would not get into his wagon.

"That," said she, "is your business—not mine." The man was completely put to his trumps—she moved not, nor would she move, or make any preparations. It was about five miles where he wanted to carry her. He was finally compelled, as a last resort, to take her in his arms, and set her in his wagon, to which she made no resistance. The friend who gave me the information, circumstantially, took his horse and followed them, to see that she met with no personal abuse; for he felt confident they never could extort an answer from her to a single question. The constable drove to the door of the office, stopped his team, and remarked, "This is Esq. F.'s office. Will you get out of the wagon, and walk in." She replied, "No; I have no business with Esq. F.; if he has business with me, let him come to me." No persuasion could make her move from the wagon; and the constable left her, went into the office, informed the magistrate of the circumstance, and asked him what he should do. The magistrate told him to bring her into the office. So he was again compelled to take her in his arms, carry her into the office, where he seated her in a chair; when the following dialogue ensued:

Magistrate. Miss Cook, inasmuch as a complaint has been entered, I have been obliged, by law, to issue a precept, and have you brought before me, not to abuse you, nor to injure your feelings, if I can avoid it; but to ask you a few questions, relative to your place of residence, means of subsistence, &c.

Miss C. You can ask me any questions you please; but I feel under no obligation to answer you, nor shall I answer any of your questions.

Mag. But will you not tell me your place of residence?

Miss C. No.

Mag. But the law requires it, madam, and I have but one course to pursue. If you will not answer the necessary inquiries, I shall be under the disagreeable necessity to commit you to jail, until you will answer.

Miss C. You can do as you please. I have seen demons in the seat of justice before now—I have a brother who acts in that capacity.

Not being able to obtain any thing like an answer to a single question he proposed, the magistrate wrote a *mittimus* for contempt of court, read it to her, and handed it to the constable.

Miss C. You have worded it right, sir, for you and all your proceedings are perfectly contemptible, in my view.

Constable. Miss Cook, will you walk out, and take a seat in the wagon?

Miss C. No.

The constable was, therefore, under the necessity of taking her into his arms again, and seating her in the wagon. He then drove to the jail, carried her into the building, and delivered her to the jailer. The keeper was a friendly man—his family resided in one part of the prison-house; and he told Miss Cook, that she was welcome to his table, and gave her liberty to visit any apartment of the prison, or other part of the building she was disposed to see. There she remained, perfectly contented and happy, for several weeks; and, while in these circumstances, she sent word to me, that she was preaching to the spirits in prison. After some weeks, finding they could neither drive nor flatter her to pay any respect to their authority, the magistrate hinted to the jailer to get rid of her the easiest way he could.[2]

, ,

Stephen R. Smith, like Stacy, diligently propagated Universalism as a circuit rider and later recorded many memories of the early days of Universalism in New York State. He writes of the year 1814.

‘ ‘

. . . Those societies which could command the regular services of a clergyman, would locate the older and more experienced ministers of the order.—And there were generally, enough of such, to supply for a greater or less proportion of the time, all the congregations which aspired to the maintenance of regular public worship. It therefore followed, that with few exceptions— every young minister was compelled to itinerate. This, though attended with many inconveniences, as well as requiring great labor, was probably best under the circumstances, both for preachers and people. It gave many congregations the means of holding an occasional meeting and inquirers an opportunity of hearing the truth, at the same time that the young preacher was acquiring experience. Societies incurred little expense, and preachers prevented from reading books, studied human nature under aspects, which never could have been contemplated in any other way. The mission of such a minister, is emphatically to all the world. Unfettered by the local considerations and attachments of the settled pastor—the itinerant feels an independence, and expresses himself with a freedom and boldness, that would startle or astonish the servant of a congregation. This therefore is the field in which germinated that species of character, for which some of the preachers of the denomination, are still distinguished; and which whatever their worth, renders them more the objects of respect than of esteem.

But while destitute and feeble congregations were assisted and often established and built up by the instrumentality of an itinerant ministry—the real wants of such preachers were sometimes overlooked and neglected. Many of the older preachers of Universalism, expended in travelling to fill their appointments, all that they received. Others who had it to spare—freely devoted the gatherings of previous years of toil; and reduced themselves to poverty. And often have these men, travelled the long, weary day, unrefreshed, from "early dawn to latest eve," to reach the place of their appointment. Poorly clad and poorly sustained—who can wonder that they were unknown by the world!

.   .   .

The violence and dogmatism with which Universalism and its ministers were assailed, during the winter of 1820–21, resulted in arrangements for a public oral debate between Mr. [Pitt] Morse and Mr. Evarts, then presiding Elder in the Black River Conference of the Methodist Episcopal Church. This took place on the first of May, 1821, at the Church in Bellville, in the town of Ellisburg. Mr. Evarts was by some years the senior of Mr. Morse—was besides, a man of some reputation as a clergyman, which was implied by his position—could and did bring an array of Methodist ministers to sustain and assist him, and to overawe his young antagonist by the double weight of numbers and the influence of public sentiment. It was arranged, that the debate should open at 9 o'clock, on each successive morning during its continuance—that it should continue till noon, when an intermission of one hour should follow—that it should be renewed at one o'clock, in the afternoon and continue till four, when it should adjourn over till the next morning—and so on from day to day, until it should finally close. The respective parties were alternately to occupy a given number of minutes, during which they were not to be interrupted—were to treat each other with respect and civility—and were to settle all arguments under the propositions in debate, by an appeal to the scriptures. The main proposition was, in substance—whether the scriptures taught the final holiness and happiness of all men, or that some men would be endlessly miserable.

The debate opened on the morning of the first day, with prayer, by one of the Methodist clergymen in attendance, in presence of a numerous auditory, that filled every part of the church. Mr. Evarts then stepped forward, and before ascending the pulpit steps—kneeled and remained a few moments in *silent* if not *secret* prayer—before the whole congregation. This ostentation of devotion, carried our minds back to the time when his predecessors in religious pretensions, thanked God that they were not like other men. God forbid, that we should be understood, as offering any objection to prayer. But we must be permitted to utter our protest, against the observance of the form, under circumstances so directly and almost exclusively calculated to excite the belief—that it is done "to be seen of men."

It were worse than useless, to attempt to give the particular arguments, proofs, assertions and assumptions, which occurred in an oral discussion of almost an entire week. Those who have read the heavy volumes that give in detail the sayings and doings on similar occasions, or have otherwise given much attention to the subject; very well know that much irrelevant matter is usually introduced, that not a few sarcasms are uttered—jokes perpetrated—some ill nature excited, and many things said in sorry keeping with the gravity and importance of the subject. In this instance, it may be said, that the discussion was conducted with about the usual amount of decorum on such occasions; and it is particularly due to Mr. Morse, to state, that though at times compelled to utter strong language and sharp rebuke, he never lost sight of the dignity of the subject nor of his own self-respect.

The arguments and proofs commonly relied on, in support of the doctrine of endless misery, were presented in every form of which the subject seemed to admit. The supposed scriptural, and all other objections that either custom or prejudice had sanctioned or could urge against the doctrine of the restitution, were presented by Mr. Evarts, with persevering and characteristic zeal. And both the faith and morality of Universalists, were assailed, as equally destructive of individual peace and public safety. On the other hand, Mr. Morse labored with very obvious success to repel the aspersions cast upon the denomination—to remove the objections to the faith of Universalism—and successfully threw back upon his opponent, the charge of maintaining dogmas, alike dishonorable to God and unworthy of sition, he proceeded to argue from various premises the necessity the faith and confidence of sensible men. Having reached his po- and the consequent certainty of the final holiness and happiness of all men, sustaining his deductions by an array of Scriptural proofs, which attracted the most intense regard of the congregation, and evidently excited the surprise of his antagonist.

Thus the discussion progressed from day to day, until Friday noon, when Mr. Evarts refused to adjourn for the accustomed intermission of an hour. His Methodist friends sustained him; and the Universalists, and more liberal part of the auditory, sustained Mr. Morse in preserving inviolate the rules of procedure originally adopted. The Methodists were accordingly left to carry on the debate as best they might, during the usual intermission. And at the close of the hour, when the Universalists returned to the house, behold, the bird had flown! During the absence of the Universalists, Mr. Evarts had called a vote from his friends, to the amount that Universalism had been triumphantly refuted and exploded; on which he declared the debate closed, when they immediately left the house.[3]

, ,

Universalists were among the most prolific of newspaper publishers—and, presumably, readers. The movement resulted in a veritable rash of newspapers, North and South. As it spread west new journals were established to cater to local tastes.

No matter where published, Universalist papers displayed certain common characteristics. They were naturally polemical sheets which sought to establish "Universalian" truth and to combat the corruptions of orthodoxy. The following pieces are from the *Star in the West*, published in Cincinnati by John A. Gurley and E. M. Pingree. As the first item (1840) shows, the Universalists, dedicated as they were to the use of reason in religion, poked fun at the claims of the revivalists. The second item (1843) displays their willingness to turn the tables on the orthodox who insisted that Universalism led to licentiousness.

‛ ‛

MR. MAFFIT AGAINST THE POWER OF GOD.

It is well known, that Mr. Maffit and his brethren, claim that the late excitement in this city was produced by the direct agency and power of God—that the conversions and shouts consequent thereon, were the results of his irresistible spirit. To show the utter fallacy of such pretensions, we propose to give a short conversation which took place a few days since between an old gentleman and a Methodist, relative to the subject. We give it as near as possible, as it came to us. The two individuals were old acquaintances, and the latter well knew that the former had no faith in their excitements—at least, had not previously believed in them. The Methodist thus accosted the Universalist.

Well Mr. ——— have you been to hear Mr. Maffit yet?

Uni. O yes, I was up to hear him the other evening.

Meth. Am very glad to hear it—how did you like him?

Uni. Like him! why, sir, I think him the greatest man in the world.

Meth. Indeed; well it does me good to hear that from you, (the Methodist thinking his old friend was perhaps converted) the power of God is certainly with him—he is doing wonders.

Uni. That he is, wonders indeed—he is certainly the most powerful man in the world!

Meth. But what do you refer to particularly friend? (the Methodist beginning to doubt a little his sincerity.) Why do you think him the most powerful man in the world?

Uni. I will tell you: On the evening I heard him preach, after sermon, the mourners were called up for prayers and soon God began to influence the people—he converted a number, was working wonderfully among them, and they were shouting at the top of their voices from the effect of his spirit, when all at once, Mr. Maffit's hand was heard, tap! tap! tap! upon the desk, and in a moment the house was so still, that you could almost have heard a pin drop in any part of it. Why, sir, was there ever such power known before in man? God himself at work with all his might, converting the people, when Mr. Maffit, stopped the whole of it in the twinkling of an eye, by the mere tap of his finger upon the desk! Most astonishing! that a man should thus be able to stop the power and direct work of Almighty God!! Whoever heard the like before? The sharp rebuke took effect, and the Methodist was silent for the space of about half an hour.

How well this circumstance proves, with many similar ones, that Mr. Maffit was the whole cause of the excitement produced, and that he was an absolute sovereign over his converts. He did with them precisely as he pleased; and just before he left, we understand, he made them form in regular columns, and marched them through the meeting house in real military order. Well, if they choose to follow his direction, we will not interfere; but for ourselves, we choose to follow the direction of a more excellent leader, even the Redeemer of men, in whom was found no sin.[4]

TRIAL FOR SEDUCTION

We have before us the 'Spirit of the Age,' published in Pittsburgh, Pa., containing the most of the testimony given in the investigation of a charge made by Eleanor Jane M'Fadden against Rev. George Marshall, Presbyterian Clergyman for seduction. The case is entitled, 'COMMONWEALTH AGAINST Geo. Marshall.' The Editor of the 'Age' remarks in reference to the matter as follows:

'This case excites extraordinary interest, and has called together an immense number of curious spectators, among whom is a large number of clergymen of various denominations, but principally Presbyterian. During the examination of the prosecutrix the court was crowded to its full extent, even the bench was invaded to such a degree, as we should think, drew largely upon the politeness of their honors the Judges of the Court.

The defendant, Mr. MARSHALL, is well known to this community, as a clergyman, and until the charge under which he is now being tried was preferred against him, has always borne an unblemished reputation.'

We think it due to the public that some notice should be taken of this trial. Justice to morality and religion require that the people should be put upon their guard against men who take the 'livery of heaven to serve the devil in.' Another fact. Endless misery is found no safe-guard against such sins. We have had many accounts of late of clerical (Orthodox) wickedness. It was only a few days since that Rev. L. Reed of Plattsburg, was exposed. He was guilty of the same villany charged against this man. He denied his sin at first, but afterwards confessed his guilt and run away. But in this case the preacher appears in Court to defend himself.—Some curious developments are made in the testimony given. For example, the young lady gives the following:

'He said he thought it was a great sin, after it was over, and wished that she would forgive him for it; he said David had sinned the same way too; recollect nothing else. My child was born on the 23d day of August, at uncle David Lyons', in St.

Clair township, she thinks.—Before the first connection had no conversation with defendant on the subject; had afterwards—about the same as we had before; said he was sorry for having done so; he gave me no book to read, turned my attention to no chapter in the Bible, in particular, only that of David; said David had sinned in the same way that he had.'

We are inclined to think that the case of David will hardly save Mr. Marshall from the just penalty of the law framed in an enlightened age. Men are always sorry after the commission of crime—then why repeat it as the girl avers was done often by Mr. Marshall. He was sensible all the time that he was committing a very great crime, but still he did not desist. And why? The following from her testimony answers.

'I told him I thought it was a great sin; he insisted upon it by saying that *we would get forgiveness if we would seek for it.'*

Ah! here is the secret of his repeated sins; his Orthodox theology taught him that by asking forgiveness all the punishment due would be readily remitted. He persuaded the poor young woman, who was a member of his own Church, to believe the same—and in this way accomplished his object. Thus, according to the testimony, he acted on that popular partialist doctrine, that there is pleasure in sin, and all its consequences may be escaped by a timely repentance. But he is now learning by sad experience, that the wicked are recompensed in the earth. The transgressor shall by *no means* escape; this is Universalism —a doctrine which the Rev. Gentleman has preached against many a time—and practised against too.

We have not all the testimony before us; but we judge from that we have . . . that Mr. Marshall is the father of the child. The Jury had not given their decision when the 'Age' went to press.[5]

, ,

Aside from newspapers, Universalists were prolific publishers of books and tracts. These books (except for the ones designed to fight internal battles) presented the faith to the world and defended it from its enemies. A whole genre was devoted to presenting the faithful both on the frontier and in the more settled areas with the ammunition necessary to ward off the slings and arrows of outrageous opponents.

Typical examples from this literature follow. The first extract is from the disciple of Hosea Ballou who, as publisher of *The Trumpet*, was to grow into a doughty defender of Universalism. Thomas Whittemore attempts to counteract two popular charges against the denomination.

' '

> "It cannot be denied, that the advocates of Universalism are mostly to be found in that class of people which the Bible denominates wicked; while nearly all the wise and good adopt the contrary belief. The intemperate, the thief, the robber, the profane swearer, the murderer, the corrupt and dissolute, are generally pleased with the preaching of Universalists; but the pious and the better portion of community deprecate the influence of such preaching. I like the society of the wise and good, better than that of thieves, and drunkards, and profane swearers."

It would be well for us all, if we would be much on our guard against the sin of self-righteousness. It is a sin that doth most easily beset us. We fear, that the author of this objection, doubtless unconsciously to himself, was under the influence of some such error. Did he not entertain a high opinion of himself? Is it not arrogating too much to himself, and those who agree with him in opinion, to say, "nearly all the wise and good" adopt the belief of endless misery? Is such a profession consistent with the spirit which led the publican to exclaim, "Lord, be merciful to me a sinner"? It rather reminds us of the case of the Pharisee, who said "Lord, I thank thee that I am not like other men." But are the allegations true, which are embraced in this objection? That those who really *feel themselves* to be sinners, and see their need of divine grace and salvation, will prize the doctrine of Universalism, is unquestionable; but this is not what the objector means. He means, that those who have no contrition for their offences,—the thoughtless, the cruel, and the debauched, are generally in favor of Universalism. In this sense the objection is false. Is it true, that the wicked are generally Universalists? Is it true, that those who take the name of God in vain, —those who are intemperate,—those who are debauched, are generally Universalists? Examine the penitentiaries. Inquire into the religious opinions of the prisoners; and in the great majority of cases, you will find, that they have been educated in the belief of endless torments. It is true, they have not paid much attention to the subject of theology, in any way; but, so far as they believe in the future state, they generally apprehend, that the doctrine of endless misery is true. Were those who have carried on persecution,—who have kindled the fagot,—who have shed rivers of human blood,—who have murdered men, and women, and children, indiscriminately, in their attempts to exterminate heresy,—have these men been Universalists? No instance of persecution can be pointed out, in all the history of the church, which can be justly attributed to those who believe, that God will at last have mercy on all. Who were the inquisitors,—those who loved to feast their eyes on writhing bodies, and to gratify their ears with the groans and unavailing prayers of the poor victims of their wrath? Were *these men* Universalists? No, not one of them; for, had they been, their doctrine would have taught them better; they would have had compassion on the ignorant, and those who are out of the way. It is a truth, which a strict observation of society will confirm, that Universalism prevails mostly in those places where crime is least known. Compare the different parts of our own country, with one another, and then inquire in which parts Universalism mostly prevails. Compare our own country with Europe, and the above remark will be fully proved. It cannot be said, in truth, that Universalism is principally to be found among those who are justly denominated the vicious.

We have already hinted at the fact, that those who really feel their sinfulness, and are exercised with contrition for their offences, will love the doctrine of Universalism. Such loved the

doctrine of Jesus, when he was on earth. The publicans and sinners drew near unto him to receive his instructions, and the
Scribes and Pharisees murmured, because he "received sinners
and ate with them."

.   .   .

> "I cannot be a Universalist, for I fear that the
> doctrine would fail me at the hour of death.
>
> 'A death bed 's a detector of the heart.'
>
> Many who have believed this doctrine while in health
> and prosperity, have, when approaching the grave, found
> it to be a false and an unsafe foundation; have been
> obliged to relinquish it, and to cry out for mercy. I can-
> not embrace a doctrine which serves its advocates in this
> manner. A doctrine which affords hope and consolation
> when we are in health, and enjoying the pleasure of the
> world, but withdraws its support when we most need it,
> is not the doctrine which a prudent man would wish to
> believe."

There is no force in this objection. It is not true that
people renounce Universalism when they come to die. Do we
not hear every day of people dying while they rejoice in that glorious faith? and have we not often heard of those who re-
nounced the doctrine of endless misery in prospect of death, and
embraced Universalism? Facts do most fully set aside the objection before us. Behold the death of the celebrated John Murray,
the early defender of Universalism in the United States. In the
last hour he dwelt with rapture on the inspiring theme which
had animated his soul for more than half his days, and on which
he had expatiated with such great effect in hundreds of pulpits
throughout the land. See the edition of his life by T. Whittemore, p. 222. The biographer of that great and good man, Elhanan
Winchester, who labored so long and so zealously in defence of
Universalism, both in this country and in Europe, assures us,
"that he continued preaching until about the first of April (1797,
then residing in Hartford, Conn.) when he delivered a sermon,

under a strong impression that it was his last, from St. Paul's farewell address to the elders of the Ephesian church. He never entered his desk again. His death was fast approaching, and he contemplated it with serenity and joy. On the morning of his decease, he requested two or three young ladies, who were sitting by him, to join in singing a hymn, observing at the same time, that he might expire before it should be finished. He began with them; but his voice soon faltered, and the torpor of death fell upon him. They were disconcerted, and paused; but he, reviving, encouraged them to proceed, and joined in the first line of each stanza until he breathed no more." The Rev. Dr. Strong, a Presbyterian clergyman, and an eminent opposer of Universalism, preached his funeral discourse, in which he gave Mr. W. an excellent character, *and bore a frank testimony to his final constancy in the doctrine which he had preached.*

The well known instances of Universalists dying in full belief of their cheering opinions, are too numerous for us to make even a reference to the tenth part of them. One or two cases must suffice. Where was the power of pure Christian faith, to sustain the soul in the trying hour, more clearly seen, than at the death-bed of our departed friend, the late Rev. William C. Hanscom, of Waltham, Massachusetts. It was the privilege of the writer of these pages, to be often at his side, during his sickness. Over and over again he assured me, of the comfort which he derived from his trust in the divine goodness, and his hope of a happy immortality for himself, and all mankind. But a few days before his death, I proposed to him the following questions: "Are you happy in your mind?" "Perfectly," was his reply. I remarked to him, "It is said Universalism fails us in the hour of sickness." He replied, "I know, from my own experience, the falsity of this statement. I believe as firmly as ever,—I have no doubt. My faith is not in the least changed. My heart and soul are at peace. Could I live, I should preach more earnestly than ever. I have nothing to regret in my short ministry, except that I have done so little in preaching what I have believed to be the truth." The day but one before his death, I was at his bedside. He probably supposed himself dying. His eyes were intently gazing upward,—his lips were moving, and by applying my ear, I recognised these words: "I am going home to my Father in heaven,—my home,—my *heavenly home.*—I am happy." * * * * * Again, in a few moments, "How sweet 't would be to die;" * * * * * and, after a brief silence, he faintly whispered,

> "While on his breast I lean my head,
>   And breathe my life out sweetly there;"

and so he did breathe his life out sweetly, reposing, with implicit trust, on the bosom of his Saviour.

Another more recent instance of the sustaining power of Universalism in the hour of death, is seen in the death-bed experience of the late Rev. A. L. Balch, of Swanzey, Massachusetts. He had been for nearly ten years a preacher of that doctrine. In an obituary notice, published a short time after his death, by the faithful friend who preached the discourse at his funeral, we find the following account of his last moments:

"But if his prospects in life were cheering, and his confidence in the truth of the salvation of the whole race of Adam strong, they were doubly so in death. His disease for the first few days was severe, but for several of his last days he was not in much distress, and was perfectly sane, and conversed upon his departure with that calmness and composure, and even joy, which the faith and hope of the gospel only can give. Many of his friends called to see him, whom he exhorted to continue steadfast in the cause of truth, and go forward in building up the glorious cause in which they had been mutually engaged. His brother, Rev. William S. Balch, of Providence, who stood by him to close his eyes in death, he exhorted to faithfulness in his calling, as a minister of the Lord Jesus Christ. And, after having said all that he could concerning his family (his wife and son), and given directions to his brother with regard to his burial, &c., and after taking an affectionate leave of all, he desired them to sing the hymn commencing,

> 'Come, thou fount of every blessing,
>   Tune my heart to sing thy grace;
> Streams of mercy, never ceasing,
>   Call for songs of loudest praise.'

"After which, he desired to be moved so that he could see the sun, which, in all the loveliness of an autumnal sunset, was just receding from his view in more senses than one;—he observed the beauty and glory of the scene, and remarked, 'I shall soon behold a brighter sun,'—and when the light of day went down, the lamp of life went out, without the motion of a muscle, or the uttering of a groan, on Monday, November 4th, 1839." [6]

, ,

Each generation of polemicists had to write expositions of Biblical words and ideas commonly misunderstood. Like the Greek words αἰὼν and, αἰώνιος, the Hebrew word *sheol* was the subject of much discussion. As long as the common understanding of "hell" prevailed, Universalists were bound to have problems. Thomas Baldwin Thayer explained its "true" significance.

' '

The word Hell, in the Old Testament, is always a translation of the Hebrew word *Sheol*, which occurs sixty-four times, and is rendered "hell" thirty-two times, "grave" twenty-nine times, and "pit" three times.

1. By examination of the Hebrew Scriptures it will be found that its radical or primary meaning is, *The place or state of the dead.*

The following are examples: "Ye shall bring down my gray hairs with sorrow to the grave." Gen. xvii. 38. "I will go down to the grave to my son mourning." xxxviii. 35. "O that thou wouldst hide me in the grave!" Job xiv. 13. "My life draweth nigh to the grave." Ps. lxxxviii. 3. "In the grave who shall give thee thanks?" lxxxvi. 5. "Our bones are scattered at the grave's mouth." cxli. 7. "There is no work, nor device, nor knowledge, nor wisdom, in the grave, whither thou goest." Ecc. ix. 10. "If I ascend up into heaven, thou art there: if I make my bed in hell, behold thou art there." Ps. cxxxix. 8. "Hell from beneath is moved to meet thee, at thy coming. It stirreth up the dead for thee," &c. Isaiah xiv. 9–15.

These passages show the Hebrew usage of the word *sheol*, which is the original of the word "grave" and "hell" in all the examples cited. It is plain that it has here no reference to a place of endless torment after death. The patriarch would scarcely say, "I will go down to an endless hell to my son mourning." He did not believe his son was in any such place. Job would not very likely pray to God to hide him in a place of endless torment, in order to be delivered from his troubles.

If the reader will substitute the word "hell" in the place of "grave" in all these passages, he will be in the way of understanding the Scripture doctrine on this subject.

2. But there is also a figurative sense to the word *sheol*, which is frequently met with in the later Scriptures of the Old Testament. Used in this sense, it represents *a state of degradation or calamity, arising from any cause, whether misfortune, sin, or the judgment of God.*

This is an easy and natural transition. The state or the place of the dead was regarded as solemn and gloomy, and thence the word sheol, the name of this place, came to be applied to any gloomy, or miserable state or condition. The following passages are examples: "The sorrows of hell compassed me about; the snares of death prevented me." Psalm xvii. 4–6 This was a past event, and therefore the hell must have been this side of death. Solomon, speaking of a child, says, "Thou shalt beat him, and deliver his soul from hell;" that is, from the ruin and woe of disobedience. Prov. xxiii. 14. The Lord says to Israel, in reference to their idolatries, "Thou didst debase thyself even unto hell." Isaiah lvii. 9. This, of course, signifies a state of utter moral degradation and wickedness, since the Jewish nation as such certainly never went down into a hell of ceaseless woe. Jonah says, "Out of the belly of hell cried I, and thou heardst me." ii. 2. Here we see the absurdity of supposing *sheol* or *hell* to mean a place of punishment after death. The hell in this case was the belly of the whale; or rather the wretched and suffering condition in which the disobedient prophet found himself. "The pains of hell got hold on me: I found trouble and sorrow." Ps. cxvi. 3. Yet David was a living man, all this while, here on the earth. So he exclaims again, "Great is thy mercy towards me. Thou hast delivered my soul from the lowest hell." Ps. lxxxvi. 13. Now here the Psalmist was in the lowest hell, and was delivered from it, while he was yet in the body, *before* death. Of course the hell here cannot be a place of endless punishment *after* death.

These passages sufficiently illustrate the figurative usage of the word *sheol,* "hell." They show plainly that it was employed by the Jews as a symbol or figure of extreme degradation or suffering, without reference to the cause. And it is to this condition the Psalmist refers when he says, "The wicked shall be turned into hell, and all the nations that forget God." Ps. ix. 17. Though Dr. Allen, President of Bowdoin College, thinks "the punishment expressed here is cutting off from life, destroying from earth by some special judgment, and removing to the invisible place of the dead" (*sheol*).

It is plain, then, from these citations, that the word *sheol,* "hell," makes nothing for the doctrine of future unending punishment as a part of the Law penalties. It is never used by Moses or the Prophets in the sense of a place of torment after death; and in no way conflicts with the statement already proved, that the Law of Moses deals wholly in temporal rewards and punishments.[7]

, ,

Religions rarely—if ever—claim to be new. Each group attempts to trace its roots back to antiquity in order to enjoy the legitimacy which age is thought to give. As the Universalist denomination began to enjoy stability and some acceptance, its thinkers sought to do the same for it. Hosea Ballou, 2d, in 1829 published *The Ancient History of Universalism.* The following year saw the publication of Thomas Whittemore's *Modern History of Universalism.*

Thomas B. Thayer displayed the same tendency in his *Theology of Universalism* when he illustrated his arguments with examples from the writings of early Christian Fathers who held universalist views.

‹ ‹

. . . Testimonies from the Bible, and many more which might be cited, reveal the general principle on which the heavenly Parent proceeds in his administration of punishments. They show that the law and the penalty are not in conflict, but one in spirit and purpose, though different in method and means; that they both are ordained, not for the good of the Lawgiver, not to secure any advantage to him; but for the good of those to whom the law is given as a rule of conduct. The penalty, or the punishment of disobedience, aims at the same thing which the law aims at, viz: to cause mankind to walk in the ways of the Lord, to do right; simply because the right leads to happiness, to the highest good of him who does it. God never inflicts punishment or pain for its own sake, as an end; but only as a means. He never rests in it as final, as the thing sought, the thing he is satisfied to make permanent and endless.

It may interest the reader, and profit him, to compare the preceding reasoning on the nature and object of divine punishments, with the views entertained by some of the Universalist Fathers of the early Christian Church.

Clemens Alexandrinus, A. D. 190, says: "Punishment is, in its operation, like medicine; it dissolves the hard heart, purges away the filth of uncleanness, and reduces the swellings of pride and haughtiness; thus restoring its subject to a sound and healthful state." *

Origen, A. D. 230. "The sacred Scripture does, indeed, call 'our God a consuming fire,' (Deut. iv. 24,) and says that 'rivers of fire go before his face,' (Dan. vii. 10,) and that 'he shall come as a refiner's fire, and purify the people,' (Mal. iii. 2.) As, therefore, God is a consuming fire, what is it that is to be consumed by him? We say it is wickedness, and whatever proceeds from it, such as is figuratively called 'wood, hay, and stubble,' (1 Cor. iii.) which denote the evil works of man. Our

* *Pedagog*, i. 8.

God is a consuming fire in this sense; and he shall come as a refiner's fire to purify rational nature from the alloy of wickedness, and other impure matter which has adulterated the intellectual gold and silver; consuming whatever of evil is admixed in all the soul." *

Titus, Bishop of Bostra, A. D. 364, says: "The punishments of God are holy, as they are remedial and salutary in their effect upon transgressors; for they are inflicted, not to preserve them in their wickedness, but to make them cease from their sins. The abyss of hell is, indeed, the place of torment, but it is not eternal. The anguish of their sufferings compels them to break off from their sins." **

Gregory, Bishop of Nyssa, A. D. 370, states his belief as follows: "I believe that punishment will be administered in proportion to each one's corruptness. For it would be unequal to torment with the same purgatorial pains, him who has long indulged in transgression, and him who has only fallen into a few common sins. But that grievous flame shall burn for a longer or shorter period, according to the kind and quantity of the matter that supports it. Therefore, to whom there is much corruption attached, with him it is necessary that the flame which is to consume it, should be great, and of long duration; but to him in whom the wicked disposition has been already in part subjected, a proportional degree of that sharpness and more vehement punishment shall be remitted. *All evil, however, must at length be entirely removed from every thing, so that it shall no more exist.* For such being the nature of sin, that it cannot exist without a corrupt motive, it must, of course, be perfectly dissolved and wholly destroyed, so that nothing can remain a receptacle of it, when all motive and influence shall spring from God alone." ***

---

* *Contra Celsum,* Lib. iv. 13; a work in which is anticipated nearly all the modern replies to infidelity; as indeed the work of Celsus, which it answers, anticipates all the attacks on Christianity from that class represented by the English infidels of the 18th century.

** *Contra Manich.* Lib. i.

*** *De Anima et Resurrectione.*

Novatus, or Novatian, who was perhaps, the rival of Cornelius for the Bishopric of Rome, A. D., 250, maintained that the "wrath and indignation of the Lord, so called, are not such passions as bear those names in man;

This perfect agreement between ancient and modern Universalists, respecting the remedial nature of divine punishments, is instructive; and suggestive of much to those who regard the doctrine of Universal Restoration as of recent origin.[8]

, ,

The ultimate in argumentation was presented by E. E. Guild when in *The Universalist's Book of Reference* (1844) he attempted to include, as his subtitle had it, *All the Principal Facts and Arguments, and Scripture Texts, pro and con, on the Great Controversy between Limitarians and Universalists.* That Universalists found it a useful mine of information is attested by the fact that it went through many editions.

---

but that they are operations of the divine mind directed solely to our purification."—*De Regula Fidei*, cap. iv. Yet he was very severe himself towards lapsed professors.—*Mosheim* i. 202.

    I shall probably have no better place than this, to call attention to the extensive prevalence of Universalism in the primitive church. A. D. 190–550 show among its advocates many of the most pious, learned, and influential of the Christian Fathers, as CLEMENT, ORIGEN, MARCELLUS, Bishop of Ancyra, TITUS, Bishop of Bostra, GREGORY, Bishop of Nyssa, DIDYMUS the Blind, one of the most remarkable and erudite men of his time, DIODORUS, Bishop of Tarsus, the birth-place of Paul, THEODORE, Bishop of Mopsuestia, FABIUS MARIUS VICTORINUS, &c. It is easy to see to what extent the doctrine must have prevailed among the lesser clergy and laity, when so many of the dignitaries of the church taught it publicly. And it is a most significant fact, little known, respecting the famous Catechetical School of Alexandria, the great Educational and Theological Seminary of the early Church (bearing to it the relation which the Andover Seminary bears to New England Theology,) that *three of its most popular and distinguished Presidents were Universalists!* Surely, Universalism was the orthodoxy of the Church at that period, or those having the church and its ministry and its youth in their charge, were culpably recreant to their duty. DOEDERLEIN, a long time ago, said, that "the more distinguished by erudition any one was in ancient Christian times, by so much the more did he cherish and defend the hope of a final termination of torments—*Quanto quis altius eruditione in antiquitate Christiana eminuit, tanto magis spem finiendorum olim cruciatuum aluit atque defendit.*"—*Institut. Theol. Christiani.* Noremberg, 1787, vol. ii. p. 199. Whittemore's Hist. p. 290.

ʿ ʿ

DIFFERENCE IN THE BELIEF
OF PARTIALISTS AND UNIVERSALISTS.

All the various denominations of professing Christians may be classed under three heads: Calvinists, Arminians, and Universalists. A chart of the agreement and the difference in the religious opinions of these three classes on the most important doctrines of Christianity may be delineated as follows:—

Calvinism.
There is one God.

> *Arminianism.*
> There is one God.

>> *Universalism.*
>> There is one God.

There is one Mediator between God and men, and that Mediator is the very and eternal God himself.

> There is one Mediator between God and men, and that Mediator is the very and eternal God himself.

>> There is one Mediator between God and men, and that Mediator is "the MAN Christ Jesus."

The one Mediator gave himself a ransom for a part only of mankind.

> The one Mediator gave himself a ransom for all.

>> The one Mediator gave himself a ransom for all.

All those for whom the Mediator died will be saved.

> A part only of those for whom the Mediator died will be saved.

>> All those for whom the Mediator died will be saved.

Calvinism.
God's purposes in the creation of the human race embraced the final holiness and happiness of a part, and the endless misery of the rest.

> *Arminianism.*
> God's purposes in the creation of the human race embraced the final holiness and happiness of all mankind.

> > *Universalism.*
> > God's purposes in the creation of the human race embraced the final holiness and happiness of all mankind.

God's purpose in reference to the final destiny of his creatures cannot be defeated.

> God's purpose in reference to the final destiny of a part of his creatures will be defeated.

> > God's purpose in reference to the final destiny of his creatures cannot be defeated.

God has the power to make all his creatures holy and happy.

> God has not the power to make all his creatures holy and happy.

> > God has the power to make all his creatures holy and happy.

God wills the salvation of a part of his creatures, and the damnation of the rest.

> God wills the salvation of all his creatures.

> > God wills the salvation of all his creatures.

God's will in reference to the ultimate destiny of his creatures will be done.

> God's will in reference to the ultimate destiny of a part of his creatures will not be done.

> > God's will in reference to the ultimate destiny of his creatures will be done.

Calvinism.
God can save all mankind, but will not.

> *Arminianism.*
> God would save all mankind, but cannot.

> > *Universalism.*
> > God can save all mankind, and will.

The object of Christ's mission to our world was to save a part only of mankind from endless misery.

> The object of Christ's mission to our world was to save all mankind from endless misery.

> > The object of Christ's mission to our world was to save all mankind from their sins.

Christ will succeed in accomplishing the object of his mission.

> Christ will succeed in accomplishing a part only of the object of his mission.

> > Christ will succeed in accomplishing the object of his mission.

All for whom Christ died will be saved.

> Some for whom Christ died will not be saved.

> > All for whom Christ died will be saved.

A glorious and happy destiny awaits a portion of the human race, and a most inglorious, unhappy and miserable destiny awaits the rest.

> A glorious and happy destiny awaits a portion of the human race, and a most inglorious, unhappy and miserable destiny awaits the rest.

> > A glorious and happy destiny awaits every individual of the entire human race.

Universalism is altogether preferable to Arminianism.

> Universalism is altogether preferable to Calvinism.

> > Universalism is infinitely preferable to either Calvinism or Arminianism.

Arminianism is supposed by thousands to be a much more consistent and reasonable system of theology than Calvinism. But who cannot see that both systems result in precisely the same thing? Arminianism damns as many as Calvinism, and the Arminian's hell is equally as horrible as the Calvinist's. What boots it then, reader, whether you go to an endless hell by the irreversible decree of the Almighty, or by the use of an agency which God gave you, and which he knew you would use to your own destruction? In other words, what difference will it make with you whether you are lost, and lost forever, because God *cannot* save you, or because he *will* not? The truth is, that between Calvinism and Arminianism there is not one cent to choose, but between either of these systems and that of Universalism the difference is infinite. And no man can fail to see that Universalism is infinitely the best.[9]

, ,

Chapter Five

Divisions Within

> If our Creator is worthy of the love and devotion of his
> rational offspring . . . it must be on account of his real
> goodness to them; and if his requirements are worthy of
> our careful observance . . . it must be because the keep-
> ing of them is enjoyment to us.

> . . . The preaching of future rewards and pun-
> ishments, for the purpose of inducing people to love God
> and moral virtue, is not only useless, but pernicious.
>
> Hosea Ballou

Universalists disagreed among themselves from the beginning concerning the likelihood of punishment for sin in the
afterlife. John Murray, like James Relly, insisted that the death
of Christ had made atonement for sin forever unnecessary.
There might be punishment in another realm for the evil angels
(devils) who had rebelled against God, but man received his
punishment on a pay-as-you-go basis on earth.

Elhanan Winchester, on the other hand, like the great
Chauncy, conceived of a limited period during which souls
would be purged of sin before being allowed to enjoy the presence of God.

Hosea Ballou wavered on the subject until 1817, when
he finally came down on the side of no punishment in the
afterlife. Man received compensation for both good and bad
deeds while still on earth, and was transformed by the power of
God's love at the time of his death as he was ushered into eternity.

148

That a long-standing disagreement should become a cause of schism at one time and not another is one of the mysteries of the world of theology. That personality as well as principle is often involved in such affairs there can be no doubt. When the debate began in Universalist circles it was due as much to resentment by some against the leadership of Ballou as to the theological issues involved.

Since Ballou was at the center of the whirlwind, it is appropriate to present excerpts from his *Examination of the Doctrine of Future Retribution* (1834), the most able of the presentations of the ultra-Universalist position.

‘ ‘

. . . It seems very evident that we always act with a hope to gain some benefit, and thereby to avoid some evil; but does it necessarily follow that the benefit which we hope to gain must be in a future state, and that the evil we hope to avoid must be there too? This is directly denied by those whose views we are now examining. They say, if the fear of future punishment were removed, and the hope of future reward taken away, there would be nothing to induce us to be religious and moral, nor any thing to prevent us from running into the practice of every vice and abomination. Then surely we could act without being incited by considerations of a future state. It would be no easier for us to commit sin without a motive, than to practise virtue without a motive. But where lies the expected benefit, which induces the vicious to sin? Does it present itself to the imagination in a future state? No one will pretend this. Then it must be given up, at once, that in order to induce men to act it is necessary to place the object to be obtained in a future world. The candid reader will now see, that the doctrine we are examining is unsound; for it depends on the supposition, that as we act from hope and fear, the good hoped for, and the evil dreaded, must both be in a future state.

If, in order further to maintain the doctrine of future rewards and punishments, its advocate should say, that although men may be induced to sin, and may become as active in so doing as possible, without the expectation of any good in the future state, yet without such expectation they cannot be persuaded to become religious and moral, he is called on to find out and assign the reason.

We have now arrived at a spot where we should do well to pause and duly consider. All the professed friends of religion and moral virtue will allow that the wicked are too active in committing sin, that they run too greedily in pursuit of forbidden indulgences; but none of them suppose that these wicked thus act in expectation of obtaining any good in a future state. Where then do the wicked expect to receive the enjoyment which they are pursuing? In this present state, to be sure.

Reader, be cautious! If the wicked are induced to commit all manner of iniquity, and to practise every forbidden abomination, by no expectation of any enjoyment but in this life, can there be any other reason assigned why they do not forsake the ways of impiety and vice, and become religious and moral, than because religion and morality do not promise them so much happiness and enjoyment, in the present world, as does the course they are now in? No one will or can doubt on this subject. Then let us ask, whether the view which the wicked have of religion and morality is a right one? To this question all will answer in the negative. We are then ready for a general and a safe conclusion. There is no necessity of promising a reward in a future state for the practice of duty in the present. All that is wanting for this purpose is to understand and to be persuaded that righteousness brings an ample reward, in the present life.

This conclusion is abundantly justified by the fact, that in room of obtaining the good which the wicked promise themselves in the paths of vice, they always meet with that degree of trouble and infelicity which constitutes a just recompense for their disobedience to the commands of God, and the dictates of conscience.

In our investigation of the force of motive to induce the wicked to push forward in wrong-doing, we must not neglect to notice the counteracting power which is overcome by it (according to common opinion). It is a fact, with which all are acquainted, that nearly all the vicious have been educated in the belief of a future state of rewards and punishments; yet notwithstanding the apprehensions which they have entertained, that by the practice of the vices in which they indulged their passions, they were exposing themselves to inconceivable miseries hereafter; the expectation of enjoyment in the present state, has carried them on in the strong current of sin, which has broken down every barrier, and furnished conclusive proof that no motive is so sure of inducing to action, as the expectation of immediate happiness.

In view of these facts, who will wonder that in these times there should be some engaged in laboring to convince men that present happiness can be obtained by being faithful in the discharge of our duty to God, to our fellow-creatures, and to ourselves, by doing justly, loving mercy, and by walking humbly, and by no other means; and that however flattering sin may appear, and however strongly our blind, fleshly passions may tempt us from duty, moral death, condemnation, and misery will be the immediate and sure recompense for unlawful indulgence?

We maintain that this view, and all the facts which we can find connected with it, are in accordance with the laws of the human mind, and will be found to agree with universal experience. By these views we arrive at the desideratum long sought for, the reason why the promises of complete bliss, in the future world, and the threatenings of most dire torments, have not accomplished the design for which they were so vehemently urged on the people. Yes, we here discover the reason why such doctrines have not been able to restrain their most zealous believers from the very sins, for which they believed these threatenings would be executed on those who practised them. Deceive ourselves as much as we may, whenever truth appears we find ourselves in pursuit of happiness, in the present world; and if we are vicious, it is in consequence of an erroneous expectation of obtaining it by wicked means; and if we are pious and virtuous, it is because we love to be so, and find ourselves richly rewarded in keeping the divine commands, and in obedience to the dictates of conscience.

·   ·   ·

There is no man so entirely ignorant of the laws of the human mind, as to suppose that we can be induced to love our Creator, either by a promised reward, or by threatened torment; and yet these motives are constantly urged on the people for this very purpose; and the arguments we are examining, in defence of a future state of rewards and punishments, contend that religion and morality depend on them.

If our Creator is worthy of the love and devotion of his rational offspring, a fact which none will deny, it must be on account of his real goodness to them; and if his requirements are worthy of our careful observance, which none will question, it must be because the keeping of them is enjoyment to us. With these simple, self-evident propositions in clear view, why should we have recourse to hereafter rewards and punishments to incite us to love God and to keep his commandments? To induce us to love God, nothing is necessary but to make us acquainted with his real character; and to persuade us to keep the divine commands, no argument need be used but to show us the interest we have in obedience.

.   .   .

. . . The preaching of future rewards and punishments, for the purpose of inducing people to love God and moral virtue, is not only *useless*, but *pernicious*. All such preaching, be it ever so well intended, not only amounts to a declaration, that God and moral virtue are, in themselves, unlovely, and unworthy of being loved, but, as far as it is believed, serves to alienate the affections from these most precious objects. We may illustrate this subject by the use of figures furnished in the Scriptures. There God is represented by a fountain of living waters. Divine truth, by waters, by wine and milk, by bread, &c. Should we be offered an immense reward for accepting these nourishing aliments, and should we be threatened with severe punishments if we refused them,—it would be natural for us to suppose, that the person who should make such proposals, and state such conditions, did not believe these things to be of any value in themselves; and the greater the zeal manifested by him from whom such proposals should come, the stronger would be the evidence to us of this forbidding fact. We see, then, that this kind of preaching is not only useless, but that it is, in fact, of a tendency the most pernicious.

· · ·

. . . I must fear *sin*, in order to prevent me from sinning. Will it be asked why I should fear sin? Answer: Because it will make me miserable if I commit it. There is no priest that I can apply to, who can prevent my suffering, if I am a sinner. If I fear a prison or a gallows, or a punishment in the future world, I may flatter myself that some way may be provided, by which I may escape them; but if I fear sin itself, I know, if I am a sinner, I must endure that evil. It is perfectly natural for a person to endeavor to avoid an evil, in proportion to its magnitude, as viewed by the mind. This being safe ground to reason on, we see at once, if we could believe that sin is the greatest evil to which we are exposed, we should be more cautious to avoid it than any other. The great and pernicious mistake, which our divines have fallen into, is that of supposing that the evil of sin is not in sin, but in a punishment which may, or may not be suffered, in the future state. It is impossible for them to exonerate themselves from having fallen into this error; for the very argument which they endeavor to maintain, and which we are now examining, is a full confession of the fact. They contend that if the fear of future punishment be removed, restraint against sin is gone. So fully confirmed are they in this most lamentable error, it is not uncommon for them to say, both in public, and in private circles, that if there be no hereafter punishment it is no matter what we do, and that if they believed in no such punishment, they would commit the worst of crimes. It is granted that they seldom go so far, unless they first become somewhat irritated in their feelings; but after all, it is only carrying out, to its full extent, the enormity of their error. What we here state we know to be true. But we do not mention it from unkind feelings towards our brethren; but solely for the purpose of making the merits of the subject plain to the reader.

· · ·

. . . All who preach the doctrine of future punishment, have relied on the terrors of that punishment, to induce men to be pious and virtuous; and yet they know that the most vicious and most abominable, in all Christian countries, have been brought up from childhood to believe that doctrine; and at the same time have been educated in the belief, that sin brings many enjoyments in this world, and is attended with great prosperity in the very things which they are taught to love; and to complete the work of iniquity, they are furnished with the means of escaping all punishment hereafter!

Thus far our investigations have been directed to ascertain, by a careful and studied reference to the moral constitution of man, and the laws by which the human mind is governed, whether true religion and genuine morality have need of the doctrine of a future state of rewards and punishments for their establishment and prosperity; and we feel satisfied that the indisputable truths, which have most evidently appeared, all harmonize in their testimony against the utility of such doctrine; and moreover, that they show, beyond a reasonable doubt, that such doctrine and preaching are of an injurious tendency. To show, still further, this unhappy tendency, on the principles of the law of mind, on which reliance may safely be placed, we here add but one fact more. It is well known, and will be acknowledged by every candid person, that the human heart is capable of becoming soft, or hard; kind, or unkind; merciful or unmerciful, by education and habit. On this principle we contend, that the infernal torments, which false religion has placed in the future world, and which ministers have, with an overflowing zeal, so constantly held up to the people, and urged with all their learning and eloquence, have tended so to harden the hearts of the professors of this religion, that they have exercised, towards their fellow-creatures, a spirit of enmity, which but too well corresponds with the relentless cruelty of their doctrine, and the wrath which they have imagined to exist in our heavenly Father. By having such an example constantly before their eyes, they have become so transformed into its image, that, whenever they have had the power, they have actually executed a vengeance on men and women, which evinced that the cruelty of their doctrine had overcome the native kindness and compassion of the human heart.[1]

, ,

One of the most able opponents of Ballou among the "Restorationists" was Charles Hudson, minister of the church in Westminster, Massachusetts. The debating ability which was later to stand him in good stead in his political career is well displayed in this series of letters addressed to Ballou which, though published earlier than Ballou's book, speak to the same issues.

' '

. . . I shall endeavor to show that *those who die impenitent will, after death, enter into a state of misery, consisting of anxiety, guilt, and remorse, which will continue until repentance or reformation is effected.* We do not believe that this misery will arise from any *external application,* but from the *internal state of the mind.* It is not our belief that this punishment will be inflicted by the immediate hand of God, and as it were, out of the common course of his moral dealings, but that it will grow necessarily out of the moral natures God has given us; that it will be the legitimate fruit of that guilt of which the mind will be conscious, in consequence of past transgressions. We know by what we feel in ourselves, and see in others, that one overt act of wickedness leaves the mind in a state of condemnation and misery; and as many commit the most atrocious crimes the instant they leave this world, it is reasonable to suppose that they will enter into a state of remorse and inquietude after death. To me this has all the force of moral demonstration. Sin always leaves the mind in condemnation. This is an established principle; it grows necessarily out of the nature which we possess. Take men as they are, and it is impossible for it to be otherwise. Now a person taken away in the perpetration of a horrid crime, must be unhappy after death. His moral nature renders immediate happiness impossible. Unless his accountability is destroyed, his consciousness done away, and his moral nature annihilated; in a word, unless man is changed into some other creature, it appears morally certain that those who depart this world in gross wickedness, will enter into a state of infelicity.

If men exist in a future state, they must retain their *identities;* that is, they must be conscious that they are the same beings who have existed in this world, and performed such and such actions. Without this consciousness, men cease to exist. If I fall asleep to-night, and awake on the morning of to-morrow without my consciousness, that is, without any knowledge or recollection of having existed before, it ceases to be myself, and becomes another being. Nothing which existed in me, and went to make up my personal identity, or individuality, is found in him; but he is as distinct and as separate from me, as Peter or Paul. The same will hold good in relation to a future state. In that state we must possess a consciousness of having existed here, or it is not we who exist, but it becomes a new creation. All then, that goes to make up an individual, must exist after death, or there is no future life to us. How do men in this world distinguish themselves from one another? It is solely because they possess an individual identity or consciousness; that is, they have a conscious knowledge that they have existed before that moment, and are the same beings who have thought, and felt, and acted thus and so. This consciousness is what constitutes an essential ingredient in an individual. Destroy this consciousness, and individuality ceases. Now if we exist in a future state, we must possess this individual consciousness, and all those principles and feelings which constitute personal identity. To talk of men's existing in a future state, without this consciousness, would be the height of extravagance and absurdity; it would be something similar to the notion that all men sinned in Adam, a position you would by no means admit. But it is no more absurd to say that men sin, without a consciousness of sinning, than it is to say that they exist, without a consciousness of existing.

It appears clear from the nature of the case, that men in a future state must retain their consciousness, and this idea receives additional support from the scriptures. Jesus Christ, who is our pattern or example, retained his consciousness after death. He knew that he was the same person who had been baptized by John, betrayed by Judas, and crucified by the Jews. He knew that he had existed before; he recognized his disciples, and commanded them to preach that gospel which he had died to establish. Hence it will be seen that Jesus Christ retained his consciousness after death. And this will be the state of all men in a future world.

.   .   .

Men are naturally selfish beings; and sin always corrupts the heart, and blunts the moral feelings to that degree that the old veteran in wickedness will feel but little remorse for the most atrocious deeds. The nature of sin is so alluring, that the old offender will almost persuade himself that his behavior is not reprehensible. Now can we reasonably suppose that a conscience thus seared and defiled will do perfect justice in all cases? It is the common consent of mankind that it would not. Would it be wise in all cases of a civil nature to place the defendant upon the bench, and let him decide his own case? Are robbers and murderers generally allowed the privilege of deciding whether they shall be executed or not? Much otherwise. And the reason is obvious. It is the common sentiment of mankind that the sinner would always favor himself at the expense of justice and equity, should he be permitted to decide his own cause. And so with a defiled conscience; its decision would partake of that selfishness which is characteristic of the sinner. The remorse we feel, arises from a just sense of our accountability to God. But the adept in wickedness has little or no sense of his accountability, and endeavors habitually to banish God from his thoughts. In the description of the wicked given by the Psalmist . . . does it appear that they had a realizing sense of their accountability to God? The farthest from it possible. The passage informs us that they set their mouth against the heavens, and say, *How doth God know? and is there knowledge in the Most High?* Here instead of admitting their accountability to God, they seem to doubt his taking cognizance of their conduct. Job also . . . represents the wicked as prosperous, and in consequence of this, they become haughty, and say unto God, *depart from us; for we desire not the knowledge of thy ways.* Thus instead of feeling their accountability, they harden their hearts, and command God to depart from them. St. Paul after the Psalmist, says of certain vile characters, *there is no fear of God before their eyes.*

Now it would be the summit of weakness to say that these characters had a realizing sense of their accountability to God, when they had no fear of him before their eyes. Who will have the presumption to say that sinners feel a just sense of their accountability to their Maker, while they have *no fear of him, do not desire his instruction, but command him to depart from them?* Since remorse of conscience arises principally from a sense of our accountability to God, and the most corrupt sinners have the least sense of their accountability, it appears morally certain that conscience does not render to every man according to his deeds. Who can believe that the selfish, mercenary being, who will destroy his neighbor's life to increase his temporal interest, will by the bar of his own conscience condemn himself to a just and equitable punishment?—But we will drop all reasoning of this sort upon the subject, for the sacred writers have decided it forever. They assure us that the conscience becomes defiled and seared, so that the most abandoned sinners, instead of feeling accountable to the divine Being, renounce his control, despise his instruction, and command him to depart from them.

If we look at the conduct of men, we shall see that the sting of conscience does not restrain them from sin. Old transgressors continue to commit sin, notwithstanding all the horrors of conscience. When tempted at any time to commit sin, they do not inquire whether they shall experience remorse of conscience; for they know that this, to a certain degree, always attends transgression. But this they are willing to bear. Should you tell an old offender, that if he continued in sin, he would experience almost intolerable remorse in every act of transgression, he would probably inform you that he was as well acquainted with his own feelings as yourself, and that if he could escape human laws, it was all he expected or desired. The principal inquiry which an old sinner makes is, not whether he shall escape remorse of conscience, but whether he shall escape human authority. We find that men are in *love* with sin, much in proportion as they practise it.

.   .   .

. . . If sin punishes itself sufficiently, then there is no need of any human laws; nay, human laws are only engines of cruelty, for they punish those who have been sufficiently punished already. Since human laws, on your system, are cruel and unjust, they ought to be repealed. No good citizen can countenance a law which inflicts a punishment upon the innocent, or, which is the same thing, upon those who are duly punished already. Your system aims a death-blow at the very foundation of all law, and consequently, of all order. It saps the very foundation of all institutions, and if it were reduced to practice, would introduce a state of general anarchy and confusion. This is the fatal, but legitimate tendency of your scheme, if reduced to practice.

But while your system has this fatal tendency, nothing of the kind can be charged upon our system. I very much doubt whether you can lay your hand upon your heart, and say in the presence of your Maker, that you believe that a future retribution corrupts the morals of society. But if your system has any salutary influence, ours has all its advantages, and others superadded. You say, that virtue is rewarded in this world; we believe in all the reward which is enjoyed in this world, and also in an additional reward hereafter. And will *increasing* the reward make people *less* virtuous? No; the reward will be greater, the motive more powerful, and consequently will be more likely to stimulate to virtue. Our system not only exhibits a greater incentive to virtue, than yours, but it lays a greater restraint upon vice. Your doctrine tells the villain who is plotting the assassination of his fellow creatures, that if he falls in his attempt, superlative glory will be his *immediate* portion; ours tells him, that if he loses his life in such a horrid attempt, he will experience a state of correction and chastisement. Armed with your system, might not the robber go forth with composure, and say to himself, I am sinning, it is true, but if I succeed I shall obtain a fortune; and if I lose my life in the attempt, I shall go in an instant to the enjoyment of heaven? In either case I shall be a gainer, he might very naturally say, therefore I will embark immediately in this bold adventure. I do not mean to signify that a belief in your system will make every man a robber. But let a person who is meditating upon this subject, and who has weighed all the other motives which have any bearing upon the point, and finds his mind in a state of equilibrium—I say, let such a person, under these circumstances, take your system into the account, and I will submit it to the judgment of mankind to determine, whether it would not encourage, rather than dissuade him from his bold adventure. Suppose a person to be in a state of trouble, would he not have an inducement to put a period to his own existence? Might he not say, and say with speciousness, that God required nothing of him but what would promote his own happiness, and by committing suicide, he might exchange the troubles of earth for the joys of heaven? I will appeal to reason to determine which system would be likely to have the most restraint upon a person who was upon a poize [sic] between virtue and crime.

.   .   .

. . . In relation to a future state, let us inquire, what your particular views are? You represent the soul of man as an *emanation from the Deity,** and contend that his future happy life con-sists in returning to the fountain from whence he came. This, as far as I am able to judge, is the common opinion entertained by the generality of those who embrace your system. Now this opinion was not only embraced by those ancient heretics, the Gnostics, but is the popular opinion of infidels at this day.* No unbeliever in divine revelation, who is not a complete Atheist, would object to a future existence on this ground. Thus we see that your sys-tem, relative to its moral influence, (the only thing wherein any system can be valuable) has little or no advantage over infidel-ity. In fact, some of the principal advocates for your system seem to admit this. Mr. Kneeland, when treating upon this very sub-ject, says, "But what is there, after all, in rational Deism, that will not *perfectly coincide* with rational Christianity?" † He fur-ther pronounces the book of Revelations a "heretical figment void of reason." He labors to point out the discrepancies be-tween the evangelists, pronounces their manner of writing careless and loose," and finally gives it as his opinion, that the

* Palmer's Principles of Nature, &c.
† Philadelphia U. Magazine.

gospels were not written by those whose names they bear, but were the *forgeries* of a later age. But while he speaks thus contemptuously of the Scriptures, he compliments the book of nature in true deistical language. His words are—Nature is "a book, in which *all* can read with the eyes of the understanding; which has not been, as we know it could not, neither indeed can it ever be, adulterated by the arts of designing men. It has neither been interpolated nor mutilated; nor can any part thereof be spurious; which cannot be said, with truth, respecting the Bible!" But the above cannot surprise us, when we consider that Mr. Kneeland joins issue with the Atheist, and contends that God is matter, and that matter is eternal. He says, that God "is an elementary principle of real matter, which inheres in caloric and oxygen, is as much material as they are, and is never separate from them!"

I will not attempt to confute these wild and antichristian notions, but will observe that they are the genuine fruits of the system I am opposing. Mr. K. is a gentleman of candor and frankness, and will fearlessly state whatever grows out of his system. And when men are prepared to reject a future retribution, we may naturally expect, if they pursue the subject to its final result, that they will embrace views like those expressed above. That system, which leads men to pronounce some of the most distinguished miracles of Christ "altogether incredible," and to assert they "surpass all belief," and "do no credit to Jesus, admitting them true," may, with no small degree of propriety, be called *another gospel.* This Mr. K. has done, and this appears to be the natural offspring of the system here controverted.[2]

, ,

An idea of the bitterness of the debate between the ultra-Universalists and the Restorationists can be gained from this reply to Hudson penned by one of Ballou's staunch supporters, Walter Balfour, who had migrated as an orthodox minister to Charlestown, Massachusetts, from Scotland. Shortly after his arrival he became persuaded of the truth of Universalism and became one of its greatest polemicists.

‘ ‘

. . . As Mr. Hudson asserts that Mr. Ballou's system is very licentious in its tendency, and his the very reverse, how shall we decide between them? I know no better course than to bring them to the following tests. 1st, To compare the morals of the two men themselves as illustrative of their systems. But I find that this cannot determine the question; for Mr. Hudson allows Mr. Ballou to be a moral man, and I presume Mr. Ballou would not charge him with being immoral. 2d, To compare the respective amount of morals, which the systems in the present day produce in those who believe them, and according to the numbers which embrace them. But here again it will be doubtful to decide. Is Mr. Hudson prepared to say that all who believe his system are moral men? Is he even prepared to say that it has a decided superiority over the other in producing good morals in those who embrace it? If he is, I confess I am not, from all I have witnessed of the temper, spirit and conduct of such as profess to believe in the two systems. I pray God all of us were more holy, and lived more in accordance with the glorious gospel of God we profess. 3d, Let us compare the two systems on a large scale, and their influence on the world in past ages. Mr. Hudson has repeatedly contended that his system of a future judgment and retribution has been believed in all ages, and in all lands, both by Jews and Gentiles. Its antiquity and universality he considers very strong proofs of its truth. We then very seriously ask him—did his doctrine produce good morals among all nations in past ages? Has it ever done this generally? He knows that the very reverse of this is the case. In the apostolic age "the world lay in wickedness," and the name of God was even blasphemed among the Gentiles, by the wickedness of the Jews. But he contends that his doctrine in that age prevailed among both Jews and Gentiles. In this last letter he might have gone off the field with flying colors, if his doctrine in past ages had only produced good morals generally among the nations of the earth. But alas! notorious, indisputable facts are here against him. Had the doctrine of his opponents—no future punishment after death, been the faith of all nations in time past, as his system has been, what would he not have said and done, to hold their system up to public scorn? He would have pointed with his finger to its effects on the nations, saying—see the horrid and licentious tendency of your system, in the fruits which it has produced. We should not very soon have heard the last about this from him. He might well say then, as he now says to Mr. Ballou and Mr. Kneeland, that their system not only leads to all manner of licentiousness, but to downright atheism. But he has all along been contending, that not their system, but his has been the universal belief of all nations. And he may now see, what has been its effects. What Mr. Hudson will say to these palpable facts against his system, in ages past, I am unable to devise. They stand as an eternal monument against his system, and ought to seal his lips forever in silence against those whom he opposes. I feel grateful to God, that whether my system is right or wrong, the heathen nations were believers in his system, not mine. If he claims kindred with the heathen in his faith, he must expect to share in the disgrace which their immorality entails, as the fruits of the system they mutually embrace. If my system had produced such fruits for so many ages, I should indeed think it was of an immoral tendency.

Mr. Hudson has been very careful to remind Mr. Ballou, that his system is but of yesterday, and glories in the antiquity as well as the universality of his own. He has told us, Mr. Ballou's system began with Dr. Huntington only about thirty years ago. He may think it has not had time yet fully to develop its licentious tendency, but when it comes to be as long and as universally believed, its effects on the world will be worse than his has been. This is a mere surmise: and I would add, that worse it hardly could be, for what system could produce more superstition, immorality, and wickedness than the one which Mr. Hudson lays claim to, in common with all nations in past ages? There can be no great risk at any rate, in discarding his, to make an experiment, if possible to produce a better state of things.

But our orthodox brethren, will likely turn the tables on Mr. Hudson, respecting what he says in this letter and many other parts of his book. I have only room for a single specimen from p. 288. They will say to him, with a slight variation of his phraseology, what he says to Mr. Ballou—"I very much doubt whether you can lay your hand upon your heart, and say in the presence of your Maker, that you believe that future endless misery corrupts the morals of society. If your system has any salutary influence, ours has all its advantages and others superadded. Your doctrine tells the villain who is plotting the assassination of his fellow creatures, that if he fails in the attempt, he must experience a state of correction and chastisement from his own mental reflections; ours tell him that if he loses his life in such a horrid attempt he must experience endless hell torments." And probably will add, "Mr. Hudson, if your mere scarecrow of a hell produces thirty fold good fruits, you must allow ours to produce a hundred. But better your hell than none; and we hope you will join your exertions with ours in getting up religious excitements by means of it. Prove your faith by your works in all time coming, by preaching your doctrine openly and fully to the world. If preaching our hell produces an earthquake, yours may produce a thunder clap, and by continuing faithfully to preach *limited* punishment you may in due time come to be of one mind with us that it is *endless*." In taking our leave of the subject, we recommend to all to re-examine the Scriptures, and see if either limited or endless punishment were the doctrines by which the apostles converted and reformed the world.

In taking our leave of Mr. Hudson, we thank him for his publication. Before it appeared we suspended judgment, not knowing certainly what the counsel on the other side had to say in defence of his cause. Now we see wherein his great strength consists, and have no fears about the issue. After his proposals were issued, we besought Mr. Hudson to take time, avail himself of every assistance, and let us have at once the strength of all he could produce in support of his system. We hope he did this, and our readers may judge for themselves between us. If he has not, we shall be happy to discuss the subject further with him. But as we did not begin, we have no desire to prolong this controversy, and therefore leave Mr. Hudson to his own choice concerning it.[3]

, ,

The mini-schism which occurred among the Universalists in 1831 as a result of the restorationist controversy was relatively short-lived. Within a dozen years most of the ministers had returned to the fold or had become Unitarians. Within twenty years the denomination was swinging away from Ballou's ultra-Universalism to a restorationist position. By the time in mid-twentieth century Universalists returned to a position of no punishment in the afterlife, many had given up any idea of an afterlife!

Abner Kneeland, mentioned by Hudson and Balfour, was an embarrassment to the Universalists generally and to the ultra-Universalists particularly. He was an old friend of Hosea Ballou. Ballou had earlier helped him fight off the lure of Deism. By 1831, however, he had abandoned Universalism and had become a pantheist, a position which his opponents apparently found difficult to distinguish from atheism.

Earlier in his career, it was said, Kneeland often found himself in the pulpit without his Bible or, on those occasions when he remembered to bring it, was unable to find the texts he hoped would prove his sermonic points. Apparently, however, he remembered to bring the Bible when he preached to his First Society of Free Inquirers in Boston. On occasion he would quote some of the more objectionable passages concerning female menstruation from the codes in the Book of Leviticus and then hurl the book across the auditorium as unfit for reading.

Kneeland was prosecuted for blasphemy by the Commonwealth of Massachusetts, the indictment being based on articles published in Kneeland's newspaper *The Investigator* in 1833. Kneeland claimed that two of the three offending pieces—which were not from his pen—were inserted in the paper without his knowledge by an assistant while he was out of town. The case, which became a cause célèbre, resulted in the conviction of Kneeland. He served a sixty-day jail term.

The third piece (included below) which got Kneeland into trouble was addressed to his old friend Thomas Whittemore for inclusion in his *Trumpet*. Point 1 below was misconstrued by Kneeland's prosecutors as a denial of belief in God. Had Whittemore published Kneeland's "Philosophical Creed," which he did not, it might have been seen that Kneeland was not denying the existence of God but rather the Universalist interpretation of the deity.

‘ ‘

Dear Sir: You observed to me the other day, that people still considered me a Universalist, and said to me 'If you will acknowledge that you are not, I will publish it.' I told you, in substance, that in some respects I am still a Universalist; but that in others I am not. I shall now answer you more at large, which I hope you will publish in full, and thereby redeem your pledge.

I still hold to universal philanthropy, universal benevolence, and universal charity. In these respects I am still a Universalist. Neither do I believe in punishment after death; so in this also I agree with the Universalists. But as it respects all other of their religious notions in relation to another world, or a supposed other state of conscious existence, I do not believe in any of them; so that in this respect I am no more a universalist than I am an orthodox christian. As for instance,

1. Universalists believe in a god which I do not; but believe that their god, with all his moral attributes, (aside from nature itself,) is nothing more than a chimera of their own imagination.

2. Universalists believe in Christ, which I do not; but believe that the whole story concerning him is as much a fable and a fiction, as that of the god Prometheus, the tragedy of whose death is said to have been acted on the stage in the theatre at Athens, 500 years before the christian era.

3. Universalists believe in miracles, which I do not; but believe that every pretension to them can either be accounted for on natural principles or else is to be attributed to mere trick and imposture.

4. Universalists believe in the resurrection of the dead, in immortality and eternal life, which I do not; but believe that all life is mortal, that death is an eternal extinction of life to the individual who possesses it, and that no individual life is, ever was, or ever will be eternal.

Hence, as Universalists no longer wish to consider me as being of their faith, and I no longer wish to be considered as belonging to their order, as it relates to a belief in things unseen, I hope the above four articles will be sufficient to distinguish me from them and them from me. I profess to believe in all realities of which I can form any rational conception, while they believe in what I believe to be mere ideal nothings to which they give both 'a location and a name.'

In giving the above a place in the 'Trumpet,' you will let me tell your readers, in my own language, what I do, as well as what I do not, believe, and thereby oblige your once brother of the same faith with yourself, and still your personal friend,

ABNER KNEELAND.

P.S. Dear Sir, If you are willing to let your readers know more fully what I do believe, please to publish also in your paper my Philosophical Creed, a copy of which, lest you should not have otherwise noticed it, I herewith send you for the purpose.

A. K.

A PHILOSOPHICAL CREED.

I believe in the existence of a universe of suns and planets, among which there is one sun belonging to our planetary system; and that other suns, being more remote, are called stars; but that they are indeed suns to other planetary systems. I believe that the whole universe is NATURE, and that the word NATURE embraces the whole universe, and that God and Nature, so far as we can attach any rational idea to either, are perfectly synonymous terms. Hence I am not an Atheist, but a Pantheist; that is, instead of believing there is no God, I believe that in the abstract, all is God; and that all power that is, is in God, and that there is no power except that which proceeds from God. I believe that there can be no will or intelligence where there is no sense; and no sense where there are no organs of sense; and hence sense, will, and intelligence, is the effect, and not the cause, of organization. I believe in all that logically results from these premises, whether good, bad, or indifferent. Hence, I believe, t God is all in all; and that it is in God we live, move, and have our being; and that the whole duty of man consists in living as long as he can, and in promoting as much happiness as he can while he lives.

Written at Hebron, N.H., May 28, 1833,

By ABNER KNEELAND.[4]

, ,

The Universalists, like the Unitarians, suffered internal difficulties as a result of the rise of Transcendentalism and rationalism in their ranks. Some of the young Universalist ministers were much taken with the ideas of the controversial Unitarian preacher Theodore Parker and began to deny the truth of the miracles reported in the Gospels. The Universalists were able to ward off this "latest form of infidelity," but only after much anguish. The controversy came to a head in the Boston Association in 1847.

The issue was couched in terms which sought to avoid the imposition of a creed but attempted to define a standard for service in the Christian ministry: "Resolved, That this Association express its solemn conviction that, in order for one to be regarded as a Christian minister with respect to faith, he must believe in the Bible account of the life, teachings, miracles, death, and resurrection of the Lord Jesus Christ."

When the votes were counted after two sessions of long and heated debate, a solid majority was recorded in favor of the resolution.

Alonzo Ames Miner, minister at Lowell, stated the continuing quandary liberal movements face when they attempt to take definite stands on issues and yet welcome to membership persons with widely divergent views. This excerpt is from a newspaper account of the session.

' '

As but 15 minutes remained before the question must be taken, and as the Moderator had had no opportunity of expressing his own opinions to the meeting, he called a member to the

Chair, and proceeded to say,—I believe the time has come when we should act. The articles of 1803 are satisfactory, when understood in their true intent. The resolution of the committee simply defines one of those articles. I would have nothing done which shall take from these brethren any of their rights. Much less would I have them persecuted. Here I apprehend is the error of former councils. They were not content with deciding upon the errors of men;—but destroyed the errorist, or shut him up in prison. True toleration does not require that we should approbate error; or that we should commend it to the world by letters of fellowship. Our government tolerates all sects; it recommends none. Nor are common charity or good-will, and christian ministerial fellowship, one and the same thing. I feel an entire good-will toward the convicts in yonder prison; but I should be quite unwilling to fellowship them as christian ministers. [Here Rev. J. M. Spear asked the speaker, if he would fellowship slaveholders?—Mr. Miner replied, Most certainly I would not.—But you *would.* Your refusal to draw any lines, would compel you to fellowship them. The slaveholder has but to say, what multitudes of them do say, that they hold the slaves for their good, and you cannot answer. Do you pretend to disfellowship them on account of their practice? But this practice is right, unless their principles are wrong. Before you can condemn slaveholding, you must condemn the conviction or faith of the slaveholder. In other words, you must draw a line which your blur-eyed charity will not allow you to do. Thus your position defeats itself.] Besides, to pursue the course recommended here, is to destroy all fellowship, and *thus* defeat the very object these brethren seek. Once let it be generally understood that Universalists fellowship rejecters of the Bible, equally with believers therein, and that fellowship will be good for nothing. Let a brother go among strangers carrying with him the fellowship of our denomination, and what influence can it have? A society of believers in Christ, in miracles, and a divine revelation, would say, this commendation is of no avail to us. [Here a clergyman, Rev. W. G. Cambridge arose, and he wished to ask the speaker a question. Do you believe that Christ cast a legion of devils out of a man? Mr. Miner. —Most emphatically, I do. Mr. Cambridge.—You are the first

Universalist I have ever heard say so. Another delegate, Rev. L. R. Paige, said, And you, (pointing to the one who interrupted Mr. M.) are the first Universalist who I ever heard question it!] We want a christian believer for a pastor, not a skeptic. But the Universalists fellowship believers and skeptics all alike. Therefore their recommendation is of no value to us. Thus, again, do these brethren destroy the very object they seek, viz: support from denominational fellowship. For these reasons, in part, I believe action called for, and I shall vote for the committee's resolution.[5]

, ,

Chapter Six

The Conscience of Universalism

> Once conceive that an Omniscient Beneficence presides
> over and directs the entire course of human affairs, lead-
> ing ever onward and upward to universal purity and bliss,
> and all evil becomes phenomenal and preparative,—a
> mere curtain or passing cloud, which hides for a moment
> the light of the celestial and eternal day.
>
> Horace Greeley

It should be expected that a gospel which preached the
ultimate salvation of every individual in the future life would be
concerned with the lot of man on earth. Some Universalists
found the reform of theology such an all-consuming task that
they had little energy left for reform of social conditions. Hosea
Ballou, for instance, was convinced that if the idea of God were
reformed all other reforms would follow.

Others were not willing to wait. Although never well organized or powerful enough to sponsor sweeping campaigns to
change American attitudes and practices on given issues, Universalism has produced its full share of reformers. The more
famous, such as Benjamin Rush, Horace Greeley, and Clara Bar-
ton, have overshadowed many others who, while achieving less
general fame, have labored within the denomination to make
Universalists responsive to the social demands of the day.

The overshadowing issue in the years before the outbreak of the Civil War was, of course, slavery and the slave trade.
But for Elhanan Winchester, viewing life in Virginia in 1774
through the eyes of a Bostonian imbued with Puritan attitudes,
slavery was the greatest of a whole catalogue of objectionable
practices. In a sermon "The Reigning Abominations" delivered
in Fairfax, Winchester held up to shame swearing, drunkenness,

171

gaming, fighting and gouging of eyes, and sabbath-breaking, among many other practices. His most stinging words, of course, were reserved for the greatest of abominations.

‘   ‘

THERE is one abomination more that prevails in this country, that calls aloud not only for sighing and crying, but for a speedy reformation and turning therefrom, if we desire to prevent destruction from coming upon us; I mean, the SLAVE TRADE.

A TRADE, conceived in iniquity, carried on in the most base and barbarous manner, productive of the worst effects, and big with the most horrid and dangerous consequences.

.   .   .

. . . The very principle upon which it is founded, from which it springs, and by which it is carried on, is one of the most base and ignoble that ever disgraced the human species:

WHICH is, *Avarice.* This mean and unworthy passion certainly has had a principal hand in this disgraceful traffic; no one can pretend that benevolence ever had, or ever can have, a hand in such a most infamous commerce. Avarice tends to harden the heart, to render the mind callous to the feelings of humanity, indisposes the soul to every virtue, and renders it an easy prey to every vice. Ought we not to be ashamed of such a commerce, that has its rise from no better principle than mere selfishness or covetousness?

.   .   .

THE most favourable construction that can be put upon the slave trade, is, that the desire of riches in general, and especially the hopes of growing suddenly rich, move men to engage therein. I say, this is the most favourable construction that can be put upon it; for I can hardly suppose, that mere wantonness, envy, cruelty, passion, revenge, or lust of power and dominion, or even ambition, can have any hand at all in this infamous traffic. And in fact, the only reason why it is not abolished, is because the interest of nations, companies, and individuals, is supposed to be connected therewith; though in the end it is more against their true interest than can be well imagined, as shall be shewn presently.

HAVING considered the principle from whence it originated, and to which its existence is owing, I pass to mention the horrible manner in which it is carried on. And here almost every vice that blackens and degrades human nature is employed; such as, deceiving, perfidy, decoying, stealing, lying, fomenting feuds and discords among the nations of Africa, robbery, plunder, burning, murder, cruelty of all kinds, and the most savage and unexampled barbarity.

BLUSH, O ye christians, to think that ye are the supporters of a commerce that employs these, and many other vices to carry it on! Could you but think seriously of the disgraceful and cruel manner in which slaves are obtained, methinks you could not attempt to justify the horrid practice. Numbers are stolen while going out on their lawful business, are never suffered to return home to take leave of their friends; but are gagged and bound, then carried on board the vessels which wait for them, never more to see their native land again, but to drag out a miserable existence in chains, hunger, thirst, cold, nakedness, hard labour, and perpetual slavery.

THINK, O ye tender mothers, how would you feel, if, when ye should send your little boys or girls to fetch a pitcher, or calabash of water from the spring, you should never see them return again! if some barbarous kidnapper should watch the opportunity, and seize upon your darlings, as the eagle upon its prey! should gagg [sic] your sweet prattling babes, and force them away! how would your eyes with tears run down! how would your souls refuse to be comforted! such is the pain that many mothers feel in Africa, and God can cause it to come home to yourselves, who contribute to such an abomination as this. Think, O ye parents, how ye would feel, if when ye sent your children into the field to watch the corn, and drive the birds away, they should be thus stolen and carried off! yet this many poor Africans experience. Many poor women take their children and go down to the rivers to wash the sand, and get gold dust; while thus employed, their foes dart upon them, take their gold and their children, nor let them return to give any account to their unfortunate husbands of the disaster. The husband comes in from the little field, to eat his chearful [sic] meal with his wife and children, whom he expects to find returned with the shining ore;—but, alas! he finds them not!—he goes towards the river—he calls—but receives no answer; at last he ventures to the shore, finds the place where the partner of his little joys was employed,—but, alas! she is gone—no more to bless his longing eyes!—he returns, frantic with rage, sorrow, and despair, and curses the authors of such horrid cruelty!

NUMBERS are decoyed, and perfidiously carried off; and by various ways the inhuman savages that are employed in this diabolical business, make up their cargoes.

BUT the great engine of all is WAR. Those who carry on this abominable trade, endeavour to foment discord among the natives; and by money, strong drink, and various articles of superfluity (which they would be better without) set one nation against another, for no other purpose than to get all the prisoners they may take, as slaves.

·   ·   ·

BUT I must proceed to consider the baleful effects of such a shocking commerce, for a little attention may convince us that it is prejudicial to our best interests. That abundance of *idleness* is introduced through the *slave trade*, is what no sensible person can deny. They who have slaves to labor for them, rarely ever labor themselves, or bring up their children to labor: and be it remembered, that IDLENESS: is one of the sins for which Sodom was destroyed, and is not only a great crime in itself, but lays men open to every temptation, and wholly unfits them for virtue and usefulness. Slavery not only encourages idleness among the higher class of people, but among the lower ranks also; for it is observed, that where it is allowed in any country the poorer sort of people refuse to labor for the rich, lest they should be put upon a footing with their slaves: so that the influence of this inhuman traffic extends its mischievous effects, in this respect, farther than one might imagine. When industry ceases, farewel [sic] to virtue, sobriety, and frugality.[1]

, ,

Dr. Benjamin Rush published, the year before the Winchester sermon, his views on the equality of blacks and whites in *An Address to the Inhabitants of the British Settlements in America, upon Slave-Keeping* (1773). Although a leading Presbyterian in Philadelphia at the time, Rush was persuaded to publish his pamphlet by the Friend antislavery leader Anthony Benezet.

‘ ‘

. . . I need hardly say any thing in favor of the Intellects of the Negroes, or of their capacities for virtue and happiness, although these have been supposed by some to be inferior to those of the inhabitants of Europe. The accounts which travellers give us of their ingenuity, humanity, and strong attachment to their parents, relations, friends and country, show us that they are equal to the Europeans, when we allow for the diversity of temper and genius which is occasioned by climate. We have many well attested anecdotes of as sublime and disinterested virtue among them as ever adorned a Roman or a Christian character.* But we are to distinguish between an African in his own country, and an African in a state of slavery in America. Slavery is so foreign to the human mind, that the moral faculties, as well as those of the understanding are debased, and rendered torpid by it. All the vices which are charged upon the Negroes in the southern colonies and the West-Indies, such as Idleness, Treachery, Theft, and the like, are the genuine off-

* See SPECTATOR, Vol. I. No. 11.

There is now in the town of Boston a Free Negro Girl, about 18 years of age, who has been but 9 years in the country, whose singular genius and accomplishments are such as not only do honor to her sex, but to human nature. Several of her poems have been printed, and read with pleasure by the public.

spring of slavery, and serve as an argument to prove that they were not intended, by Providence for it.

Nor let it be said, in the present Age, that their black color (as it is commonly called), either subjects them to, or qualifies them for slavery.* The vulgar notion of their being descended from Cain, who was supposed to have been marked with this color, is too absurd to need a refutation.—Without enquiring into the Cause of this blackness, I shall only add upon this subject, that so far from being a curse, it subjects the Negroes to no inconveniencies, but on the contrary qualifies them for that part of the Globe in which providence has placed them. The ravages of heat, diseases and time, appear less in their faces than in a white one; and when we exclude variety of color from our ideas of Beauty, they may be said to possess everything necessary to constitute it in common with the white people.†

' '

* Montesquieu, in his Spirit of Laws, treats this argument with the ridicule it deserves.

"Were I to vindicate our right to make slaves of the Negroes, these should be my arguments.

The Europeans having extirpated the American Indians, were obliged to make slaves of the Africans, for clearing such vast tracts of land.

Sugar would be too dear, if the plants which produce it were cultivated by any other than slaves.

These creatures are all over black, and with such a flat nose, that they can scarcely be pitied.

It is hardly to be believed that God, who is a wise being, should place a soul, especially a good soul, in such a black ugly body.

The Negroes prefer a glass necklace to that gold, which polite nations so highly value: can there be a greater proof of their wanting common sense.

It is impossible for us to suppose these creatures to be men, because, allowing them to be men, a suspicion would follow, that we ourselves are not Christians."

Book XV. Chap. V.

† "Quamvis ille niger, quamvis tu candidus esses.
————Nimium ne crede colori.
Alba Ligustra cadunt; Vaccinia nigra leguntur."
Virgil.

"I am black,—but comely."
Song of Solomon.

Abolition of slavery was just one of Dr. Rush's multitude of reform interests. The variety of his social interests can be gauged from these brief excerpts from pieces published after he had become an active Universalist.

‘ ‘

It has been said, that the horrors of a guilty conscience proclaim the justice and necessity of death, as a punishment for murder. I draw an argument of another nature from this fact. Are the horrors of conscience the punishment that God inflicts upon murder? why, then, should we shorten or destroy them by death, especially as we are taught to direct the most atrocious murderers to expect pardon in the future world? no, let us not counteract the government of God in the human breast: let the murderer live—but let it be to suffer the reproaches of a guilty conscience: let him live, to make compensation to society for the injury he has done it, by robbing it of a citizen: let him live to maintain the family of the man whom he has murdered: let him live, that the punishment of his crime may become universal: and lastly let him live—that murder may be extirpated from the list of human crimes!

.   .   .

Judges, attorneys, witnesses, juries and sheriffs, whose office it is to punish murder by death, I beseech you to pause, and listen to the voice of reason and religion, before you convict or execute another fellow-creature for murder!

But I despair of making such an impression upon the present citizens of the United States, as shall abolish the absurd and un-Christian practice. From the connection of this essay with the valuable documents of the late revolution contained in the American Museum, it will probably descend to posterity. To you, therefore, the unborn generations of the next century, I consecrate this humble tribute to justice. You will enjoy in point of knowledge, the meridian of a day, of which we only perceive the twilight. You will often review with equal contempt and horror, the indolence, ignorance and cruelty of your ancestors. The grossest crimes shall not exclude the perpetrators of them from your pity. You will *fully* comprehend the extent of the discoveries and precepts of the gospel, and you will be actuated, I hope, by its gentle and forgiving spirit. You will see many modern opinions in religion and government turned upside downwards, and many new connexions established between cause and effect. From the importance and destiny of every human soul, you will acquire new ideas of the dignity of human nature, and of the infinite value of every act of benevolence that has for its object, the bodies, the souls, and the lives of your fellow-creatures. You will love the whole human race, for you will perceive that you have a common Father, and you will learn to imitate him by converting those punishments to which their folly or wickedness have exposed them, into the means of their reformation and happiness.

.   .   .

Among the defects which have been pointed out in the Federal Constitution by its antifederal enemies, it is much to be lamented that no person has taken notice of its total silence upon the subject of an office of the utmost importance to the welfare of the United States, that is, an office for promoting and preserving perpetual peace in our country.

It is to be hoped that no objection will be made to the establishment of such an office, while we are engaged in a war with the Indians, for as the War-Office of the United States was established in the *time of peace*, it is equally reasonable that a Peace-Office should be established in the *time of war*.

The plan of this office is as follows:

I. Let a Secretary of the Peace be appointed to preside in this office, who shall be perfectly free from all the present absurd and vulgar European prejudices upon the subject of government; let him be a genuine republican and a sincere Christian, for the principles of republicanism and Christianity are no less friendly to universal and perpetual peace, than they are to universal and equal liberty.

II. Let a power be given to this Secretary to establish and maintain free-schools in every city, village and township of the United States; and let him be made responsible for the talents, principles, and morals, of all his schoolmasters. Let the youth of our country be carefully instructed in reading, writing, arithmetic, and in the doctrines of a religion of some kind: the Christian religion should be preferred to all others; for it belongs to this religion exclusively to teach us not only to cultivate peace with men, but to forgive, nay more—to love our very enemies. It belongs to it further to teach us that the Supreme Being alone possesses a power to take away human life, and that we rebel against his laws, whenever we undertake to execute death in any way whatever upon any of his creatures.

III. Let every family in the United States be furnished at the public expense, by the Secretary of this office, with a copy of an American edition of the BIBLE. This measure has become the more necessary in our country, since the banishment of the bible, as a school-book, from most of the schools in the United States. Unless the price of this book be paid for by the public, there is reason to fear that in a few years it will be met with only in courts of justice or in magistrates' offices; and should the absurd mode of establishing truth by kissing this sacred book fall into disuse, it may probably, in the course of the next generation, be seen only as a curiosity on a shelf in a public museum.

IV. Let the following sentence be inscribed in letters of gold over the doors of every State and Court house in the United States.

THE SON OF MAN CAME INTO THE WORLD, NOT TO DESTROY
MEN'S LIVES, BUT TO SAVE THEM.

V. To inspire a veneration for human life, and an horror at the shedding of human blood, let all those laws be repealed which authorise juries, judges, sheriffs, or hangmen to assume the resentments of individuals and to commit murder in cold blood in any case whatever. Until this reformation in our code of penal jurisprudence takes place, it will be in vain to attempt to introduce universal and perpetual peace in our country.

VI. To subdue that passion for war, which education, added to human depravity, have made universal, a familiarity with the instruments of death, as well as all military shows, should be carefully avoided. For which reason, militia laws should every where be repealed, and military dresses and military titles should be laid aside: reviews tend to lessen the horrors of a battle by connecting them with the charms of order; militia laws generate idleness and vice, and thereby produce the wars they are said to prevent; military dresses fascinate the minds of young men, and lead them from serious and useful professions; were there no uniforms, there would probably be no armies; lastly, military titles feed vanity, and keep up ideas in the mind which lessen a sense of the folly and miseries of war.

VII. In the last place, let a large room, adjoining the federal hall, be appropriated for transacting the business and preserving all the records of this office. Over the door of this room let there be a sign, on which the figures of a LAMB, a DOVE and an OLIVE BRANCH should be painted, together with the following inscriptions in letters of gold:

PEACE ON EARTH—GOOD-WILL TO MAN.
AH! WHY WILL MEN FORGET THAT THEY ARE
BRETHREN?

Within this apartment let there be a collection of plough-shares and pruning-hooks made out of swords and spears; and on each of the walls of the apartment, the following pictures as large as the life:

1. A lion eating straw with an ox, and an adder playing upon the lips of a child.

2. An Indian boiling his venison in the same pot with a citizen of Kentucky.

3. Lord Cornwallis and Tippoo Saib, under the shade of a sycamore-tree in the East Indies, drinking Madeira wine together out of the same decanter.

4. A group of French and Austrian soldiers dancing arm and arm, under a bower erected in the neighbourhood of Mons.

5. A St. Domingo planter, a man of color, and a native of Africa, legislating together in the same colonial assembly.[2]

, ,

It was Rush, of course, who was assigned the task of working over the Articles of Faith, Plan of Church Government, and Recommendations which were adopted by the Convention of Universalists in Philadelphia in 1790. Aside from the advanced position in regard to slavery and the slave trade, it should be noted that Section IV indicates a tender regard for the Philadelphia Friends and probably for those converts to Universalism who brought with them certain Quaker attitudes.

Section V should be read as support for the form of government which had come into being under the new Constitution the year before. In addition to this resolution of support, the Convention addressed congratulations to President George Washington on his assumption of office and received his cordial good wishes in return.

‛ ‛

RECOMMENDATIONS.

Sect. I. Of War.

ALTHOUGH a defensive war may be considered lawful, yet we believe there is a time coming, when the light and universal love of the gospel shall put an end to all wars. We recommend, therefore, to all the churches in our communion, to cultivate the spirit of peace and brotherly love, which shall lead them to consider all mankind as brethren; and to strive to spread among them the knowledge of their common Saviour and Redeemer, who came into the world, "not to destroy men's lives, but to save them."

Sect. II. Of going to Law.

We hold it unbecoming for Christians, who are members of the same church, to appeal to courts of law for the settlements of disputes. Such appeals too often ingender malice, beget idleness, and produce a waste of property. They are, therefore, contrary to the spirit of the gospel. In disputes of all kinds, and with all persons, we recommend appeals to arbitrators appointed by both parties, where it is practicable, in preference to courts of law.

Sect. III. Of holding Slaves.

We believe it to be inconsistent with the union of the human race in a common Saviour, and the obligations to mutual and universal love, which flow from that union, to hold any part of our fellow creatures in bondage. We therefore recommend a total refraining from the African trade, and the adoption of prudent measures for the gradual abolition of the slavery of the negroes in our country, and for the instruction and education of their children in English literature, and in the principles of the gospel.

Sect. IV. Of Oaths.

We recommend it to all the members of our churches to inquire, whether oaths do not lessen the frequency of truth in common life; whether they do not increase profane swearing; whether they be not contrary to the commands of our Saviour and the apostle James; and lastly, whether they do not lessen the dignity of the christian name, by obliging professors of christianity to yield to a suspicion of being capable of declaring a falsehood. And as we are indulged by the laws of all our states, with the privilege of giving testimony by simple affirmation, we submit it to the conscience of our members, whether that mode of declaring the truth should not be preferred to any other oath.

Sect. V. Of Submission to Government.

We recommend to all the members of our churches a peaceful submission to the higher powers, not for wrath, but for conscience sake, &c. We enjoin, in a particular manner, a regard to truth and justice, in the payment of such duties or taxes, as shall be required by our rulers, for the maintenance of order, and the support of government.[3]

Whatever hope was held for an expeditious solution of the problem of slavery was dashed by the introduction by Eli Whitney of the cotton gin in 1794, which made the demand for slave labor greater.

The abolitionist agitation begun in Boston with the publication of William Lloyd Garrison's *Liberator* in 1831 was to spread into Universalist circles with the help of Sylvanus Cobb. Cobb, after an itinerant ministry in Maine, held pastorates in Waterville, Maine, and Malden, Massachusetts. It was in this latter position that he became interested in temperance and abolition. His autobiography recounts his adventures as an agent for the Middlesex Temperance Society (1836–38).

‘ ‘

The labors of these three years in the Agency of the Middlesex Temperance Society were enormous. The lectures were not little thirty minute essays. In that stage of the temperance reform, there were ignorance, and prejudice, and hostility to be encountered;—and old customs of all classes, good, bad and indifferent, were to be revolutionized; and the necessary argument could not be compressed within a shorter space of time than an hour. Generally my lectures exceeded an hour, and were of necessity uttered in what I felt, an earnest spirit. I circulated the pledge, the "Teetotal" pledge, at the close of every lecture, and, in all, thousands of names were won, and many new societies were organized. I worked over even the old Temperance societies, advancing them from the partial pledge, discarding distilled spirits only, to the thorough pledge, discarding, as a beverage, all intoxicating liquors, distilled and fermented. And, besides my public lectures, I labored much in conversation with individuals at their homes. And I called upon most of the taverners, victuallers and grocers in the county, and labored with them on the subject of their voluntary abandonment of the liquor-traffic. They treated me respectfully, and generally professed a desire to be rid of that branch of their business. "But," each one would say, "if I refuse to supply my customers with liquor, and others around me sell it, my customers will go to others, not only for their liquor, but with all their custom; so that I shall suffer loss without any good result, as no less liquor will be sold. But prohibit the business by law, and it will be impartial; and will relieve me from liability to complaint from my customers." But, when such just and impartial law obtained, it did not please them.

There was quite a rowdy set of tippling hangers-on about the tavern in Bedford Village. One evening when I had a lecture in the Unitarian Church in that Village, as I was about to commence the services, I observed the entrance into the vestibule of a company of rough-looking men, with shouldered canes, deploying in military style, and separating into two parties, which took their stands at the two doors opening from the vestibule into the Church. It was obvious to my perceptions that mischief was intended. I arose and offered a few introductory remarks, solemnly stating the purpose of the meeting, and recognizing the relations sustained by the people present, as husbands, wives, fathers, mothers, children, brothers, sisters, and members of society,—and the duties and privileges which appertained to all those relations, with the due observance and improvement of which was associated peace, prosperity and happiness,—and from the disregard of which proceeded wretchedness and ruin. These suspicious characters looked, and looked, with raised faces and parted lips; and one after another moved softly in and took seat in a pew, until one was left standing alone, who turned and went away. I learned after the dismission of the meeting that my suspicions did the party no injustice. They agreed (about a dozen of them), in the tavern, to go into the Church and break up the meeting, by annoying me, and irritating me to some words or acts which they would make an occasion for dragging me out. But we had an exceedingly happy and profitable meeting.

, ,

By 1839 Cobb had become convinced of the need within the Universalist denomination for a newspaper that would deal with slavery and temperance, and other burning reform interests of the day such as abolition of capital punishment. He agreed that the Universalist papers already in existence were doing a good job extending the faith but—for that very reason—they did not include controversial "political" material. When he launched his *Christian Freeman and Family Visiter*, [sic], published in Waltham and Boston, he was immediately assailed by the editors of these other papers and by friends, one of whom commented, "I am sorry you could not make up your mind to give us a good Universalist paper without meddling with Rum and Niggers!"

‹ ‹

We salute the Christian public with good wishes, and proffer them fraternal counsel, and kind instruction. We present them with a new weekly periodical, which shall stand forth among them a true *Christian Freeman*, and a good *Family Visiter*. May God aid and bless us in our long contemplated and arduous undertaking. . . .

When we engaged as a public lecturer for the Middlesex County Temperance Society, it was predicted by some of our kind and well beloved brethren, that this service would diminish our interest in the gospel, and in the work of the Christian ministry. We then felt that they knew not what they said; and now we know it. The more the servant of Christ imitates his Master in going about, observing the blindness, the wants, and the sufferings of mankind, and doing good as opportunity offers, the more he will feel engaged in all those great and good principles of truth, which shall promote virtue and happiness.

Of these principles the gospel stands pre-eminent. Indeed the Christian religion comprises all that is excellent in faith and practice. Its faith, the faith which rests in the infinite wisdom, goodness, and power of God, and nourishes the hope, sweet, soul-satisfying hope, of the universal emancipation and glory of the human race through Jesus Christ, is peculiarly fitted to elevate and reconcile the mind to God, and to produce the love of God and holiness. If we forget this faith, or neglect to propagate and defend it, let our right hand forget its cunning. It shall be borne by this *Family Visiter* to the abodes of all our readers, and applied in its adaptedness to work the reconciliation and comfort of the mind under every earthly circumstance.

But the Christian religion does not alone apply to our hope for ourselves, and others, beyond the grave. It applies to the infinite variety of duties and interests of our present diversified relations. And to the nature of some of these relations, and the manner of some of these interests, and the verity of some of these duties, the prejudices, passions, and supposed interests of many may blind them, while they can stoutly argue, and may even quite feelingly believe, the leading doctrines of the Christian faith. And in respect to this point, our travels and labors have brought us in the way of such observation, as has often told us of the need of a public journal, which should go forth as a *Christian Freeman*, laboring not only to convert unbelievers, but also to remove remaining darkness from the minds of believers, in any and every case where they are blindly or inconsiderately giving their influence to perpetuate the causes of reigning evils.

"Ye shall know the truth, and the truth shall make you free," is the language of the Saviour. It will make us not only free from the slavish fear of human creeds, but free also to do good. "To do good and to communicate, forget not," is the admonition of the Christian apostle.

. . . The Universalist who will neglect, in any obvious case, "to do good and to communicate," because certain others see not eye to eye with him, gives practical sanction to the precise principle of action which he so loudly denounces in others, who make it their rule in matters of religious faith to ask, not "what is truth?" but "what will secure me favor with the popular voice?"

But our brother tells us that he should like the plan of our Family Visiter, if we would exclude all matter touching the subject of slavery. Then he would have us doff our caption, "*Christian Freeman.*" God forbid that we should do it. For us to preach, and pray, and sing praises to God, upon the theme of that blessed gospel which we prize above earthly riches, the gospel of Him who lived, and labored, and died, and reigns on high for all,—for Jews and barbarians, bond and free; the gospel which teaches us that God is the Father of all, and that all we are brethren; and yet for us at the same time to look upon a portion of our brethren, in our own country, held as cattle, as goods and chattels, the property of others, where knowledge is danger, and ignorance is the only hope of safety,—and here to insist that not a word must be spoken, not a thought indulged, not an inquiry breathed, whether some means may not be devised, some moral influence put in motion, which shall meliorate the condition of these poor, unfortunate, unhumanized fellow beings,—this does indeed to us seem monstrous. If our brother can persevere in his efforts to smother investigation, and to foster slavery as an undisturbed institution, until it shall break forth in horrible destruction upon its proprietors, with their wives and innocent little ones,—and yet feel that he can lift up holy hands, and pray God to prosper him in these efforts, he is to us an insolvable enigma.

.   .   .

The question is often gravely asked, "What can we, in the North, do towards the abolition of Slavery in the South?" I will answer so far, at the present time, as to mention two things which we can and ought to do, by a candid and manly discussion; the first relating to the North, and the second to the South. The first thing to be done, and that relating to the North, is, to vindicate and establish the principle of free discussion, and deliver a large portion of the community from the slavish fear of looking at a great moral subject. When I look at an evil in our country, in view of which one of the greatest of southern patriots has been moved by the spirit of prophecy to exclaim, "I tremble for my country, when I reflect that God is just,"—and when, upon some good citizens proposing to deliberate ways and means to save the country, ere it be too late, from a judgment more intolerable than that of Sodom and Gomorrah, I see the community up in arms to suppress all investigation touching the subject, I feel ashamed for my native and beloved New England. And I view the restoration to the people, of this one principle—the principle of free, open, frank, ingenuous, fearless, manly, Christian investigation, of this, and all subjects involving the rights, duties, interests and privileges of mankind,— worth a firm persevering labor to attain it. Let this great principle be, by all, conceded,—and then, though there may yet be difference of opinion on the question of ways and means, there will be that general good feeling, that harmony of spirit in the community, which can never be brought about by the childish cries of those who are feeding the feverish spirit of division, by essaying to stop discussion with forever sounding upon the *fear* of divisions! Divisions! No Christian should ever speak, write, or print a word, which shall express the thought of a possibility of division among *Christians*, (a division as to Christian union, I mean) by the free candid discussion of any subject touching moral principles. If it be said that all discussion on the subject of slavery has not been candid, I answer, neither has all discussion on religion, or any other subject, been candid. We are never to condemn a good cause for the errors of some of its friends. . . .

The owners of slaves are objects of our commiseration; their case demands the exercise of charity. They are blinded by supposed, but mistaken interest, as keepers of dram-shops have been, in this section. But, after all, if we will be their true friends, while we exercise that charity which "suffereth long and is kind," we must remember that the same charity "rejoiceth not in iniquity, but rejoiceth in the truth." And if such were the elevated tone of moral sentiment in the non-slave-holding States, that when their southern brethren step within their borders, they should feel that they breathe an atmosphere in which the very principles of slavery must blight and die, as the accursed fig-tree by the word of Jesus, this state of public sentiment with us would, in spite of all menacing and scolding, gradually move upon them to pass the inquiry around, "What shall we do to raise ourselves to our proper moral elevation? What shall we do to be saved!" But when they feel that the institution of slavery is approved and cherished by the popular sentiment of the whole country, this circumstance constitutes an additional bond to hold the slave in his chains, and the master in his error.[4]

, ,

It was the constant agitation of Sylvanus Cobb and other reformers which was responsible for an upsurge of reform activity among the Universalists in the generation before the Civil War. 1841 saw the publication of a petition signed by a large group of ministers protesting slavery because it "denies the eternal distinction between a man and property, ranking a human being with a material thing." In September of 1843 the United States Convention of Universalists meeting in Akron, Ohio, passed the following resolution with but one dissenting vote.

‘ ‘

Resolved, That we rejoice in the knowledge of the truth that the doctrines of Christ have for their end the holiness and happiness of all mankind; and that the faithful inculcation and acceptance of those doctrines must lead to the overthrow and extinction of all institutions, observances and relations, however ancient or firmly fortified, which are contrary to righteousness, to human well-being, and thus hindrances to the full establishment of the true and glorious kingdom of God on earth.

Resolved, That in the light of this truth we feel constrained to bear testimony against the slavery of the African race, now maintained in a portion of our country, as contrary to that gospel which is destined to break every yoke and lead captivity captive; as especially subversive of that golden rule which teaches us to do unto others as we would that they should do unto us; as contrary to the plainest dictates of natural justice and Christian love; and as every way pernicious alike to the enslaver and enslaved.

Resolved, That, regarding the whole human family as in the larger sense our brethren, joint heirs with us of our Father's love and the immortality of blessedness revealed through our Saviour, we are constrained both by duty and inclination to regard with peculiar sympathy and affection the oppressed, the benighted, the down-trodden, of our own and other lands, and to labor for their restoration to the rights and blessings of Freedom, Light and Truth.

Resolved, That, while we regard the holding in bondage of our brethren for whom Christ died, or the treatment of any human being with obloquy, harshness, or any indignity on account of his color or race, as contrary to righteousness, inconsistent with Christianity, and especially with that doctrine of Universal Grace and Love which we cherish as the most important of revealed truth, we are well aware that many worthy and upright Christians have sustained the relation of slave-holder in ignorance of its true character or from inability to relieve themselves therefrom; and while we earnestly entreat all Christian and especially all Universalist slave-holders to consider prayerfully the nature and tendencies of the relation they sustain, we recommend or countenance no measures of indiscriminate denunciation or proscription, but, appealing to the gospel, to humanity, and to their own consciences, we await in implicit confidence the perfect working of the principles of Divine and Universal Love.[5]

, ,

By 1849 the momentum in behalf of various reforms had so increased that a Universalist General Reform Association was established. This organization allowed members from various state and local reform committees to compare notes and learn from each other new forms of agitation and education.

On the whole Sylvanus Cobb pursued a moderate course in his campaign against slavery. But as the Mexican War opened up the prospect of vast new territories being turned over to slavery, his tone became less conciliatory. The heated congressional discussion of the Compromise of 1850 with its hated Fugitive Slave Law is reflected in this editorial in which Cobb looks into the gun barrel of secession without flinching.

‘ ‘

POLITICAL CROAKING. THE COMPROMISE.

We do protest against the present style of croaking, by the political press of the North, in relation to the dissolution of the Union. Almost the entire political press indulges in a tone of alarm in respect to the safety of the Union, and with Northern members of Congress, suffers itself to be diverted to the discussion of ways and means for averting such a catastrophe. This is just the slavish business to which our Southern masters wished to put us.

It is mortifying in the extreme to see our Representatives in Congress condescending to go into a discussion of *compromises* and *surmises* for saving the Union, and our political journals applauding their wisdom and patriotism in making "*discretion their better valor.*" What are they sent to the Capital to do? It is to deliberate and legislate for the right and the good, for the present and permanent interest of the country. If they have a measure which is wrong and mischievous, or which infringes upon the constitutional rights of sister States, let there be no compromise, but an utter abandonment of their project. But if they have a measure to urge which is constitutional and right, and which is demanded by the law of republican liberty and happiness, let them not consent to compromise it away, but firmly, calmly, seasonably, justly, labor for its consummation.

But what if secession is threatened by a sister State as the price of such a measure? What? Pass it as the idle winds, which you respect not,—and keep about your business. If we cannot have our holiest sentiments represented in our national legislature, and we may not perform our highest duties there as branches of the Federal Republic, for fear of the bowie knife, the pistol, or the secession of States, then the sooner the great bubble bursts, the better. We would not consent to occupy so degraded a position, as to sit in Congress as mere dotards, to do as any spoiled child may bid us do, under the threat of dashing out its own brains if we refuse. Depend upon it, every indulgence which Southern members extort by their threats, *endangers* the Union; for it fosters in them the spirit of tyranny, encourages further encroachments, and settles a precedent on which they will argue a prescriptive claim for such indulgence. In this way the Union will soon be made too shameful a thing to bear its own weight. It will decompose by its own putrescence.

What is the question now? It has been pleaded by the

apologists for slavery as it is, that they, and even *Southerners*, generally, are as much opposed to slavery *in the abstract* as we are. The introduction of slavery, they say, was a wicked transaction, and if it were not in our country, they would by no means have it entered. But as it is in the Southern States, and the present generation had no agency in introducing it, they are not to be blamed for its existence.

Well, what is the question now? It is, whether we as a republic, we of the Free States even, will blast and curse the now free territories of our domain with the terrible sin and evil of slavery: Or, which is the same, whether we will open the doors of those territories to the influx of this evil. Every principle of religion and morality, of reason and nature, of republicanism and common sense, of social and political economy, forbids it. How many thousands in the slave-blighted States of America have cursed the memory of King George, for his agency in the introduction of slaves into our country. Shall we, under the light and the profession of those doctrines of human rights which King George had never studied, give the same occasion for posterity in those new and fertile countries to curse our memory? No hotspur gasconade can render it justifiable in us.

Suppose you are in a productive business co-partnership. A member of the firm comes to you with the project of an extensive murder and robbery for the increase of capital. You refuse to participate in the scheme, or to be accessory to it. He then attempts to procure your concurrence, by the threat that otherwise he will withdraw from the partnership! Would this threat constitute a justification of your confederacy in the robbery?

No, let not our Representatives in Congress, nor our political journals, set up their praises of a compromise of *principle*. Be deliberate, calm, firm, persevering in the right. And if any turn their gasconade into an overt act of insurrection, let the Executive take care of them.

We speak not as a political partisan; nor do we speak ought that bears against any one political party. We speak as a man, an American citizen, a Christian, a father, whose posterity are to enjoy or suffer, according to the preparations we provide.

And we speak unto wise men, for none but wise men would be patrons of the *Christian Freeman*. Judge ye what we say.

, ,

     The wave of interest in utopian communities which swept the United States in 1840 led Emerson to write Carlyle, "We are all a little wild here with numberless projects of social reform. Not a reading man but has a draft of a new community in his waistcoat pocket." Adin Ballou was one of those with a plan. Adin, a distant relative of Hosea Ballou, was one of the leaders of the Restorationists in their opposition to Hosea's ultra-Universalism. It was out of the Restorationist Association, after its defection from the main body of Universalism, that the impulse for the Hopedale Community was to come. Adin Ballou, a Christian pacifist and socialist, insisted to the last that Hopedale, Massachusetts, stemmed from a different spirit, grounded in the precepts of Christ, than the other utopian communities of the day. In various of his later writings he recounted the rise and fall of Hopedale and the lessons to be learned therein concerning human nature.

‹ ‹

     Christian Union. An interesting religious movement bearing this designation originated in central New York. Its rallying cry was "Union of all Christians: Away with Sectarianism." Among its progenitors and leading promoters was a no-less-distinguished personage than Gerritt Smith, a world-renowned philanthropist, who, a few years before, had distributed a hundred thousand acres or more of his vast landed possessions among free negroes and other poor people, whereon to build homes for themselves and earn a livelihood. It had come to have so much of a foothold in central and eastern Massachusetts that in the summer of 1840 a general convention of its friends and those sympathizing with its declared sentiments and objects was called to meet in the town of Groton on the 12th day of August. One Rev. Silas Hawley seemed to be its chief representative in this part of the country and a prominent mover in getting up the Groton convocation. The call for it was addressed "To all the friends of the Redeemer and of Reform." Our little group of Progressives, though doubtful of a cordial welcome on account of what might be regarded as their theological heresies, were in a mood to hope something from such an ostensibly well-meant and philanthropic enterprise, and resolved to lend it, in a general way, their sanction. The meeting was accordingly announced with favorable comments in the *Practical Christian*, and immediately after a pleasant conference of our own in Southborough, most of us repaired to Groton—myself and wife among the number. We were kindly received, respectfully treated, and so far had no cause of complaint.

But such a heterogeneous gathering assembled as can hardly be imagined, made up, as it was, of Christian Unionists proper, Perfectionists, Transcendentalists, Comeouters, and nondescript eccentrics of widely varying types and peculiarities. The whole number of enrolled members of the convention was about 275. Dr. Amos Farnsworth (residence unknown) was chosen president, and Edmund Quincy of Dedham, Oliver Johnson of Boston, and Lucius M. Burleigh of Plainfield, Ct., secretaries. The parties interested in calling and providing for the meeting found themselves so involved with erratic and chaotic opinionists that they had hard work to control the proceedings or utilize the occasion to the advantage of their special cause. Many unacceptable subjects were introduced and warmly discussed; generally, however, in good temper. There was a large number of earnest talkers who dispensed profitable thoughts and suggestions as well as unprofitable ones, but few satisfactory conclusions were reached. Finally, as I recollect, the Christian Unionists succeeded in making their favorite and distinctive affirmations. These in condensed form were that Sectarianism is abhorrently anti-Christian and that the divided branches of the professed Christian church ought to come at once into harmonious fellowship. How this was to be done was not stated, nor was it found practically possible to realize it, even among those present. Could it have been accomplished there and extended thence throughout Christendom, it would have produced little improvement in the popular theology or ethics, or in the characters and lives of men. Names and externals might have been changed, but not *evil things*. I tried to be just and generous to these self-styled reformers, but was obliged to conclude that their aims and claims were comparatively superficial, and that, whatever their merits, we of the Practical Christian household of faith could derive no special edification from them.

Soon after the publication of our "Standard of Practical Christianity," my mind began to be exercised with the question of how it could be actualized. How could the principles and sentiments it contained be made the basis of individual and social life? I could not suppress this inquiry on my own part and my brethren were burdened with the same problem. To treat our declaration of principles and duties as a mere speculation or rhetorical flourish would be alike false to our highest convictions and "disobedient to the heavenly vision"—it would be both inconsistent and wicked. We must not only preach but live by what we had received as truth, or else renounce it honestly as impracticable. Conscience and a proper self-respect forbade its renunciation. There was no honorable retreat for us; we must go forward. But if we went forward, to whom could we look for cooperation and support? With whom could we affiliate in carrying our declared theories into effect? We had broken with the existing social system in three fundamental respects—in respect (1) to the non-resistance of evil with evil, (2) the serviceship of superiors, and (3) the fraternization of property. And we could not suppose for a moment that those who believed in and were a part of the existing order of society would encourage and aid us in preaching what was in its very nature opposed to and subversive of that order, or in any attempts we might make to establish and build up one that was radically different from it and designed in due time to supersede it in the administration of human affairs. We had nothing whatever to hope for from that quarter, either in the way of maintaining our ministry in the promulgation of the principles we had avowed, or in any effort we might put forth to apply and carry out those principles to their logical and moral results in life's varied interests and concerns. We must therefore depend on ourselves under divine providence and on the converts we could make to our cause in both its theoretical and practical aspects.

Here, then, we took our stand. For us there was no other alternative. Upon the Practical Christian platform which we had adopted and given to the world, we must try to build a new civilization radically higher than the old, which should hold inviolate the distinctive principles of truth and duty·just enumerated and declared by us to be essential to the realization of a divine order of human society founded on the great ideas of the fatherhood of God and brotherhood of man.

.   .   .

For a few months, my coadjutors and myself as their leader entertained and discussed somewhat indefinitely the plan of purchasing a common farm, settling upon and running it as a means of mutual physical self-support—making it a sort of missionary post whence our preachers might go forth to localities where an opportunity was offered us, like the apostles of old, and proclaim an untrammeled gospel as we understood it in its application to all the affairs of life. This plan, after much consideration, grew into the more ample one of a community, which should be composed of a considerable number of persons sympathizing with us and representing a variety of interests pertaining to the welfare and prosperity of society. Having deliberated sufficiently, as I thought, upon the subject, I issued in the *Practical Christian*, the 15th of September, 1840, an article entitled "communities," in which I announced and explained our private discussions and the result to which they brought us, viz: *The desirability of establishing a colony of persons pledged to the principles of our standard, for mutual encouragement and support in proclaiming and exemplifying those principles before the world.* In that communication I endeavored to answer many questions which would naturally be asked by persons of a practical turn of mind concerning such an undertaking, even going so far as to present a *suggestive constitution* for its general management. I also, in closing, set forth what I thought would be the advantages of the proposed scheme, as follows:

"Such a community would furnish a happy home to

many pure-hearted Christians now scattered abroad, insulated from each other, ignored or maligned by a corrupt church, and oppressed by the unregenerate world. It would enable them to secure, with less severe toil and more certainty, a comfortable subsistence for themselves and their dependents. It would render it much easier for them to reform many pernicious habits of living and to promote the true physical health and comfort of themselves and families. It would remove them from the dominion of many corrupt and demoralizing influences to which they are now exposed. It would enable them to set up and maintain a purer religious worship, a holier ministry, a more salutary moral discipline, and altogether a better spiritual state of things than they now enjoy. It would enable them to send forth true-hearted religious, moral, and philanthropic missionaries into the surrounding world for its conversion; men and women who would not be bribed or frightened into subserviency to popular iniquities, and who, when weary, might return, like Noah's dove, to the window of a peaceful ark and find repose. It would enable them more effectually to prosecute every branch of moral reform and human improvement by means of the press, of well-ordered schools, and of teachers qualified to go out and inculcate our holy principles wherever people might welcome them. It would enable them to bring up their children 'in the nurture and admonition of the Lord,' free from those loose and corrupting influences so prevalent elsewhere. It would enable them to establish asylums for the orphan, the widow, and the outcast, in which they might be duly cared for and directed into the paths of life. In fine, it would be a powerful concentration of moral light and heat, which would make 'Practical Christianity' known and felt by the world."

.   .   .

It is a somewhat singular fact that our "Fraternal Communion" originated altogether independently of the general agitation referred to, and of the movements mentioned, as it did in utter unconsciousness of the existence of any published expositions of the general subject of social reconstruction. It grew primarily out of New Testament Christianity as we understood it, as a practical issue of its essential spirit, principles, and precepts; though our general reading and acquaintance with what was going on in the world soon advised us of the broader field of discussion and experiment which others, in this and foreign lands, were occupying. When this occurred, we availed ourselves of the opportunity of examining their theories and suggestions, hoping to get some light not before obtained upon the problem we were earnestly trying to solve. But to little profit. For after comparing the various schemes accessible to us with our own, we preferred the latter with the peculiarities which distinguished it from each and every other brought to our notice.

A very kindly feeling sprang up between us and our Brook Farm neighbors, and there was much friendly conference and correspondence between us, looking to a union of the two movements. Mr. Ripley and his associates were very cordial and earnestly urged us to join them at West Roxbury. The temptation was strong for us to do so. We were few, poor, and comparatively unlearned. They were more numerous, rich, and scholarly. In these respects they could be of great service to us and our children. On the other hand, we could be a help to them in more ordinary ways. But there were serious, insuperable objections to anything of the kind proposed. Their transcendentalism and individualistic independence made them quite averse to our views upon historic and authoritative Christianity, to our positive ethical position on several important points of doctrine and duty, and to our uncompromising religious and reform pledge. On our own ground, which we had carefully and conscientiously chosen, we were equally averse to their extreme views of personal liberty and their noncommittalism. Such being our incompatibilities, neither party being able to yield to the other without giving up some things it regarded as most sacred in principle and most vital to success, we wisely decided to close all negotiations in peace and mutual good will, and go our own respective ways.

In proceeding to get ourselves into proper working order, it seemed desirable to abridge and modify somewhat the fundamental basis of our association as expressed in the constitution of our "Fraternal Communion." Our prolix "Standard of Practical Christianity" was consequently condensed into the following "Declaration," to be openly made by each individual entering our membership:

"I believe in the religion of Jesus Christ as he taught and exemplified it according to the scriptures of the New Testament. I acknowledge myself a bounden subject of all its moral obligations. Especially do I hold myself bound by its holy requirements never, under any pretext whatsoever, to kill, assault, beat, torture, rob, oppress, persecute, defraud, corrupt, slander, revile, injure, envy, or hate any human being—even my worst enemy; never in any manner to violate the dictates of pure chastity; never to take or administer an oath; never to manufacture, buy, sell, deal out, or use any intoxicating liquor as a beverage; never to serve in the army, navy, or militia of any nation, state, or chieftain; never to bring an action at law, hold office, vote, join a legal posse, petition a legislature, or ask governmental interposition *in any case involving a final authorized resort to physical violence*; never to indulge self-will, bigotry, love of preeminence, covetousness, deceit, profanity, idleness, or an unruly tongue; never to participate in lotteries, games of chance, betting, or pernicious amusements; never to resent reproof or justify myself in a known wrong; never to aid, abet, or approve others in anything sinful; but, through divine assistance, always to recommend and promote with my entire influence the holiness and happiness of all mankind." [7]

, ,

What then did produce the fatal crisis? Why was it deemed necessary to suspend the operations of our combined industry, surrender our Joint-Stock holdings, and dissolve our peculiar associated relations, going back to the assumption of strictly individual interests and responsibilities, to the old competitive, unfraternal, unchristian business methods and to the long-established usages, maxims, customs, and institutions of the world at large? It was because, as a whole, we lacked the Christ-like wisdom and virtue necessary to the successful prosecution and final triumph of such an undertaking,—those qualities of mind, heart, and character, without which any comprehensive, all-sided movement for the individual and social uplifting of humanity—any organized attempt to realize the divine kingdom on the earth in a radical form, must, in the nature of the case, prove abortive. Our experiment was born out of due time. It was scores and perhaps hundreds of years ahead of the age in which it was put on trial. The world, even the best part of the world, was not ready for it—was not at the stage of moral and spiritual development in which it could understand, appreciate and supply the appropriate atmosphere for a work so thorough, so all-embracing, so superior to all the ordinary aspirations and ambitions of men, so antagonistic to the selfishness, pride, arrogance, contention, belligerancy, and barbarism that characterize existing society;—to say nothing of its indisposition and lack of desire to enter into, sustain, and carry such a work forward to triumphant issues. And not only was the world, or the best part of the world, notwithstanding all its professions of intelligence, virtue, philanthropy, piety—of Christian love and loyalty—not ready for such an undertaking, but we ourselves, who had assumed to enter upon it, were not ready. We had too many of the infirmities of the carnal nature about us, we were too much under the dominion of the worldly mind, we entered too little into the Spirit of the Master, and were entangled with too large a number of the errors and follies of the prevailing religion of the church to win the success of which our cause was intrinsically worthy. We lacked the wisdom, the grace, the large-mindedness, the generosity, the nobility of soul, in a single word, the Christlikeness that was requisite to the end we sought, that qualified us to be the builders of a temple on every stone of which was to be inscribed "Holiness to the Lord." Probably the best of us lacked these qualities in too great a degree, and it may be that those most wanting in them were as true to their light and capability as their more favored brethren. I judge no one in this matter but refer all judgment, whether of approval or condemnation, to Him who cannot err and whose verdict is righteous and irreversible.

Some have been disposed to censure severely and blame

without reserve the Brothers Draper for their course in the matter
—for their agency in bringing on the fatal crisis, charging them
with treachery to the cause they had espoused and with infidelity to their brethren. I have never sympathized with such impu-
tations. To be sure, these men unitedly owned three-fourths of
the Joint-Stock of the Community and had a constantly increasing income from their own private business, which was carried
on outside of Community superintendence, though in accord
with its established polity. To be sure, it was their decision to
withdraw their portion of the common funds from the treasury
that precipitated our overthrow. And it is also true that they
were enabled to erect upon the foundation which had been laid
by us with much study, labor, self-denial, and prayer, an enterprise that yielded them personally an ample fortune and enabled
their successors to rise to a commanding place among the opu-
lent capitalists of their day and generation. But I could never
yield assent to any charges, open or implied, of infidelity or be-
trayal of trust that may have been preferred against them, usually from outsiders; certainly not of perfidy or injustice towards
their brethren; nor could I count them sinners above all others
in the competitive, money-making, self-seeking world. For the
reason, that neither of them ever sought to enrich himself at the
Community's expense, or took advantage of its necessities, or
shirked his share of its burdens, or tried to absolve himself from
any of its obligations. On the contrary, both helped it in many a
time of need, by augmenting its capital, by enhancing its credit,
by co-operating cheerfully with their brethren in maintaining its
honor, and not infrequently, especially in the case of the elder,
by making it important and gratefully-received donations.

I did at the time greatly deplore the decisive step on
their part by which our associated endeavors were brought to an
end. I longed to have them and all my associates prize the cause
as I did, see the matter as I saw it, feel as I felt, and be willing
and happy to do with their means as I should have done had I
been favored as they were—use them for the good of our body
and for the continuance and advancement of the work to which
we were all sacredly pledged. And I then had, as I have now, no

doubt, that if these two brothers had been so minded, the Community would have gone on prospering and to prosper for many years after its career was terminated.

But as the movement rested wholly on the basis of the inherent and indefeasible individual rights of its members—rights of conscience, of private judgment, of personal possession of property, and of voluntary action in the management of our common affairs, I always held these sacred, and never attempted or desired to dictate, coerce, overrule, or over-persuade any one, even to save the Community from dissolution. I never could respect or love or have confidence in any social experiment that was not undertaken by intelligent, free-minded, willing-hearted men and women—persons sincerely and reverently obedient to divine moral principles, and not blindly subservient to mere human authority of any sort whatsoever. Much as I desire and pray for a true Community, I want none for the sake of merely temporal and worldly advantage, and none in which the individual member loses his identity in the general mass and is made less a man or woman by socialistic organization or polity. Perish all plans of social reform—all devices, expedients, schemes, systems, that destroy or dwarf the human personality, that limit or enthrall any of the capabilities or possibilities of the children of the infinite Father of all mankind. I do, however, sincerely believe in the practicability and coming actualization of a social order, or system of communal life, under which those capabilities and possibilities shall be exercised, unfolded, and enjoyed illimitably. Only that attainment is far more difficult and demands a far higher development of character and a far fuller and richer experience of the life of God in the soul of man than I formerly conceived.

Moreover, I am now able to see from my present point of observation, that, if the Brothers Draper had been of the same mind as myself—had been willing to devote their rapidly accumulating property to the further development, growth, and prosperity of the Hopedale Community, it would have sooner or later failed; and for the same general reason already given; on account of the same lack of moral qualification which existed at the time of its suspension, and which, I repeat, will

forever prove fatal to any enterprise of like character and purpose at any period of the world's history. I at present see no
ground for believing that, with the prevailing currents of society
setting so strongly in the direction of the accumulation of
wealth, of political preferment, of fashionable display, of easy-
going morality, and of a religion still studiously careful not to
offend too seriously the popular taste, or habits of the multitude
by arraigning and condemning giant wrongs and unchristian
practices in social, civil, and national life,—I see no ground for
believing under these circumstances that the membership of the
Community would up to this moment have been raised to a
higher moral and spiritual level than it occupied at that time,
even had it been possible for it to have maintained its then existing integrity and standing before the divine law and in the
presence of Him who is of purer eyes than to look upon iniquity
with favor, and whose kingdom in this and all possible worlds is
righteousness and peace and joy. No Community can be a success except its membership consist of persons the like of which
the world even now possesses very few.[8]

, ,

In the same year, 1840, while Adin Ballou and his associates planned their withdrawal from the cold realities of an increasingly industrial, materialistic American society, Abel C.
Thomas and Thomas B. Thayer, ministering to the churches of
Lowell, Massachusetts, sought to confront the problems of that
burgeoning textile town. To keep the young maidens who came
from the farms to the industrial town from the temptations inevitably present, they formed "Improvement Circles," one result
of which was the world-famous *Lowell Offering*. Thomas' autobiography provides the details.

‹ ‹

The first number of the 'Lowell Offering' was issued in
October. That unique magazine made some stir in its day, which
will justify a few paragraphs relating to its history.
During the previous months of the year, Improvement

Circles were held in the Session-rooms of our two churches. Improvement in composition was the principal aim, and whosoever felt disposed, was invited to furnish original articles. These were corrected by the Pastors, (who were severally in charge of the Circles,) and publicly read at the meetings, with suggestive comments, to large assemblies. By this process, surprising advancement was visible among those who persevered, and several persons of extraordinary talent were discovered, mostly females.

Why should we not make a selection of the best articles, and present them to the public in print? The suggestion became a reality in four occasional numbers, the expenses being paid by sales of copies.

Why should not the suggestion be extended to a monthly publication, with a regular list of subscribers? This also became a reality, the projector being both editor and publisher. The peculiarity of the magazine was in the fact, that all the articles were written by Females employed in the Mills—or, as they are popularly called, 'Factory Girls.'

It was decidedly 'a new thing under the sun'—and meritorious also, without any reference to the position of the writers. The articles were *bona fide* what they professed to be, and editorial corrections were very few and unimportant. All sectarianism was rigidly excluded from the work, while it was under my control, and my name was inserted only once, namely, at the bottom of the last page of the second volume. The succeeding volumes were issued under other auspices.

The magazine was highly commended by distinguished authors of America and England. In the latter country, a selection was published in book form, entitled '*Mind among the Spindles*'—with the understanding of course, that it was the mind of a population not degraded into factory-fixtures—the active mind of New England—mind having the advantage of an admirable system of Common Schools—and even *that* mind brought out in cultivation by the Improvement Circles of Lowell.

No department of our pastoral work (I speak for Mr. Thayer no less than for myself) is more pleasurable in the remembrance, than the attention we devoted to the young people, in the way of social and intellectual culture. Generally, they were far from home, among strangers, and busily occupied during the day. They needed recreation and yearned for proper companionship. The Circles referred to answered these necessities, and at the same time cultivated thought and promoted facility in its expression—all these influences and tendencies being made subservient to religious trust.[9]

, ,

Also addressing the needs of an industrializing society was Edwin H. Chapin, a leader among the reform preachers of the period. Chapin, one of the most accomplished orators of his day, addressed a New York congregation which included such notables as Horace Greeley and Phineas T. Barnum.

Concerned with the shocking conditions of the thousands of immigrants who were being crowded into New York slums, Chapin published in 1853 a series of lectures he had delivered on the moral aspects of city life.

‘ ‘ ‘ ‘ ‘ ‘ ‘ ‘ ‘ ‘ ‘ ‘ ‘ ‘ ‘ ‘ ‘ ‘ ‘ ‘, ‘ ‘ ‘ ‘

. . . These *Lower Depths* comprehend two conditions not necessarily identical; the condition of abject vice, and of destitution. Far be it from me to confound honest poverty with anything that looks like moral obliquity; or to say that because one is reduced to the last strait of physical need, and is compelled to herd with the vilest, he therefore, of course, is vicious. And yet one of the very points that I must bring out is the too-common connection which actually *does* exist between these conditions. But, however separate they may be in moral respects, socially they are at the bottom of the scale—they present the most wretched features of humanity; they unfold the most awful problems of civilization. And, therefore, I treat them together.

The Lower Depths of Vice in this Metropolis! Who would unfold all their lineaments and drag them here into the public light, if he could; who could, if he would? As there are certain wonders in nature which no man can completely reproduce, either by the pencil or by words, so there are immensities of human degradation which require the eye-witness to apprehend. You, yourself, must walk through those reeking labyrinths; must breathe that fetid air; must see into what shapes of moral abomination and physical disgust man can distort himself; must learn from inspection how intellect, and soul, and heart, can all collapse into a mere lump of animality, a condition ten-fold lower than the brute's, because of the hideous deformity and the unmistakable contrast. You, yourself, must go into lofts and cellars, where all the barriers of shame are broken down and childhood confronts the coarsest spectacles of infamy—into the apartment bare of every thing except the deadly bottle, and the rags where the father cuddles in his drunken sleep, or the mother among her babes lies prostrate in her drunken helplessness. You, yourself, must witness the frolicsome hell of midnight, where the lowest vices, the grossest conceits of the heart, put on bodily shapes and dance together—the presence of dishevelled womanhood, worse in its degradation than man can be—the unclean laughter, the quarrel, the artillery of blasphemy. And, then, while it is like letting you down into a nether world, and giving you a lurid revelation of horrors you had not conceived, you did not think could exist in a land of refinement, and churches, and homes, you can carry away with you only the terrible impression, the swimming mist of hideous transactions, and hideous faces— you cannot describe to others. And, probably, it is well that it is so. There is no edification in the mere details of vice. And for the young and the innocent, it is a good thing, slight as these brick walls are, that they are thick enough to shut out this abominable reality. Nevertheless, it is necessary we should know that these Lower Depths do exist—opening down close by us—in the midst of the Great City. And whatever facts shall help us to realize that thus not a few but a vast army of our fellow-men, our neighbors, are existing—that down in those black pools, affections, minds, souls, are sweltering and perishing—that there men, and women, and children, are matted together in the very offal of debasement—that up against the walls of our dwellings heave surges of moral death out from human hearts, and dashed back by our indifference upon those hearts again—any facts that will help us to realize this, must be welcomed and urged, whatever may be our squeamishness or our horror.

.   .   .

One of the most obvious things in contemplating these Lower Depths of Vice and Poverty, is the fact that mere *Education* is not a sufficient remedy. Religious teaching is not enough. Do not think, for a single moment, that I under-estimate it. I know that the moral power which religion imparts is mighty over external circumstances, and that there is no true reformation unless its regenerating life strikes into the very centre of the heart. In the hour of temptation nothing else can be depended upon. Do not accuse me of being merely an outside reformer, holding the theory that all man requires to make him stand erect is a few circumstantial props. I hold to no such thing. But it is sheer cant to accuse those who say with me—"give to the poor and the vicious physical and immediate help"—it is sheer cant to accuse them of holding any theory of mere circumstances. We do say, that tracts, and Bibles, and religious conversation, will be but little heeded by those who are numb with cold, and perishing with hunger; that in order to get at their inner nature, a thick crust of physical misery must be removed; that foul alleys, and fetid apartments, have a bad moral influence, and that the gospel itself has far less efficacy than in the clear light and the sweet air. And this was the way our Master worked. He laid hold of the evil that was closest at hand—touched the blind eye, the fevered brow, the withered limb, and would not dismiss those whom he had fed with the richest Spiritual food, fasting for want of material bread, lest they should "faint by the way." So these, in the Lower Depths of the great City, who are fainting by the way, must be restored with bread and meat; these who are shivering with the winter's frost, must be warmed and clothed; and we must reach their deepest nature—intellectual and moral—by removing that cramp of physical position, that craving of physical need, which they most distinctly feel.

.   .   .

. . . Not attempting now any philosophical speculations upon this subject, and passing by the consideration of overcrowded spheres of activity, and direct agencies of temptation, like the innumerable dram-shops which throw down as fast as the philanthropist can set up; there are three points, going beyond the mere giving of alms, which I would urge upon those who give any heed to the question—"Who is my neighbor?"

And, first, I may say to the rich that they can do much in clearing out these Lower Depths, by the erection of a class of dwellings divided into compartments, each of which shall be a complete home, cheap enough for the humble laborer, and yet furnished with the accessories of pure air, fresh light, and clean water. I need not dwell upon the effect which the kind of habitation has not only upon the physical, but also the moral welfare of men. The seeds of vice, as well as of suffering, are nurtured in foul atmospheres and crowded rooms. The scheme which I propose to the rich capitalist is no "lending to the Lord," but a dollar-and-cent matter, and those who act shrewdly upon it will not only put their wealth to a noble use, and rank among the benefactors of the age, but will, I doubt not, find it in a business sense profitable. And remember, it opens an opportunity for thousands who now do not fairly breathe and live.

My next remark concerns not only the capitalist, but people of moderate means, who are willing to give, and every year do give something, for the relief of poverty and the eradication of vice. To these I would say, so disburse your money that it will not feed a recumbent idleness, but excite the poor to maintain themselves. I have said that those who dwell in the Lower Depths require not charity, but justice. They have a right to room enough, and facilities enough, in this world, for the development of their own humanity, and what many of them seek is not food or money, but work. Let us then encourage any system which proceeds upon this plan of enabling the needy to help themselves. My friends, I represent no society here to-night, I am the mouthpiece of nobody's scheme, but there is an Association in this city which well illustrates the idea I am now endeavoring to enforce. I allude to "The Shirt Sewers' Union." This association employs from seventy to one hundred women in a spacious and comfortable work-room, free from all evil contact, with a certainty of punctual payment and steady employment. Now our means should go to create and encourage some such system as this, or that which a noble missionary is endeavoring to carry out in the most degraded region of this metropolis. More than food or raiment or shelter for the poor, is needed employment, for it strikes at the deepest sources of suffering and guilt.[10]

, ,

Some leading Universalists in the years before the Civil War were concerned with reform within the denomination itself. While they appreciated the movement's beginnings among the unlettered and its early dependence on relatively uncouth and uneducated preachers, they feared for the future of the denomination now that its members were much higher on the socioeconomic ladder. The more cultured might slip away and find places in other denominations.

A persistent advocate of the establishment of institutions of higher learning was Hosea Ballou, 2d, grandnephew of the first Hosea. In 1847 he delivered the occasional sermon in New York to the United States Convention of Universalists. Ballou outlined the need for moral reform: temperance, slavery, prison conditions—and education. He sparked the beginnings of a new drive in behalf of higher education. It was appropriate that Tufts College (founded 1852), the first of the institutions to result from this activity, engaged Hosea Ballou, 2d, as its first president.

‘ ‘

Has not the time arrived, my brethren,—I do not say when it becomes our denomination to act in this cause, but when it is dangerous any longer to neglect acting in it? Have we not all felt that it was our duty, years ago? that we had the means, and that we ought to have the work done? that we needed, deeply needed, the fruits? It does not appear safe to remain in such a state of criminal inactivity. There are consequences growing out of it. We have already suffered some of the evils, in a form that may well alarm us: in the want of regular mental discipline among those who must be our future teachers; and in the consequent flightiness of those lively imaginations, that are among God's choicest gifts, were they but trained and balanced by any systematic education. 'These are the beginning of sorrows;' the end is not yet. We have suffered some of the consequences, too, in the well-known tendency among the more cultivated minds, who once belonged with us, or whose families belonged with us, to seek other forms of religious ministration. We may declaim against the frivolousness of their motives, and sometimes, perhaps, with much justice; but I cannot help asking, Who is to blame, in the first place, for it? Why do we leave these powerful temptations to drive them away? Happy shall we be, if we take warning from these first signs of impending danger, and apply ourselves to the work of removing the offence. Otherwise, we need not be told that the evils will multiply with increasing rapidity, till they end in 'the abomination of desolation.'

I beg your forbearance with the tone in which I speak. I do not know that it is proper. But the suggestions themselves are so plainly true, that I cannot suppress them. I once indulged the confident expectation that I should live to see Universalists doing their duty, in this cause,—founding well-endowed Academies, and at least one College, placed on a permanent basis. I have so long solaced myself with the anticipation of sharing in the work, that it is hard, my brethren, it is hard to part with all hope. But the night is coming down, in which no man can work.—The shadows of age are already on these eyes; and nothing is done. If we make an effort, it is like men striving in a troubled dream.—There is a night-mare on our limbs; the muscles will not move at our volition. When shall we awake from our frightful slumber!—Shall we ever throw off the smothering incubus, which has held us so long that it threatens death?

We have existed, now, as a body, more than 60 years. We have increased, as we boast, almost beyond precedent. We number 18 State Conventions, 80 Associations, about 700 preachers, more than 1000 Societies; and probably 700,000 people nominally belong to our Connexion. We have made our presence felt and recognized by the world; we have drawn the public observation upon us. And the inquiry is now growing louder, on every hand, 'What are the actual results of this numerous and increasing community, on all the important interests that such a body naturally has in charge?' With our 700,000 in number, with abundant means, in our hands at least, if not in our will, we do, and we must, stand forth before the world, either as the active patrons, or the practical discouragers, of general improvement. And which of these characters we shall bear, will be determined, not by what we say, but by what we accomplish. Let it once be discovered that when we can do, we will not; that we have no tendency in the direction of real, sober, intellectual progress; that we but suffer ourselves to be dragged on by others in the pursuit of general knowledge and in the cultivation of mind,—let it be seen that such is the course we are permanently to hold; and can you wonder at, or severely blame, that part of the community which is attached to the cause of learning, if it gives up its hopes of us, and turns to some other quarter, where a more commendable spirit prevails? I speak the more plainly on this subject, because I am confident, from a long series of observations, that all which is necessary, now, for us to do, in order to begin a better state of things, is to lay this matter distinctly before the people, so as to fix their attentions upon it. They are more ready to act, than we are to give them a proper opportunity. Only touch the sleeping giant, and the night-mare spell is broken.[11]

, ,

Universalists, as was seen in the case of Maria Cook in Chapter IV, were early to break with the tradition, based on St. Paul's injunction that women should be still in church. The Universalists ordained the first woman minister in the United States in 1863. Olympia Brown was to be the first of many. Understandably, among her various reform activities she always maintained an interest in the higher education of women.

‘ ‘

. . . If boys after leaving school went home to be supported, and devoted themselves to needle-work and novels, we should look for no noble manhood, and only when girls cease to do this and seek some business of life whereby to independently support themselves, and benefit society, can we look for the truest womanhood. But, says some objector, women will no longer be angels when brought in contact with the rude world. Alas! the United States of America in 1874, is not a favorable place for angels, nor are the men of the nineteenth century suitable companions for them. An angel in American society at the present time, would be sadly out of place and very uncomfortable. Even that hymn by which little girls are made to sing,

> "*I want to be an angel*"

adds,

> "*And with the angels stand.*"

Nobody wants to be an angel, and stand with unsuitable companions. Since women are placed here in this very practical and matter-of-fact world, it is well for them to make the best of the situation, adapt themselves to the occasion, and do the duty of the hour, and leave all angelic airs, until, by a life of loving service to humanity, they shall have won for themselves crowns brighter than those of angels. Since they are surrounded by fallible, suffering mortals, let them give themselves to the work of the world, that they may alleviate the evils which they see about them, and in so doing, work out their own salvation.

And this is the great argument in favor of the enfranchisement of women; it is not so much the repealing of wicked laws, or the establishment of justice, although these are important, as it is that women should gain that self-respect and independence which is the characteristic of the free. Not till women share in the responsibilities, and enjoy the privileges of the enfranchised citizen can it be expected that they will gain the highest excellence.

Freedom and responsibility have in all times, been

thought essential conditions of mental growth in men; they are not less essential to the development of women. Nor does this larger life militate at all against those duties which are peculiar to women. The position of wife and mother will be far better filled by one whose mind is enlarged by a great knowledge of affairs, and whose character is matured by the discipline of life, than by one whose sympathies and whose knowledge extends no farther than the half dozen or more rooms which she calls her home.

It can be no possible advantage to a man that his mother was socially a toy, financially a dependant, politically a slave. On the contrary, the stream can not rise higher than its source, and if women are fettered, dependent, ignorant, their sons will be narrow in mind, craven and cowardly. When women are free and independent, and by experience in the business of the world, shall have grown into the stature of true womanhood, then, indeed, we may look for a race of noble men such as the world has never seen. The larger woman's experience is, the better is she fitted for every duty, the more intelligently can she take any position to which she is called.[12]

, ,

Ordained the same year (1863) as Olympia Brown, another of the several Universalist women ministers to be active in the woman suffrage movement was Augusta J. Chapin. An organizer of the Woman's Congress in New York in 1873, Miss Chapin labored in other reform causes as well. When she wrote of women in the ministry, it was the result of a full career which included years of itinerary from Allston, Massachusetts, to San Francisco: "I attended the first [Universalist] State Convention ever held in Oregon and did nearly all the preaching." She was also an organizer of the World Parliament of Religions in Chicago in 1893.

‘ ‘

. . . Let us consider . . . what, being already in the ministry, woman can and ought to do therein. Shall she preach a little by way of experiment merely? There are those who are fond of claiming that all this is an experiment of doubtful issue. Is it so? My own experience, extending through fifteen years of uninterrupted pulpit and parish work; years of work in the rural villages and neighborhoods of the West; years of work as a settled pastor in a large and growing parish; personal acquaintance with hundreds of parishes east and west in a dozen different States of the Union; all this, together with years of study in college as a direct preparation for the work, has not led me to feel that it is at all an experiment. When I see as many of the wise, powerful and good, and as many of the poor and needy crowding to hear the glad tidings from the lips of my sister as from those of my brother; when I see as many converts bow at the one altar as at the other; when I see churches reared, debts paid, and all good works going on and prospering through the blessing of God, in her hands as in his, and this through a succession of years in the same parish, it does not seem an experiment, nor do the people blessed by such ministry so regard it. How is it practically? Here is a congregation, gathered from the different homes and solitary places of the world. Among them, one is struggling with the powers of darkness, and has come as to a place of refuge, vaguely hoping that he may get help to resist the awful strength of the tempter; one is overshadowed by gloom, and hopes for a ray of light; one is bewildered in the crooked ways and needs to be directed; one walks over rough places and needs support; one mourns almost without hope, and one stands on the very brink of the river of death and asks of the life beyond. And so all over the house each one has come with a special need and a special burden. And here is a woman with earnest, loving heart, who knows just what needs to be said to these waiting souls, and just how to say it. She speaks the needed word, in the same spirit as she would, in the name of Christ, hold a cup of cold water to the lips of the thirsty. Is this an experiment? Whatever blind prejudice or unthinking conservatism may say, the good sense and heart of humanity will refuse to judge it so.

Those who fear that women cannot endure the fatigue of the work may be referred to the fact, that among the hundred or more women preachers now in the field, in the various denominations, we hear less complaint of fatigue and ill-health than among an equal number of men doing equal work.

If it be said that women cannot sustain the ordinary relations of life and preach the gospel, we must reply that women are doing it. In our own denomination, there are more recognized, ordained women preachers than in any other branch of the Christian church, yet of all the number only two are unmarried, and neither of these seems to be any more successful in the work than the rest of the sisterhood. The houses of these women preachers are as well arranged, and as well kept as those of their neighbors who do not preach. You can find in New England as cosy, pleasant, and well-kept a little home as there is within all her borders, in which you shall see a babe, as bright, healthy and happy as ever blessed a household, and on every Lord's day morning the mother is found in her pulpit speaking the words of life, comfort and hope to all who will listen. In the pews before her are other mothers whose children are also at home. They spend equal time in the house of God, one speaking, the others listening, and their little ones are equally well cared for during the brief absence. And so while the faithless, and conservative, so called, are assuring us that this cannot be done, lo, it is done! and done, not by women who are exceptional and peculiar in their temperament and disposition, but by earnest, devoted Christian women like a hundred of those whom everybody personally knows. Women who are simply doing in their own way and as best they can the work that their hands find to do in the Lord's vineyard.[13]

, ,

Looking back over his career, Horace Greeley saw definite connections between his belief in Universalism and his multitude of reform interests. In addition, he attributed the more humane treatment of man by his fellow man to the enlightened outlook promoted by Universalism.

In his autobiography (1868), Greeley estimated that he was about ten years old (he was born in 1811) when he was stimulated to ponder the nature of God by his reading in Greek history. He was amazed by the magnanimous treatment of Athens by Demetrius I of Macedonia (Poliorcetes, "Destroyer of Cities," 336–283 B.C.) who spared the city although, according to every previous standard of warfare, he should have taken vengeance for Athens' earlier refusal to provide him refuge when he needed it.

‘ ‘

Reflecting with admiration on this exhibition of a magnanimity too rare in human annals, I was moved to inquire if a spirit so nobly, so wisely, transcending the mean and savage impulse which man too often disguises as justice, when it is in essence revenge, might not be reverently termed Divine; and the firm conclusion to which I was finally led, imported that the old Greek's treatment of vanquished rebels or prostrate enemies must forcibly image and body forth that of the "King immortal, invisible, and only wise God."

When I reached this conclusion, I had never seen one who was called, or who called himself, a Universalist; and I neither saw one, nor read a page of any one's writings, for years thereafter. I had only heard that there were a few graceless reprobates and scurvy outcasts, who pretended to believe that all men would be saved, and to wrench the Scriptures into some sort of conformity to their mockery of a creed. I had read the Bible through, much of it repeatedly, but when quite too infantile to form any coherent, definite synopsis of the doctrines I presumed to be taught therein. But, soon after entering a printing-office, I procured exchanges with several Universalist periodicals, and was thenceforth familiar with their methods of interpretation and of argument; though I first heard a sermon preached by one of this school while passing through Buffalo, about 1830; and I was acquainted with no society, and no preacher, of this faith, prior to my arrival in New York in August, 1831; when I made my way, on the first Sunday morning of my sojourn, to the little chapel in Grand Street, near Pitt,—about the size of an average country school-house,—where Rev. Thomas J. Sawyer, then quite young, ministered to a congregation of, perhaps, a hundred souls; to which congregation I soon afterward attached myself: remaining a member of it until he left the city.

I am not, therefore, to be classed with those who claim to have been converted from one creed to another by studying the Bible alone. Certainly, upon re-reading that book in the light of my new convictions, I found therein abundant proof of their correctness in the averments of patriarchs,* prophets,† apostles,‡ and of the Messiah§ himself. But not so much in particular passages, however pertinent and decisive, as in the spirit and general scope of the Gospel,—so happily blending inexorable punishment for every offence with unfailing pity and ultimate forgiveness for the chastened transgressor,—thus saving sinners from sin by leading them, through suffering, to loathe and forsake it; and in laying down its Golden Rule, which, if of universal application, (and why not?) must be utterly inconsistent with the infliction of infinite and unending torture as the penalty of transient, and often ignorant, offending, did I find ample warrant for my hope and trust that all suffering is disciplinary and transitional, and shall ultimately result in universal holiness and consequent happiness.

In the light of this faith, the dark problem of Evil is irradiated, and virtually solved. "Perfect through suffering" was the way traced out for the great Captain of our salvation: then why not for all the children of Adam? To say that temporary affliction is as difficult to reconcile with Divine goodness as eternal agony is to defy reason and insult common sense. The history of Joseph's perfidious sale into slavery by his brethren, and the Divine overruling || of that crime into a means of vast and permanent blessing to the entire family of Jacob, is directly in point. Once conceive that an Omniscient Beneficence presides over and directs the entire course of human affairs, leading ever on-

* Gen. iii. 15; xii. 3.

† Isa. xxv. 8; xlv. 23–25.

‡ Rom. v. 12–21; viii. 19–21; 1 Cor. xv. 42–54; Eph. i. 8–10; Col. i. 19–21; 1 Tim. ii. 3–6.

§ Matt. xv. 13; John xii. 32.

|| Gen. xlv. 5–8.

ward and upward to universal purity and bliss, and all evil becomes phenomenal and preparative,—a mere curtain or passing cloud, which hides for a moment the light of the celestial and eternal day.

I am not wise enough, even in my own conceit, to assume to say where and when the deliverance of our race from evil and suffering shall be consummated. Perceiving that many leave this stage of being depraved and impenitent, I cannot believe that they will be transformed into angels of purity by the intervention of a circumstance so purely physical and involuntary as death. Holding that the government of God is everywhere and always perfect (however inadequate may be our comprehension of it), I infer that, alike in all worlds, men will be chastised whenever they shall need to be, and that neither by suicide, nor any other device, can a single individual escape the penalty of his evil-doing. If man is punished because he needs to be,—because that is best for him,—why should such discipline be restricted to this span of life? While I know that the words translated hell, eternal, &c., in our version of the Bible, bear various meanings which the translators have befogged,—giving hell, the grave, the pit, &c., as equivalents of the one Hebrew term that signifies the unseen home of departed souls,—and while I am sure that the luxuriant metaphors whereby a state of anguish and suffering are depicted were not meant to be taken literally,—I yet realize that human iniquity is often so flagrant and enormous that its punishment, to be just and efficient, must be severe and protracted. How or where it will be inflicted are matters of incident and circumstance, not of principle nor of primary consequence. Enough that it will be administered by One who "doth not willingly* [that is, wantonly] afflict nor grieve the children of men," but because their own highest good demands it, and would be prejudiced by his withholding it.

. . . In our age [universalism has] been affirmed and systematically elucidated by the calm, cogent reasoning of Ballou, the critical research of Balfour, the fervid eloquence of Chapin, and hundreds beside them, until it is no longer a feeble hope, a trembling aspiration, a pleasing hypothesis, but an assured and

* Lam. iii. 33.

joyful conviction. In its clear daylight, the hideous Inquisition, and all kindred devices for torturing heretics, under a libellous pretence of zeal for God, shrink and cower in shame and terror; the revolting gallows hides itself from public view, preliminary to its utter and final disappearance; and man, growing ashamed of all cruelty and revenge, deals humanely with the outcast, the pauper, the criminal, and the vanquished foe. The overthrow of a rebellion is no longer the signal for sweeping spoliation and massacre; the downfall of an ancient tyranny like that of Naples is followed by no butchery of its pertinacious upholders; and our earth begins to body forth and mirror—but so slowly, so faintly! —the merciful doctrines of the meek and loving Prince of Peace.[14]

, ,

Chapter Seven

The Challenge of Modernism

> *That a certain thing has been taught by the Church in*
> *all ages does not guarantee its freedom from error. Repeti-*
> *tion, though obstinate and clamorous, cannot turn false-*
> *hood into truth. . . .*

Marion Shutter

In confronting the issues raised by Darwinism and Higher Criticism of the Bible in the decades following the Civil War, the Universalists were fortunate to be able to count among their number one of the outstanding New Testament scholars. Orello Cone, professor at St. Lawrence University and president of Universalist Buchtel College (now the University of Akron), counted among his many books *Gospel-Criticism and Historical Christianity* (1891), reputed to be the ablest American work on Higher Criticism. In its pages he confronted a generation of Americans with the issues that, misunderstood, were to create schisms and heresy trials in some of the leading denominations. His own attitude toward criticism and its uses can be surmised from his dedication of the book:

> *To the Believers who Fear Criticism*
> *and*
> *To the Unbelievers who Appeal to it.*

‘ ‘

That criticism tends to invalidate historical Christianity is a prevalent popular impression. But like many another popular impression, this is a popular misapprehension. A prejudice, or perhaps it were better to say a sentiment, is the root of this error. What is established, what is venerable with age, what has served noble ends, and nurtured great virtues, naturally calls forth the conservative interest, the devotion, even the zeal and fanaticism of mankind. Accordingly, when even the soberest and most reverent criticism is directed upon revered documents or institutions with the sincere purpose of reconstructing the one or improving the other, it is confronted by a sentiment which can see in its performance only a menace or a work of destruction. Against a criticism which is merely negative and destructive, it must be conceded that this sentiment is a wise provision of nature. It is not, however, until the discriminating judgment is applied to the matter that a justifiable opposition to the critical procedure can even seem to be established. Now, at the first glance there does appear, indeed, to be ground for a rational judgment against criticism as hostile to historical Christianity, for the reason that in its name many excesses have been committed, and many conclusions reached which tend to dissolve the historical contents of the Gospels by making it appear that these writings are composed mainly of myths, or of creations of the imagination, or of "tendency-" speculations. But it is evident that criticism, as a whole, can no more fairly be condemned for its excesses than science or theology, as a whole, for its errors. Besides, criticism has always tended to correct itself, exposing and repudiating the errors which have been committed in its name. Great critics have alone been found competent to deal with the most masterly perversions of criticism. So Strauss had his Weisse, and Baur his Hilgenfeld within his own school, and his Ewald and Meyer outside it. Accordingly, the history of criticism shows a tendency towards quite sober and sound conclusions, a tendency, in fact, to construct rather than to destroy, to establish rather than to overthrow, historical Christianity.

Now, since criticism proceeds upon the principle that the Gospels are to be treated as literature, as productions of men affected by the spirit which came forth from Jesus, indeed, but also by the influences which their age threw around them, who dealt with their materials in a wholly sincere and earnest way, it must seek the grounds of the credibility of the historical kernel of these writings, or, in other words, the basis of historical Christianity, in the documents themselves and in the data which history furnishes. No other course is indeed open to it, since it is one of its fundamental principles that no claims which may be dogmatically set up in favor of the infallibility of the writers of the Gospels can be allowed before they have been tested by its processes. Such claims, then, cannot be suffered to determine its conclusions. In fact, if it should admit them its occupation would be gone, its whole work superfluous.

.   .   .

Criticism appears, then, on its own grounds and by its own methods to contribute to the confirmation of historical Christianity, if to establish the general credibility of the synoptic Gospels as to the essential teachings and the character of Jesus be to do this. It must be acknowledged, however, that if by historical Christianity is meant the whole body of doctrines, or a certain considerable number of them, which have been and are taught in the name of Christianity, then criticism does not give it support. If it is made to include such doctrines as the infallibility of the records, original sin, total depravity, the trinity, imputed righteousness, a vicarious atonement, and endless punishment, then so far criticism is unfriendly to it. If, however, it means that Jesus of Nazareth lived; that he was a personality of unsurpassed moral and spiritual greatness; that he taught a morality and religion founded upon the doctrine that God is the Father of men, and all men are brothers, the central, practical precept of which was love to God and man; that he lived a blameless, worshipful life of consecration and service in which his great teachings were eminently illustrated; that he performed some works which in his age were regarded as wonders; that after an amazing and brilliant career of a few months in Galilee he was crucified at Jerusalem; and that he was thereupon in some way manifested to those who had loved and followed him as victorious over death; if these are the essential contents of historical Christianity, then it finds in criticism not an opposing and destructive agent, but a helpful ally. The relation which some of the important conclusions of criticism hold to it remains to be considered.

The criticism of the text of the Gospels shows that these

writings were exposed to the fortune which has attended all the literary productions of ancient times; that the autographs were early lost; that the text was corrupted and interpolated; that a considerable time elapsed between their composition and the appearance of careful and accurate quotations of them, during which the changes to which the text was subjected are indeterminable; that there appears to be no reason for assuming that a regard for them as other than human productions preserved them from the perils to which they were exposed, nor any grounds for believing in a divine intervention for their protection; that, however, alterations, corruptions, and interpolations have not, in all probability, materially affected their essential, historical contents—that is, their accounts of the great teachings of Jesus and their representation of his life and character. These results are not prejudicial to historical Christianity; for if Christianity is properly called historical—that is, a religion which has had a history, its development belongs to the ordinary course of human affairs, and no supernatural intervention can be assumed in its interest, such as would be a miraculous preservation of its documents against the common fortune of ancient writings.

The critical study of the canon of the Gospels shows them in the stream of human history amidst a great number of other writings to which the powerful impulse proceeding from the personality of Jesus gave rise, left to make their way to public recognition chiefly by their own merits. It finds that, along with the oral tradition and these other writings, they were for a considerable time regarded as ordinary human sources of information as to the life of Jesus; that this tradition was thought by an important witness near the middle of the second century to be an authority superior to them; that down to a period which marks the lapse of nearly one hundred years from the composition of the oldest of them they were loosely and inaccurately quoted without mention of their supposed authors; that they appear to have attained recognition largely by reason of internal qualities, their historical character, and general excellence in comparison with other similar writings; that the opinion prevailed in the primitive Church that believers in Jesus were in general inspired, and that no especial inspiration was supposed to be possessed by those who wrote; that other writings than those now contained in the New Testament were then believed by some to be inspired; that not until about the end of the second century were our four Gospels ascribed to their reputed authors, and recognized as the works of specially inspired men which were to be received as exclusive or canonical sources for the life and teachings of Jesus; that the dogma of the inspiration of these writers, resting on no claim made by them in their works is to be regarded simply as a dogma which had an historical development, and admits of a genetic explanation; that the traditions current in the second century respecting the origin of the Gospels must be critically sifted, and are to be accepted only when confirmed by the criticism of these writings themselves; and finally, that the writers of that century, commonly quoted as "witnesses" to the canon, often give no reasons, or only trivial ones, for their opinions, show little or no evidence of having critically examined the matter, and accordingly furnish testimony which is to be received only with caution and discrimination. These are precisely such phenomena as one would expect to find in the natural, historical development of a religion under the conditions of the age in question; and they are rather favorable than otherwise to historical Christianity, since they show its records to have come to recognition and authority in the ordinary course of events on their intrinsic merits, and accordingly to have been able to dispense with a divine supervision to determine their selection as canonical. The question of the inspiration of their writers is not vital to historical Christianity, for their infallibility was not necessary to insure general accuracy and credibility in their works, which is all that a system of belief calling itself historical can reasonably claim for its documents. So far, then, as criticism tends to establish such an accuracy and credibility in the essential contents of the Gospels, it comes to the support of historical Christianity, and sustains its claims in the only way in which they can be sustained. For if Christianity is based upon the assumption of the inerrancy of the writers of its records, it is likely to be rejected entirely when this assumption is found, as sooner or later it must be, to be unsupported by the facts in the case.[1]

, ,

Like Albert Schweitzer, then a young Biblical scholar thinking through the problems presented in his *Quest of the Historical Jesus* (1906), Cone was to reject the notion that Jesus and other early Christian leaders had a specific "social programme." Cone in *Rich and Poor in the New Testament* (1902) tackled the most difficult of the problems of the Christianity of his time: the relevance of early Christian social ethics to the modern day.

‘ ‘

On whatever a *priori* grounds we may believe in the authority of the New Testament, we have practical demonstration of it in the experience that in the matter of religious faith it furnishes principles adapted to promote the highest perfection of the spiritual nature, and in the matter of life such impulses and ideals as tend to the best possible individual and social achievement. Our experience thus reproduces that of the great teachers of the New Testament, so far as their objects of faith and their ideals and impulses become our own. We see that they became what they were, and taught as they did, because they had a true insight into the laws of the spirit and the principles of the social order. It is characteristic, then, of the modern estimate and use of the New Testament that men are searching its pages rather for ideals and inspirations than for systems of belief and outlines of social polities. Thus it is becoming in the hands of teachers and learners more a Book of Life and less an arsenal of the weapons of dogmatic warfare.

Under this limitation must the New Testament be regarded and treated as an authority in the social question of to-day, so far as it is at all appealed to in this relation. To Jesus and Paul and the writer of the Epistle of James* the social ques-

---

* See the writer's article, "James, Epistle of," in the *Encyclopoedia Biblica*, ii.

tion did not present itself, in the complexity in which it confronts us in this age, as a problem that they felt called upon to solve. They looked upon the rich, selfish, grasping, and hardhearted, and upon the poor, labouring, weary, and heavy-laden, primarily with reference to their susceptibility to repentance and their capacity for the righteousness required for the impending kingdom of God. In view of the catastrophe of an age that was hastening to its end and in the dazzling splendour of the new era of the divine rule, the light of which to the intense prophetic vision was already on the horizon, there could hardly be a clear perspective of a social order struggling from generation to generation with the solution of its mighty problems.

With reference to the great Teacher in this relation I will quote the words of a scholar well known to students of current German theology for his caution and candour: "How different are the general relations with which we have to deal from those to which Jesus referred his message I do not need to point out in detail. Jesus reckoned on an impending end of the existing course of the world, therefore he did not take into consideration the task of a dutiful care for the remote future and also the task of a gradual reform of human relations—tasks that press themselves upon the moral consciousness when that presupposition is absent." *

If, accordingly, one will seek in the New Testament an authority for the social life of men in this age, for the construction of a new or for the reform of the existing social order, one must first have a clear idea as to the kind of authority that is sought. The kind of authority that is to be looked for is of course precisely and only the kind of authority that is there to be found by a right interpretation of the New Testament. The indispensable first step for the inquirer who seeks such instruction is that he put himself in the place of the teachers to whom he would appeal, and endeavour to understand the environment, the dominant ideas, and the purposes that determined or at least influenced their social teachings. He must decide whether they are to be judged and interpreted primarily as social philoso-

---

* Wendt, "Das Eigenthum nach christlicher Beurtheilung," in *Zeitschrift für Theologie und Kirche*, 1898, 2tes Heft, p. 114.

phers or as preachers of righteousness, as scientific political econ-omists or as heralds of the kingdom of God; whether their environment simply appealed to their sympathies, or suggested a radical reconstruction of the social order; and whether they purposed such a reconstruction, or merely endeavoured to inspire men to live in the existing society more in the spirit of kindness, charity, and fraternity.

Such an inquirer, if he would make his search fruitful, would be led to ask himself whether he is to regard most of the teachings relating to earthly possessions, to riches and poverty, and to the relations of rich and poor, as sayings of the occasion, adapted to existing relations and necessities, or as the expression of principles having perpetual validity and applicable to human society in all ages and regions. He would have to determine whether such directions as "Be content with your wages"; "He that hath two coats, let him impart to him that hath none"; "Sell all that thou hast, and distribute unto the poor"; "Sell that ye have, and give alms," and others of like import, are to be re-garded as binding everywhere and upon all—whether, in a word, they are at all to be taken as principles that can be made con-trolling in human society.* He would raise the question whether the mode of life adopted by Jesus and required of his disciples in their ministry is to be regarded as binding upon his followers in the ministry in all times and places,—that they who go forth "to preach the kingdom of God" are to "take nothing" for their jour-ney, "neither staff nor wallet, nor bread nor money, neither have two coats," **—and whether the social relations of all Chris-tians should be governed by the direction not to invite to their houses at a feast their friends, kinsmen, and rich neighbours, but the poor, the maimed, the lame, and the blind.***

The consideration of these passages and others of a simi-lar character leads the student to seek for a method of interpre-tation that shall be just to their original intention. If a principle of exegesis can be adopted that will assign them to their true relation in the New Testament as a whole, it should serve to

* Luke iii. 11, 14; xii. 33; xviii. 22.
** Luke ix. 3.
*** Luke xiv. 12 f.

show in what sense the New Testament may be taken as a guide in the social affairs of men. It is unwarrantable to have recourse to "figurative language," "hyperbole," or "Oriental style," since the passages contain nothing of the kind. The only legitimate exegesis of the passages is one that assigns to them their obvious literal meaning. Nothing else could have been intended. In no other sense could they have been understood by the original hearers or readers. But we have not done with them when we have reached this conclusion. The one important matter remains to be considered—how are they related to us? Do they "find" us at all, and if so, how? Obviously it is impracticable for us to carry out these directions in their actual import. Equally obvious is it that they do not express principles of a permanent and universal social order. The question, then, that the inquirer is constrained to ask is, whether they are therefore to be disregarded as wholly worthless for us.

The matter of paramount importance is that such of these injunctions as concern riches and poverty express an *attitude* toward these two conditions in society. They denote a sympathy and a want of sympathy with the poor on the one hand and the rich on the other. More than this, there is an unmistakable implication of a *duty* of the rich toward the poor that includes interest, kindness, and helpfulness. This is in general terms the underlying truth in these passages and others of kindred import. This is the spirit of the texts, and it is life-giving everywhere and always. With the letter, the ministry of which is death, we may well have nothing to do. If, then, these precepts cannot, in the present social conditions, be carried out according to a strict interpretation, it happens with this part of the gospel of Jesus as with all the rest of it, that though its outward form may perish, its inward, essential truth remains, and that in every age it is fruitful only as it is adapted to the changing needs of the times. If in the circle of the ages some things fail of application and fall away, those things that remain are found to be no less effective and potent on that account.

If the foregoing considerations furnish the right key to the interpretation of the somewhat "rough requirements of renunciation" made by Jesus of the rich men of his time, of the exaltation of poverty, and of the favourable disposition toward the poor, they may serve as a means of correcting many gross perversions of his teachings that show themselves to be erroneous because they run counter to the entire spirit and intention of his gospel. Such words as, "Lay not up for yourselves treasures upon the earth"; "If any man cometh unto me, and hateth not his own father and mother and wife and brethren and sisters, yea and his own life also, he cannot be my disciple"; and, "So therefore whosoever he be of you that renounceth not all that he hath, he cannot be my disciple," * have been appealed to as sanctioning the ascetic principle and enjoining asceticism as a mode of life. In supposed compliance with them men have thought themselves commanded to withdraw their interest and activity from the world, to renounce the natural duties to their kindred, and to spend their lives in ascetic self-mortification and degrading poverty.

Yet Jesus was manifestly no ascetic, and did not require of his disciples an ascetic mode of life.** His gospel commands, moreover, that men love their neighbours instead of isolating themselves from them in monkish seclusion and indifference, and thus presupposes a life of helpful activity in their midst. Such sayings as those quoted above are not to be regarded as inflexible directions for the conduct of life or as principles of the social order in general. They can be brought into relation with the social question in every age only as they are adapted according to a right sense of their spirit to the existing situation and needs. If some of them do not admit of application and use, these may be disregarded as belonging to the transient elements of Jesus' teaching, the temporary character of which by no means impairs the value of those that are permanent and universal. One might doubtless find better uses of wealth than bestowing it in alms. One could certainly render it more helpful to the poor than by making them pensioners upon one's bounty to the loss of their self-respect. Moreover, riches can be accumulated and employed to such beneficent ends that their possessor by his wise and helpful use of them lays up treasures in heaven.

* Matt. vi. 19; Luke xiv. 26, 33.
** Matt. xi. 19; Mark ii. 18 f.

Who will say that the man who in such ways fulfils the spirit of these requirements, which is sympathy with the poor and opposition to selfishness and greed, is not as truly a follower of Jesus as if he were to attempt to observe them according to the letter of the texts? [2]

, ,

The problem of adapting Christian Universalism to the Darwinian mode of interpreting life was confronted by many theologically attuned ministers and laymen. Universalist journals in the last forty years of the nineteenth century devoted endless pages to the debate.

Marion Shutter's *Applied Evolution*, based on a series of lectures he delivered in Minneapolis, was widely appreciated as one of the most popular attempts to reconcile science and religion. By 1900, the year the book was published, Universalists had pretty much settled the issue for themselves. The "monkey trial" of Dayton, Tennessee, and like fundamentalist inroads on freedom of belief was still twenty-five years in the future.

‘ ‘

It is related, we know not with how much truth, that a certain Brahmin once shivered a microscope to pieces, because it revealed the fact that every drop of water contained innumerable minute insects; thus showing that the commandments of his religion, which forbade the destruction of living creatures, were broken whenever any one took a draught of water, and must inevitably be broken unless men were to perish of thirst. So long as that microscope remained, the Brahmin argued, his religion was insecure. Whether the story of the Hindoo be correct or not, the illustration will serve. Very similar is the panic of superstition everywhere at the advance of scientific discovery. Many have felt that the Christian religion was not safe in the presence of the astronomer's telescope and the geologist's pick and hammer.

This fear, however, has largely passed, or is passing. We

are beginning to see that the long battle between Science and Religion was, to a certain extent, upon both sides a mistake.

. . . Not only is there no real conflict, when we come to understand the subject, but religion, or religious thought, so far from suffering disaster at the hands of science, has been the actual gainer. Religious thought has been helped by its once seeming foe. It has lost nothing but some unscientific notions that were long, but erroneously, supposed to belong to religion. It is better without them. It stands upon solider footing. It can make stronger appeal to the human intellect.

The first distinct gain that Religious Thought has made from Science is its quickened sense of truth, its awakening to the real nature and value of truth, and the right methods for its discovery. Science has taught theology to look at facts as they are, and not as it wishes or hopes or imagines or guesses them to be.

Theology has learned something of the value of evidence. Religious thought has rested too much upon the authority of Church or Book. The time-honored formula of the theologian has been, "This is God's truth; your controversy is with God and not with me. This you must believe or be damned." Nothing is quite so revolting to the sincere, inquiring mind, as to be met in this fashion—to ask for proofs and be answered with dogmas. Suppose the question concerns the origin of man: it is no longer sufficient to say, "The Bible teaches that he was formed from the dust of the earth, and by creative edict instantly endowed with life." We may still demand how the writer of the account in the Bible obtained his information, and whether his statement is in harmony with facts that have since been ascertained. To say that a scientific or historical statement is in the Bible, settles nothing. Who put it there? Where did he get it? What are his proofs? These questions must still be answered as if the statements were found in any other books. Science has taught us to push our investigations beyond the literature of Genesis. Or, if we are told that this has been the teaching of the Church in all ages, we may justly require the Church to show upon what ground she bases her claim to speak with authority upon that particular subject. That a certain thing has been taught by the Church in all ages does not guarantee its freedom from error. Repetition, though obstinate and clamorous, cannot turn falsehood into truth; antiquity cannot pass muster as evidence; "gray hairs cannot make folly venerable!"

Science has taught Theology something about right methods of reasoning. "Religion," says Mr. Munger, "will never cease to be a matter of intuition and revelation, but so long as it is only such, it will be overspread by unreason and superstition." Every vagary that dances through the brain will be mistaken for reality substantial as the everlasting hills. The mind is not divided. There are not two distinct methods of reaching objective truth. We cannot receive by direct revelation that which depends upon study and research. We cannot accept by faith that which contradicts our common sense. Historical and scientific assertions made in the name of religion and in relation to religious subjects must be submitted to the same methods of reasoning and the same processes of investigation to which we devote all other statements upon all other subjects. Some one has made the astonishing declaration that he could, by an act of religious faith, believe in the story of the flood: that the animals came two by two, of all kinds, from all quarters of the earth,—traversing continents and crossing seas, to offer themselves to Noah for his projected voyage in the ark,—but that, as a historical or scientific fact, he could not believe it at all. If a man cannot believe that story as a historical or scientific fact, he has no right to believe it at all. Either such an occurrence took place or it did not. If there is not sufficient evidence to establish it as a historical or scientific fact, no man has a right to incorporate it into his creed or accept it as a matter of religious belief. The story of the flood was no more a revelation from heaven by supernatural agency than the story of the Discovery of America is a revelation from heaven. It is no more a matter of intuition than the story of George Washington's life is a matter of intuition. It is no more a flash of inspired vision than is the story of the Spanish Conquest of Mexico. He who thinks the account of the flood can be established in any other way than any of the facts of history and science are established, is on the way to permanent confusion of thought. He who accepts without evidence or in the teeth of evidence is guilty of intellectual immorality. He allows the supposed necessities of his creed to destroy his mental integrity. Faith itself must be founded on evidence.

Science is also delivering Theology from the wretched habit of defending doctrines on account of their supposed usefulness. The sole object of Science, as announced by her votaries, is "To discover truth." The scientific spirit has been defined as "the love of truth for truth's own sake." The late Mr. John Tyndall said: "In science the first condition of success is an honest receptivity and a willingness to abandon all preconceived opinions, however cherished, if they be found to contradict the truth." This is the aim and spirit of Science. Not very long ago while a certain unforgotten controversy was raging, a prominent layman of the city of Plainfield, New Jersey, said: "Nobody believes in a certain confession, but it ought not to be revised or disturbed in any way because our Church is founded upon it." A gentleman of national reputation said once: "The common doctrine of hell is all nonsense and educated people do not need it; but it ought to be preached to hold the ignorant in check." A distinguished novelist and lecturer, said after one of his trips through a certain section, "The leading denominations do not seem to ask, 'What is true?' but 'What can we teach the negro that will make it safe for us?'"

Is it any wonder, with such facts as these staring us in the face, that people so often distrust the sincerity of the Church and the reality of religion itself? The best thing for all classes is truth. The safest thing—the only safe thing—is truth. The best thing in this world for the ignorant is enlightenment. The best thing for the humblest devotee at the altar, as well as for him who ministers thereat, is knowledge. It is as good for the one as for the other. It is as good for the pew as for the pulpit. How can teachers in the church expect to train in the way of duty the consciences of those who look to them for instruction, when they play tricks with their own integrity? How can they preach, "Be true," when they themselves tamper with what, in their inmost hearts, they believe to be falsehood?

May we not hope that the influence already being exerted upon Theology by Science will grow, until religious teachers everywhere will think no longer about what may be useful or safe; will no longer study in new fields simply to confirm old prejudices; will no longer play upon the fears of superstition to perpetuate ecclesiastical power, but will say among themselves, "Let us emulate the men of science; let us go forth through the realms of nature and life to search for truth; let us abandon old errors when the new light of investigation shall have shown us to be wrong; let us be candid with our fellow-men, no longer proclaiming to them doctrines and creeds we reject in our inmost souls!"

We talk about revivals of religion. We generally mean more prayers and sermons and excitement. But a revival of common honesty in our churches; a revival of the spirit of truth that would consume, in the flames of a higher enthusiasm, the pious frauds and falsehoods we have been proclaiming to the world; that would reduce to ashes the outworn creeds and dogmas that hold their places, solely by virtue of their antiquity, and burden and crush the living thought of to-day; that would purge away the pious phraseology of the past, as well as its ideas,—words and phrases that are dead and empty to-day, as shells on the sea-shore,—and make way for honest modes of expression as well as of thought,—such a revival would give our common Christianity such a power and influence and standing, as never yet have the centuries witnessed!

.   .   .

There are two theories of the universe, which may be illustrated as follows: Take an artificial flower.* The stem was made by itself, the petals were cut out, each one separately. The leaves were fashioned in the same way. None of these parts had any relation to each other. The leaves and flowers did not grow out of the stem. They were made piece by piece and put together afterwards. They were made and put together by some power outside of them. They were not produced by any interior force, by any power acting from within. This illustrates the first theory of the universe, that of special creation.

* Used by Dr. Lyman Abbott.

In other words, the earth and all that it contains were called into being at no very remote period of the past, by the creative word or touch of Jehovah. The entire work was completed in six days,—although modern interpreters stretch without warrant the six Scriptural days into long geologic periods, trying to save their Science and their Scripture, and making bad work of both. Each species of animal, creeping, walking, or flying, was made as we find it to-day by some special word or act, and added to all the rest. No two bear any relation to each other. They are separate and independent, as the leaves of the artificial flower, until placed in juxtaposition by some external force. Man's body was made at once out of the dust of the earth, and stands entirely unrelated to any other beings that went before. The spirit was flashed into it in an instant. When the flood came, the family of Noah was preserved in the ark, together with specimens of all the other living things that had been originally created. From those the present races of men and the present species of animals have sprung. Calvin stated the theory very succinctly when he said: "All species of animals were created in six days, each day made up of an evening and a morning, and no new species has ever appeared since." This was the main theory of the universe from the earliest years to more recent times.

Let us now turn from the artificial plant to a real one, which will help us understand the new theory of evolution. This plant was not made outright. It grew. It grew from a very small germ into its present size, complexity, and beauty. It put out branches from the original stem upon the right hand and upon the left. These, in turn, subdivided, and produced leaves and blossoms. Each part of this plant is vitally related to every other part. The flower at the very top is connected with the roots. In the unfolding of this plant from the seed, there were constant changes; these changes went on without interruption; they were progressive. The unfolding of this plant took place by means of a force that was wrapped up in the plant itself. The growth was from within.

This illustration will pave the way to a better understanding of that classic definition by Le Conte: "Evolution is continuous, progressive change, according to certain laws, and by means of resident forces."

EVOLUTION IS "CONTINUOUS, PROGRESSIVE CHANGE."

This theory is the result, not of theological dogmas based upon the letter of an infallible book; it is the result of patient study and research on the part of scientific men,—men who take nothing for granted,—and who believe that nature and nature's processes can only be learned by the most thorough study of nature itself.

The conclusions of these students of the universe and the life which it contains and which has recorded itself in the earth, is this: All things that exist, the earth upon which we stand, the plants that grow in its soil, the animals that roam its forests and swim its seas, man himself the crown of the whole, have not been created just as we see them, all at once, or each by some definite act, but have become what they are by a long and gradual succession of changes. Evolution means that the earth, instead of being flung into space a ready-made sphere from the hand of God, took its rise in nebulous mists and clouds, and by a process of whirling and condensing and cooling, through countless ages, became the globe of to-day. Evolution means that, whatever the ultimate origin of life, the plants and flowers and grasses and trees which clothe the earth, were not made at once, as we behold them now, but began in the simplest and fewest germs; and by slow and gradual changes, under varying conditions, attained the variety, luxuriance, and beauty which wreathe the brow of the planet. It means that the members of the animal kingdom, in all its departments, were not—each kind—called into being in a moment, and in fixed and definite and unvarying and unchanging species; but that the whole kingdom began countless ages ago in a shapeless mass of jelly, and has developed from one form to another up to man. There has been no break or crack or flaw in the entire process. Professor Wilson says: "There can be no evolution for one group, and special creation for another. There can be no evolution for the lower races and creation for the higher forms of animal life, or for man himself. Uniformity and sequence exist wholly or not at all." These changes were progressive, from lower forms to higher, from simple to complex. They were continuous. With nature it was no six days' task, with a seventh for rest. With tireless energy has nature wrought, and pursues her work to-day with undiminished vigor after the lapse of unnumbered centuries.

.   .   .

While the scientific man has simply to do with the methods and facts of nature, the religious man, when these are discovered, need not abandon his belief in a wise and loving power back of all that the eye can see and the hand handle. We can no longer believe in special creations. But the religious man, instead of fearing that God is read out of his universe, ought to feel that God is identified all the more closely with his universe. The scientific man shows us the processes of nature; the religious man may see in them the methods of God. He no longer appears as a carpenter standing outside, building a fabric or constructing a machine; but he is the very life and soul of his universe, animating every part, guiding from within and not without, all things to

> "One far-off, divine event,
>   To which the whole creation moves."

But the religious man may go farther and he may say to the scientist: "You tell me of resident forces; you tell me of life and power manifested in every atom of this great universe; and I believe it all. But to me that life which is behind the plant in its unfolding, the animal in its development, and man in his growth to perfection, is none other than the Living God himself, to whom I cry with the Psalmist, 'Before the mountains were brought forth, or ever thou hadst formed the earth and the world, even from everlasting to everlasting thou art God.'" Science compels us to change some of our notions about God; but does not rule out of the universe an infinite power, intelligence and love.

Equally groundless are the fears of those who think that evolution completely materializes man. Carlyle, who never tried to understand the question, stigmatized it as a "brutal philosophy."

Every argument for the soul of man that ever had any force in it still remains. Nothing in that department of thought is abated. We may discredit the old story of man's creation from the ground, and yet believe that he has become a living soul. Indeed, the doctrine of evolution but adds to the dignity and worth of man. We measure man to-day by all the processes that have gone to produce him. In the light of an infinite past, we hold him up. The crown of the universe, the consummate flower of the ages, what honor and glory are his!—how vastly superior to the being of a few thousand years, created at the pinnacle, and ignominiously fallen to the base, covered with the dust of humiliation and disheartened by the original defeat. The new theory shows man with the roots of his life deep struck in the soil of the eternity past,—assurance that the blossom of his life shall go on unfolding in the light and air of an eternity to come!

.   .   .

Does it seem a degradation to have ascended from the animal? It enhances the dignity and grandeur of man, to think of the ages that went to produce him, of the marvelous processes of which he is the crowned and glorious outcome. We may exclaim with more wonder and greater knowledge than did Hamlet: "What a piece of work is a man!" "Those who know the Cathedral of St. Marks," says Professor Henry Drummond, "will remember how this noblest of the stones of Venice owes its greatness to the patient hands of centuries and centuries of workers, how every quarter of the globe has been spoiled of its treasures to dignify this single shrine. But he who ponders over the more ancient temple of the Human Body, will find imagination fail him as he tries to think from what remote and mingled sources, from what lands, seas, climates, atmospheres, its varying parts have been brought together, and by what innumerable contributory creatures, swimming, creeping, flying, climbing, each of its several members was wrought and perfected. What ancient chisel first sculptured the rounded columns of the limbs? What dead hands built the cupola of the brain, and from what older ruins were the scattered pieces of its mosaic work wrought? Who fixed the windows in its upper walls? What winds and weathers wrought strength into its buttresses? What ocean beds and forest glades worked up its colorings? What love and terror and night called forth the music? And what life and death and pain and struggle put all together in the noiseless workshops of the past, and removed each worker silently when its task was done? How these things came to be, biology is one long record. The architects and builders of this mighty temple are not anonymous. Their names and the work they did are graven forever on the walls and arches of the human embryo. For this is the volume of that Book in which man's members were written, which in continuance were fashioned when as yet there was none of them."

.   .   .

When the great man has been produced he himself becomes a factor in the development of the race. The world's inventors and discoverers help on its material progress. It was an epoch in the history of the race, when one day, in the primitive forest, a savage found out that rubbing two sticks together, or striking two flints, would produce fire. The age of steam was in that first spark. The Newtons and Darwins have enlarged our knowledge. The Homers and Shakespeares have added worlds of beauty to the world of invention and the world of knowledge. But higher than those who have struck the harp, higher than those who have searched for truth and found it, higher even than those who have died for truth, stand those "who were ready to die for men, if only thereby they might improve their lot."

Jesus was not an inventor, philosopher, or scientist. His sphere is the moral and spiritual. Great as were man's other needs, he saw that the needs of the soul were greater. To the soul his life was devoted; and his death crowned and made glorious his life. He made an epoch in the religious history of the race. The mission of Jesus must be re-read in the light of what evolution shows us concerning the origin and nature of man. If we are not fallen, and under the wrath of God, then Jesus as an atoning sacrifice is not needed. If we have come up from the animal, with a brute inheritance that wars with our higher aspirations and aims, then we need some one to help us in the moral struggle thus precipitated. We want to get rid of the lingering vestiges of serpent and tiger, and ape and hyena. We want to bring into the ascendant those higher qualities whose feeble germs date also back to the remote past. How can this be done? What methods shall we use? What motives will prompt us? What leadership will go before us to show us the way? What inspiration or incentive shall we have?

Here the mission of Jesus becomes apparent. At a certain point in history the religious genius of the Jewish nation produced its highest example and illustration. Jesus was born at that point where he could best develop; at the time when his influence could be most widely diffused. Wherever his teachings spread, men said, "That is the word we need." Wherever the story of his life was told, they said, "That is the light to guide us!" And his truth is still the word we need; his life is still the light that shines upon our perplexed and uncertain pathways.[3]

, ·, , , , , ,

The blending of science and religion into a modernist synthesis is well illustrated by the article that Henry Blanchard, one of the radical Universalists who had taken part in the formation of the Free Religious Association in 1867, addressed in 1889 to the faculty of his old alma mater, Tufts.

‘ ‘

"To be religious is to feel that God is the Ever-Near," said F. W. Robertson, one of the most spiritual teachers the world has yet received. And Daniel Webster said, "Religion is a necessary element in every great human character." I have no reverence for culture which does not culminate in religion. I cannot value highly a college course which does not send forth men into the world who are religious. "Haunted forever by the Eternal Mind," said Wordsworth. That is the condition of mind which I would have every graduate possess. To obtain this, I see great power in the modern study of science. I am profoundly impressed by the great possibilities of development of the consciousness of God, the Ever-Near, the Infinite Life, the Infinite Mind, which are in the power of science to-day. I would not make the study of science less. I would not ask men to turn away from Astronomy, Geology, Chemistry, Biology. These can make us wonder and adore. These can show us that science is the handmaid of Religion. But I am profoundly convinced that it is the power of a great soul which does most toward making men religious. Of the greatest known in History, Jesus Christ, we learn in the New Testament. Of the next greatest, the apostle Paul, we learn in the same volume. To know these two men thoroughly is to receive mightiest help in the religious life. Others will help,—the great law-giver of Israel, the great prophets— Isaiah, Ezekiel, Habakkuk, Micah, so that as we study the biographies of the heroes of the Old and New Testament, we shall find ourselves lifted into communion with Him who created the heavens and the earth and the multitude of men and who rules over all things for good. For the Scriptures are pre-eminent in this,—the wealth of biography of men who felt God as the Ever-Near. I know full well the need of wise discrimination. I can see how young men may turn away from characters eulogized as "Men of God." To praise David without criticism, to offer a Samson as one to be revered, is foolishness and will create disgust. But modern scholarship shows that men are to be judged by their times, that a man may be a hero and yet have serious faults. The one great underlying fact of Biblical characters is their consciousness of God, their passion that His righteousness shall prevail.

I should not dare to use these Scriptures if I were a believer in the old theories concerning them, but in all the freedom and wisdom of modern knowledge, all the characters of the Scriptures can be used to inspire or to warn. In this new knowledge, also, the greatest teacher comes to us as a man and a brother, imitable, inspiring, saving, bringing us into union with God. I know what nature can do to make men religious. From the summit of College Hill, I have looked on sunsets and night

skies that have made me feel the mystery of the universe and
God and Man, and have lifted me into communion with my
Maker. I know what the revelations of science are doing, as in
the magnificent story of evolution there is shown the Infinite
Mind and the Infinite Power at ceaseless work. I know what history does as she, unrolling her scroll which tells of rise and fall of
nations, makes us feel that "through the ages one increasing purpose runs." Reverence, wonder, awe,—all these will come as we
feel the play of vast cosmic forces in vast cosmic fields. But it is
the great human soul, undaunted by the mysteries of life and
universe, wrestling with evil, longing for righteousness, living in
God who lifts us up to that height, on which standing, we too
can say, "And yet I am not alone, because the Father is with
me."

I have long been persuaded that biography has great
power to ennoble men. It is the knowledge of noble lives which
inspires to noble living. I can ask men to study the lives of other
heroes than those found in the Scriptures. I think Carlyle wise
in calling the histories of nations their Bibles.[4]

The one seriously jarring note in this period of adaptation to evolutionary and higher critical ideas was the suspension
from fellowship by the Minnesota State Convention of Herman
Bisbee in 1872. Bisbee, a controversial preacher in Minneapolis,
had taken a very advanced position regarding biblical criticism
and evolution and had upset many not prepared to move as fast
as he. It was easily proved that he did not stand by the principles stated in the Winchester Profession of 1803.

It seemed for a while that the horns which Noah Murray
had warned the convention of 1803 would grow on the creedal
calf had indeed been sprouting and had begun to hook.

In addition, an evolutionary age could no longer accept
the idea, stated in the Winchester Profession, that man would
finally be restored to holiness and happiness. This implied fall
from grace did not sit well with a generation that believed man,
having started from very low beginnings, was evolving to greater

heights. A quarter-century of bickering finally produced a statement which avoided this pitfall and also took into account the new views of the Bible by avoiding any implication of a literal acceptance of the Scripture while at the same time asserting belief that the Bible contains "a" revelation from God. This statement of the conditions of fellowship adopted in Boston in 1899 is a masterpiece of theological dexterity.

‘ ‘

The conditions of fellowship shall be as follows:

1. The acceptance of the essential principles of the Universalist Faith, to wit: 1. The Universal Fatherhood of God; 2. The Spiritual authority and leadership of His Son, Jesus Christ; 3. The trustworthiness of the Bible as containing a revelation from God; 4. The certainty of just retribution for sin; 5. The final harmony of all souls with God.

The Winchester Profession is commended as containing these principles, but neither this nor any other precise form of words is required as a condition of fellowship, provided always that the principles above stated be professed.

2. The acknowledgment of the authority of the General Convention and assent to its laws.[5]

, ,

Chapter Eight

The Old and the New Universalism

Conduct is three-fourths of life. The present life is the great pressing concern.

P. T. Barnum

Universalists are freemen. Therefore they should be in the front rank of the daring few who are fighting the battles of social emancipation. They have pledged themselves to break the tyrannies of the mind, and strike the shackles of tradition from the soul.

Clarence R. Skinner

Intimately connected with the development of modernism in American Christianity was the rise of the social gospel between the Civil War and World War I. The social gospel sought to shift organized religion from its all-engrossing concern with the fate of the individual soul to a concern with the fate of society as a whole. Spurred by the tawdriness of the Gilded Age and the brutalization of American society by the rise of industry, it hoped to set the Christian conscience loose on the problems confronting society.

A concomitant of the social gospel was a lessening of doctrinal and denominational concern. The various denominations tended to minimize their peculiar points of view and to stress a common concern with the uplift of American life.

Phineas T. Barnum, entrepreneur of the "Greatest Show on Earth," and Horace Greeley, as delegates to the Universalist Centennial Convention in Gloucester in 1870, supported the funding of the Universalist Publishing House. The Publishing House was naturally delighted to be able to publish in the 1880's in pamphlet form the great showman's reasons for being a Universalist. Barnum gives several doctrinal arguments to support his belief; however, his statement is chiefly interesting for the stress he puts on the need to live a virtuous life in the here and now.

‹ ‹

I base [my] belief—for my belief and hope are one—on the attributes of God as admitted by all Christians. Infinite Wisdom knows the end from the beginning, and will not in the beginning create what will defeat the end. Infinte Power is able to control all things toward a desired end. Infinite Love, as expressed in the words "Our Father," will do the best for its children. What shall we say of the attribute of justice? No attribute has been so belittled as this. We once heard that since man's sin was infinite, justice demanded infinite punishment; now it is changed to the statement, if men sin endlessly, justice demands they be punished endlessly. Both these statements are an abortion, a caricature of justice. No finite man can commit an infinite sin. If any man sin endlessly, justice cannot be satisfied, but only endlessly thwarted. Justice demands obedience to just law. It is never satisfied with less. As God is a just God, so nothing is ever settled until it is settled right. There are other attributes. "God is a consuming fire." His wrath and anger are spoken of. These attributes express the Divine hand raised against sin. If the Divine hand is raised against sin one must yield, and I don't believe it is the Divine hand. God is a consuming fire, not a fire burning forever in empty rage. He consumes man as the refiner's fire does the ore, burning the dross and bringing forth the good, as gold tried by fire.

I base my hope on the office and character of Jesus Christ. I see in his life no clumsy mechanical device of vicarious atonement. He did not shed blood to appease an angry Deity. The Deity does not want blood, He wants obedience. The life, and teachings, and death of Jesus are the supreme appeal to all mankind, "Be ye reconciled to God." God never needed to be reconciled to them, save in some such sense as any loving father might feel a barrier between himself and a prodigal son. Blood cannot remove it. Only the son coming back penitent can. The character and purpose of Jesus are most comprehensively stated in the parables of "The Lost Sheep," "The Lost Piece of Silver," "The Prodigal Son." The final declaration of his purpose he told when he declared, "I, if I be lifted up, will draw all men unto me." The completion of this purpose, man's rebellion may delay but cannot disappoint or annul.

I base my hope on the trend of Scripture. It is well known that a comparatively small portion of Scripture bears on this immortal life and the great end of our course. Conduct is three-fourths of life. This present life is the great pressing concern. A very large portion of the Old Testament dwells on righteousness and its earthly temporal rewards or sin with its temporal punishments. The New Testament is a great appeal to men to build character, seek eternal life, and "now is the accepted time." A solemn reserve is thrown over the future life; the great emphasis is on the present time. This is precisely as it should be. Not a few threats of judgment and promises of joy have been stupidly and persistently thrust over there which belong here.

Now and then, however, scattered through the Bible, its writers looked into the future, and spoke of the great consummation. There are enough such passages to give every believer warrant for his hope of immortal life.

Take, then, these passages which speak of the great end and consummation—on the point in question, of course, many others bear—and what is the trend of these Scriptures? Without an exception that I know of in these passages is a great song of joy, a great shout of triumph. I can cite but one: "Then cometh the end, when he shall have delivered the kingdom to God, even the Father; when he shall have put down all rule, and all authority and power. For he must reign till he hath put all enemies under his feet. . . . And when all things shall be subdued unto him, then shall the Son also himself be subject unto him that put all things under Him, that God may be all in all." (I Cor. XV. 24–28).

I base my hope on the Word of God speaking in the best heart and conscience of the race—the Word heard in the best poems and songs, the best prayers and hopes of humanity. The ages have been darkest when this hope was lowest. It cannot be successfully controverted that out of the six theological schools of the Early Church four taught the doctrines of Universalism, only one annihilation of the wicked, and one their endless punishment. To-day no preacher in his fiercest sermons approximates to such utterances as those of Jonathan Edwards. If he did he would not be tolerated a year. The Christian pulpit is silent on the doctrine of endless punishment, or else denies it, as . . . a great multitude of greatest minds have done.[1]

, ,

The social gospel within Universalism came into full bloom in the career of Clarence R. Skinner. Skinner was consumed with a passion to make Universalists responsive to the social needs of the day. As professor of Applied Christianity (later as dean) of the School of Religion of Tufts College he inspired a generation of young preachers to bring social problems into the pulpit and into the activities of the church. As a founder of the Community Church of Boston, he sought to go beyond denominationalism by shifting the concerns of the church from doctrine and sectarian politics to the problems surrounding it.

In 1915, on the eve of America's involvement in the worldwide conflict which was to be so painful to Skinner because of his staunch pacifism, he published a passionate statement of *The Social Implications of Universalism.* Skinner's concern was to connect religion and society so intimately that an expression by an individual of the former would inevitably involve him in the problems of the latter.

‘ ‘

Universalists are freemen. Therefore they should be in the front rank of the daring few who are fighting the battles of social emancipation. They have pledged themselves to break the tyrannies of the mind, and strike the shackles of tradition from the soul. If they are true to the spirit of their faith, they pledge themselves to free humanity from the economic degradation which fetters it, body, mind and soul, in this twentieth century. The logic is relentless, the implication clear. Universalism, by its very genius, is led into the great social maelstrom, because it is essentially a battle for the freedom of the common man. It is a struggle for complete emancipation.

It is easy to gain the right to palliate when charity is popular. It is easy to boast of the similitude of social freedom, to hide slavery behind the mask of relief. But it is hard to win the freedom to eradicate, to blaze the trail, to risk prestige, popularity, ease, in a fight against the causes of misery. There is no issue in religious life today of more fundamental import than the freedom of the churches. The cause of vital religion will fall or rise as the cause of true freedom is lost or won. . . .

All great social problems involve theological conceptions. We may divorce church from state, but we cannot separate the idea of God from the political life of the people. So intimate is the connection between religious and social development, that the history of tribal and National evolution reveals the fact that a particular type of theology is an almost inevitable concomitant of a particular type of society. There is a constant interaction between ideals of economic and political life on the one hand, and ideals of God on the other. As man attains increasing democracy, he conceives God as being more universal, more just and more intimately associated with life; and as God is conceived to be more universal, just and intimate, the idea begets more democracy among men. Social action and theological reaction are equal, and in the same direction.

In the olden times God was conceived to be aristocratic, imperious, partial, because the people were so; and the commonly accepted notions of deity never rise higher than the common social experience. Our religious terminology and imagery smack of imperialism and aristocracy. Therefore we find the old sacred literatures full of such statements as this, which in the Bhagavadgita is attributed to the Creator: "The fourfold division of castes was created by me according to the apportionment of qualities and duties." God is here imagined as dividing his human creatures into four distinct classes, each with appropriate powers. This supposed fiat of a partial deity became the constitution for the caste system of social, political and economic life which has held sway so universally and so imperiously among the peoples of the Orient. A caste system created a caste God and a caste God spread its sanction over a divisive and aristocratic society. Government used the church as a reinforcement for the execution of its tyrannies.

The Old Testament record of the dramatic struggle between the worshipers of Yaweh and Baal is illustrative of the clash between a democratic people with a democratic idea of God and an aristocratic people with an exploiting God. Prof. Lewis Wallis, author of "The Sociological Aspects of the Bible," has ingeniously but clearly shown the deep economic and political significance of this struggle. The Israelites were born to the rugged freedom of the hill country, inheritors of a rich social idealism, worshipers of a God, Yaweh, who stood for justice. The Amorites were a commercial people, with traditions of a slave class, worshipers, therefore, of Baal, who became the shekel raised to the nth power, a God who condoned greed and injustice. Professor Wallis therefore rightly calls the victory of Yaweh worship by the Israelites over Baal worship by the Amorites the first great victory of the common people, for it meant the establishment of the religious sanctions to democracy, brotherhood and freedom.

So the struggle has gone on through the course of history, a democratic people projecting into their idea of the deity those social and spiritual qualities which were most highly developed in themselves. Each nobler and more just conception of God, therefore, becomes evidence of a new level of political life, and is in turn a *magna carta* of liberties yet to be won.

In the light of this undoubted law, the problem of theology in the twentieth century becomes twofold. First, the problem of imagining attributes of deity which are at least as democratic as the attributes of the most highly socialized man; and second, creating an idea of God which shall bring man up to a newer and finer level of social experience.

The old ideas of a God who created a spiritual aristocracy, who maintained partiality, whose sympathies were not as wide as the whole of humanity, are patently inadequate to meet the new needs. There is no mistaking the democratic instinct in the new man. He passions after freedom and brotherhood. He lays bare his heart and mind to the great human currents and exults in the tides of feeling which pour upon him, enriching and enlarging him. There is no mistaking the widening of sympathies, the greater sense of inclusiveness, the new solidarity of humanity. Such a humanity will no longer brook the imperious and fastidious God who has scorned the fellowship of most of his creatures in the past. A democratic people demand a democratic God, a robust deity who likes his universe, who hungers for fellowship, who is in and of and for the whole of life, whose sympathies are as broad as the "rounded catalog, divine, complete". . . .

The Universalist idea of God is that of a universal, impartial, immanent spirit whose nature is love. It is the largest thought the world has ever known; it is the most revolutionary doctrine ever proclaimed; it is the most expansive hope ever dreamed. This is the God of the modern man, and the God who is in modern man. This is no tribal deity of ancient divisive civilization, this is no God of the nation or of a chosen people, but the democratic creator of the solid, indivisible world of rich and poor, black and white, good and bad, strong and weak, Jew and Gentile, bond and free; such a faith is as much a victory for the common people as was the passage of the Fourteenth Amendment to the Constitution. It carries with it a guarantee of spiritual liberties which are precedent to outward forms of governmental action.[2]

, , , , , , , , , , , , , , , , , , , ,. , , , , ,

The concern of Skinner and the other social gospelists among the Universalists seemed to come to fruition with the adoption of "A Social Program" at the General Convention in October 1917. But the previous April the United States had declared war on Germany and was gearing up for its battles on the Western European front. Universalists, like other Americans

caught up in a frenzy of hate which was to make the world safe for democracy, had to postpone their noble social aspirations.

‘ ‘

The Universalist Church recognizes the fact that no individual and no nation can live a completely effective Christian life in an unchristian social order. We therefore declare the primal task of the church of to-day to be the reconstruction of the world's civilization in terms of justice, peace and righteousness, so that the spiritual life of all may develop to its fullest capacity.

To this end we submit the following working program:

Through all the agencies of the church we shall endeavor to educate and inspire the community and the nation to a keener social consciousness and a truer vision of the kingdom of God on the earth.

We want to safeguard marriage so that every child shall be born with a sound physical, mental and moral heritage.

We want to guarantee to every child those conditions of housing, education, food and recreation which will enable him to become his best.

The standard and plane of living for all should be such that deterioration becomes impossible and advancement becomes limited only by capacity.

Democracy, in order to be complete, must be economic and social as well as political. We therefore declare for the democratization of industry and of land, and for the establishment of co-operation.

We would condemn those forms of private monopoly which make it difficult or impossible for men to attain their common share of the common heritage of earth, and especially do we condemn those forms of exploitation which in time of national stress and suffering make the few wealthy at the cost of the many.

No democracy can be real which shuts out half the people. Women should therefore have equal economic, social and political rights with men.

Free discussion is the soul of democracy and the guaran-

tee of our liberties. It should therefore be maintained in our churches, colleges and public platforms, and limited only by mutual self-respect and courtesy.

We recognize in the use of narcotic habit-forming drugs an imminent peril to social welfare, and we are particularly alarmed at the extent to which tobacco, in the form of cigarettes, is undermining the health and character of American youth. We therefore recommend action toward securing national prohibition of the manufacture and sale of alcoholic liquors, and such progress in restriction of the manufacture of cigarettes and the sale of tobacco as public welfare shall require and public sentiment support. We particularly commend the tobacco laws of Kansas as a model for all the states.

While co-operating to the fullest extent possible with the various forms of charity, relief and correction, we recognize that they do not eradicate fundamental causes. We would mobilize the forces of our church against the causes which create misery, disease, accidents, ignorance and crime, and summon all our strength to the establishment of justice, education and social righteousness.

Some form of social insurance should gradually replace the present individualistic and inadequate methods of charitable relief.

War is brutalizing, wasteful, and ineffective. We therefore pledge ourselves to work for the organization and federation of the world, that peace may be secured at the earliest possible date consistent with justice for all.

The Universalist Church offers a complete program for completing humanity:

First. An Economic Order which shall give to every human being an equal share in the common gifts of God, and in addition all that he shall earn by his own labor.

Second. A Social Order in which there shall be equal rights for all, special privilege for none, the help of the strong for the weak until the weak become strong.

Third. A Moral Order in which all human law and action shall be the expression of the moral order of the universe.

Fourth. A Spiritual Order which shall build out of the

growing lives of living men the growing temple of the living God.[3]

, ,

Ardor for society's improvement cooled by the first World War, Universalists felt the need to work toward a new formulation of the faith. L. B. Fisher stressed in his book, *Which Way?* (1921), that there was no possibility of standing still.

‘ ‘

Universalists are often asked to tell where they stand. The only true answer to give to this question is that we do not stand at all, we move. Or we are asked to state our position. Again we can only answer that we are not staying to defend any position, we are on the march. No Protestant Church to-day can tell where it stands or what position it defends.

We are not stationary nor are we defending any final position. The Church of Rome is the only Church that stands to-day and defends an unchanging position. Even this old and conservative body now and then shows signs of growing pains, but it counts these as dangerous symptoms to be sharply suppressed. Most people, being conservative, or under the same law of inertia that prevails in matter, are therefore attracted to the old Mother Church, and this fact gives to her great numerical strength and enables her to present an imposing front.

But no Protestant Church to-day is as sure about finalities as is the Catholic Church, and for this reason Protestants suffer in numbers and in solidarity.

We do not stand still, nor do we defend any immovable positions, theologically speaking, and we are therefore harder to count or to form into imposing bodies. We grow and we march, as all living things forever must do. The main questions with Universalists are not where we stand but which way we are moving, not what positions we defend but which way we are marching. Our main interest is to perceive what is true progress, and to keep our movements in line with that, and not to allow ourselves to move round and round in circles simply, like Fabre's insects, or like a squirrel in its cage. Of course we can always say that we stand for God and man, for Jesus Christ and the Holy Spirit, for the Bible and the immortal soul, for redemption from sin, and for a human race that, in some day yet to be, shall learn to move on in harmony with God. But all these words and phrases take on new meanings, and therefore need new definition, in each succeeding age. Nothing is clearer than the fact that the old definitions do not meet the needs of the new day, or that the old theologies do not function for the new occasions. Our worn phrases are always losing their old meanings, and must forever be finding new meanings in the light of new experiences.

All good men and women to-day want a gospel that functions for the individual and for society, but the gospel that functioned for these yesterday fails to-day, and the gospel for to-day will have to meet the enlarging knowledge and experience of to-morrow.

What may probably be more disturbing to minds that tend to inertia, which are dreading changes, and stoutly demanding final and authoritative statements and definitions, is that they will never get what they want in this or in any other possible world. What such people think they want is not what they truly need. No human word ever has reached or ever will reach finality of meaning. Each living age always has defined religion in the light of its own experiences, and all ages to come will do the same.[4]

, ,

Fisher's description of Universalism, elsewhere in his book, as a faith dedicated to Jesus made it clear that there was little to distinguish Universalists in the 1920's from the mainline denominations of the day. The old distinctiveness was, if not gone, at least submerged.

When the Congregationalists made overtures regarding a possible merger of the two denominations it is understandable that the Universalists would display more than a casual interest. When Dr. John van Schaik, Jr., editor of the *Universalist Leader*, was "urged" in 1925 by his friend, the editor of the *Congregationalist*, to write an article on "Universalists of Today" he produced a piece which tried to minimize the old distinctions and to make the old heresy palatable to his fellow Protestants.

‘ ‘

. . . I realize that it is just as dangerous to say "all Universalists are this or that" as it is to make sweeping statements about Jews or Germans or Chinese or Congregationalists.

The one thing which characterizes practically all Universalists is their faith that "what ought to be will be."

One of our writers for the encyclopedias describes this as "the belief that in a sane and beneficent universe the primacy belongs to Truth, Right, Love—the supreme powers." Universalists are optimists. They not only hope, but they confidently assert, that this universe is so organized that good will be the final result, that man has the power to work out his own salvation and learn by doing it, and that he can no more fail in doing it, things being as they are, than he can separate himself from the universe.

This optimism might be attacked as "unreasoning" and "foolish" if it were not that it is based upon faith in a God who is not limited either in Power or in Goodness. In the study of Universalism past and present this is the nub of the whole matter. From the beginning Universalists took their stand on the character of God. That character they asserted to be Beneficent. Everything in their theology started here. If God is a Father, man is His child and the race is one family. If He is infinitely wise and good, He will not fail with His universe or with any individual in it. If, like the old Scotchman, we "postulate God," "immortality follows," and we do not need to indulge in endless speculations on that subject. . . .

This same largeness of view characterized Universalist ideas of Christ. The purpose of his great mission included all souls within its scope. He must reign until he has put all enemies under his feet. If he is "lifted up" he "will draw all men" unto him.

Sometimes Universalists have stated their belief in Christ according to Trinitarian, and sometimes according to Unitarian, formulas. There never was a time when a vast majority of Universalists did not give him some kind of primacy among the sons of men. Always he has been a special revelation of God. The Parable of the Prodigal Son and the Parable of the Lost Sheep have been held up in Universalist pulpits for a hundred and fifty years to teach the great Christian truth that God is not passive in the matter of the salvation of man, but is "a seeking, searching, striving God," "standing at the door of our lives and knocking," waiting to come in. But both the words Trinitarian and Unitarian are generally regarded by Universalists of to-day as inadequate to express the larger thought of God or the true Gospel of Christ. Dimly they begin to see that He must be vastly more than the most devout man ever has been able to put into either word. And they accept "the spiritual authority and leadership of Jesus" because they are convinced he saw clearly both the Infinite Resources of God and the Infinite Possibilities in Man.

Universalists of to-day emphatically teach and preach a doctrine of hell. They claim that it is a more stern and severe doctrine than the old fire and brimstone teaching because of its inevitableness. There is "certainty" in it. No scapegoat can carry away the sin and punishment. No Savior can bear the penalty in our place. Each soul is under the operation of invariable law. The instant violation occurs penalty begins. It all is rooted in love. It has a divine purpose. But it is inescapable. "Whatsoever a man soweth that shall he also reap" is a favorite Universalist text. Another is, "Though hand join in hand, the wicked shall not go unpunished," and still another is, "The wicked shall be turned into hell, and all the nations that forget God."

There never was a time when Universalists taught, as was charged, "that it makes no difference how a man lives here; at death all will go shouting off to glory." . . .

Universalists to-day probably will have to be classified among the more practical Christians. The application of Christ's principles here and now, the Christianizing of institutions and men, the abolition of war, the establishment of social justice, the relief of misery, the uniting of races and nations in constructive work, take the time and strength of modern Universalists much more than speculations about the hereafter.[5]

, ,

When the flirtations between Congregationalists and Universalists came to nought, the Unitarians breathed a sigh of relief. They had made occasional overtures to the Universalists since 1899, but to no avail. In 1931, however, probably because of the threat posed by the Congregationalists a joint commission was appointed, which led to the Free Church Fellowship—an organization designed not to merge the denominations but to transcend them. The only practical result of this effort was a hymnbook of high quality.

The Bond of Fellowship proposed in 1933 and adopted in 1935 illustrates the extent to which Universalists had melded into the social-gospel Protestantism of the day. The social gospel had made much of the "Kingdom" Jesus had supposedly sought to achieve on earth. That it looked forward to the "progressive establishment" of such a kingdom by men capable of overcoming "all evil" indicates the extent to which evolutionary ideas had become accepted. No explicit indication is given of a distinctive belief in universal salvation.

‘ ‘

The bond of fellowship in this Convention shall be a common purpose to do the will of God as Jesus revealed it and to co-operate in establishing the Kingdom for which he lived and died.

To that end we avow our faith in God as Eternal and All-Conquering Love, in the spiritual leadership of Jesus, in the supreme worth of every human personality, in the authority of truth known or to be known, and in the power of men of goodwill and sacrificial spirit to overcome all evil and progressively establish the Kingdom of God. Neither this nor any other state-

ment shall be imposed as a creedal test, provided that the faith
thus indicated be professed.[6]

, ,

The controversy over humanism which swept the Unitarian and Universalist denominations revealed a greater common concern than had been apparent. "The Humanist Manifesto," of 1933, issued at the depth of economic depression, was
the work of ministers, professors, and other leaders who expressed a renewed faith in man's ability to overcome the
multitude of problems facing him.

' '

The time has come for widespread recognition of the
radical changes in religious beliefs throughout the modern world.
The time is past for mere revision of traditional attitudes. Science
and economic change have disrupted the old beliefs. Religions
the world over are under the necessity of coming to terms with
new conditions created by a vastly increased knowledge and experience. In every field of human activity, the vital movement is
now in the direction of a candid and explicit humanism. In
order that religious humanism may be better understood we, the
undersigned, desire to make certain affirmations which we believe the facts of our contemporary life demonstrate.

There is great danger of a final, and we believe fatal,
identification of the word *religion* with doctrines and methods
which have lost their significance and which are powerless to
solve the problems of human living in the twentieth century. Religions have always been means for realizing the highest values of
life. Their end has been accomplished through the interpretation of the total environing situation (theology or world view),
the sense of values resulting therefrom (goal or ideal), and the
technique (cult), established for realizing the satisfactory life. A
change in any of these factors results in alteration of the outward forms of religion. This fact explains the changefulness of
religions throughout the centuries. But through all changes reli-

gion itself remains constant in its quest for abiding values, an inseparable feature of human life.

To-day man's larger understanding of the universe, his scientific achievement, and his deeper appreciation of brotherhood, have created a situation which requires a new statement of the means and purposes of religion. Such a vital, fearless, and frank religion capable of furnishing adequate social goals and personal satisfaction may appear to many people as a complete break with the past. While this age does owe a vast debt to the traditional religions, it is none the less obvious that any religion that can hope to be a synthesizing and dynamic force for to-day must be shaped for the needs of this age. To establish such a religion is a major necessity of the present. It is a responsibility which rests upon this generation. We therefore affirm the following:

First: Religious humanists regard the universe as self-existing and not created.

Second: Humanism believes that man is a part of nature and that he has emerged as the result of a continuous process.

Third: Holding an organic view of life, humanists find that the traditional dualism of mind and body must be rejected.

Fourth: Humanism recognizes that man's religious culture and civilization, as clearly depicted by anthropology and history, are the product of a gradual development due to his interaction with his natural environment and with his social heritage. The individual born into a particular culture is largely molded by that culture.

Fifth: Humanism asserts that the nature of the universe depicted by modern science makes unacceptable any supernatural or cosmic guarantees of human values. Obviously humanism does not deny the possibility of realities as yet undiscovered, but it does insist that the way to determine the existence and value of any and all realities is by means of intelligent inquiry and by the assessment of their relation to human needs. Religion must formulate its hopes and plans in the light of the scientific spirit and method.

Sixth: We are convinced that the time has passed for

theism, deism, modernism, and the several varieties of "new thought."

Seventh: Religion consists of those actions, purposes, and experiences which are humanly significant. Nothing human is alien to the religious. It includes labor, art, science, philosophy, love, friendship, recreation—all that is in its degree expressive of intelligently satisfying human living. The distinction between the sacred and the secular can no longer be maintained.

Eighth: Religious humanism considers the complete realization of human personality to be the end of man's life, and seeks its development and fulfillment in the here and now. This is the explanation of the humanist's social passion.

Ninth: In place of the old attitudes involved in worship and prayer the humanist finds his religious emotions expressed in a heightened sense of personal life and in a co-operative effort to promote social well-being.

Tenth: It follows that there will be no uniquely religious emotions and attitudes of the kind hitherto associated with belief in the supernatural.

Eleventh: Man will learn to face the crises of life in terms of his knowledge of their naturalness and probability. Reasonable and manly attitudes will be fostered by education and supported by custom. We assume that humanism will take the path of social and mental hygiene and discourage sentimental and unreal hopes and wishful thinking.

Twelfth: Believing that religion must work increasingly for joy in living, religious humanists aim to foster the creative in man and to encourage achievements that add to the satisfactions of life.

Thirteenth: Religious humanism maintains that all associations and institutions exist for the fulfillment of human life. The intelligent evaluation, transformation, control, and direction of such associations and institutions with a view to the enhancement of human life is the purpose and program of humanism. Certainly religious institutions, their ritualistic forms, ecclesiastical methods, and communal activities must be reconstituted as rapidly as experience allows, in order to function effectively in the modern world.

Fourteenth: The humanists are firmly convinced that existing acquisitive and profit-motivated society has shown itself to be inadequate, and that a radical change in methods, controls, and motives must be instituted. A socialized and co-operative economic order must be established to the end that the equitable distribution of the means of life be possible. The goal of humanism is a free and universal society in which people voluntarily and intelligently co-operate for the common good. Humanists demand a shared life in a shared world.

Fifteenth and last: We assert humanism will: (a) affirm life rather than deny it; and (b) seek to elicit the possibilities of life, not flee from it; and (c) endeavor to establish the conditions of a satisfactory life for all, not merely for the few. By this positive *morale* and intention humanism will be guided, and from this perspective and alignment the techniques and efforts of humanism will flow.

So stand the theses of religious humanism. Though we consider the religious forms and ideas of our fathers no longer adequate, the quest for the good life is still the central task for mankind. Man is at last becoming aware that he alone is responsible for the realization of the world of his dreams, that he has within himself the power for its achievement. He must set intelligence and will to the task.[7]

, ,

Although the economic panaceas indicated in the Manifesto have proved of ephemeral interest to most religious liberals, the faith in man's capacities remained a constant conviction despite a second World War, with its attendant horrors in German death camps, and the rise of neo-orthodoxy in religion.

Dr. Clinton Lee Scott, a signer of the Manifesto, was to be one of the persistent advocates of humanism within the Universalist church. The following selections from a series of radio talks published in 1949, when he was Superintendent of the Massachusetts Universalist Convention, display the straight-talk of a native of Vermont and a logic reminiscent of Ballou.

ʿ ʿ

"What does it mean to be religious?"

In more than a quarter of a century of teaching religion and dealing with all sorts of people, old and young, of various religious backgrounds, and living under a variety of circumstances, I have learned that there are many persons who feel that if they ever had religion they have somehow lost it. A young woman came to her minister in deep distress. She thought she had become an atheist and that she was no longer religious. Talking with her, the minister discovered that this young woman was not an atheist, but that she had been doing some thinking, and her mind had outgrown her childish ideas about God. This is the situation with regard to many persons who have outgrown a religion which no longer makes sense, and who have not yet found a religion helpful and satisfying to the mature mind.

Here is a man, honest and upright in his business dealings. He pays his debts, is a good neighbor, a faithful and kind man in his home, but he looks back upon his early Sunday school experience with a kind of horror. He was taught religious ideas which simply do not make sense in practical life. Here is a woman who lives on a plane of high moral standards. She is interested in her family, and in the education of her children. She gives time to community affairs. Religion as she understands it, however, leaves her cold. The religious ideas to which she has been exposed seem to her fantastic and impractical. They do not make sense.

Here is a young man who, during early childhood, attended dutifully his church and Sunday school. There he learned of a world of supernaturalism, of miracles, and of theological doctrines that are the product of an age before the dawn of science. His subsequent learning in high school and college is of a different world—a world of causes and consequences, of unchanging natural laws never set aside for special privileges. He learns that his freedom and welfare are to be found within these natural laws and not outside them. The result of this conflict is that, unless he develops that strange mental habit of keeping his religious thinking in a separate compartment of his mind, he finds in his school studies a contradiction of his church instructions. He is forced to choose between religious ideas on the one hand and scientific ideas on the other. Usually it is religion that goes out the window.

. . . There is confusion over the relative importance and the meaning of theology and religion. Theology deals with theory and is often deeply involved over things about which nobody knows and only theologians make guesses. But real religion is simple, easy to understand, though difficult to live. The teachings of Jesus are simple teachings; but Christian theologians have obscured simplicity with doctrines which have no more reasonable grounds for acceptance than that which rests upon ecclesiastical authority. As a matter of fact, no preacher, priest, bishop, or other professionally religious person has any inside information. Truth is discovered by the ministers of religion. It is also discovered by scientists, poets, prophets, garage mechanics, and housewives. And always by the one way of human experience! Over the long road mankind has come, ways of living have been found which are productive of personal and social good. These ways have been recorded in such writings as the Ten Commandments and Jesus' Sermon on the Mount. God's laws have not been given exclusively to any church. God's laws are the ways of living found to be good for us. Truths are derived from the experiences of men and women living, not apart from the world, but within it—in all the temptations, problems, and perplexities of the daily round of human relations.

It is in this round of the common everyday life that to many of us religion must have meaning, if it is to have any meaning at all. Not in formal observances, not in creeds or doctrines, however long ago proclaimed, but in the lives we live, in the home, in the community, and in the world, is the religious way of life to be found. A religious person is one who fulfills his highest function as a human being in his relations with other persons.

.   .   .

All our individual and civil liberties stem from the belief in human worth. The free churches, like the American representative government, are founded upon this principle. A government which denies its citizens the right of free discussion, tells them how to vote, and taxes them without giving them voice in political affairs is readily recognized as a dictatorship, whatever its officials may call it. A church which denies its communicants the right of free thinking, tells them what they must believe, is a dictatorship, whatever its officials may call it. Moreover, there is ample evidence that these areas cannot be kept separate. Political tyranny and religious tyranny go hand in hand. Wherever one prevails the other is bound to follow. Democracy is a way of life wherever life is lived, in state or in church. Some of us like dictatorship as little in religion as we like it in politics, and for the same reason; it violates the principle of private judgment, the right of individual opinion necessary in order to give meaning to personal human values.

The value we place upon man depends in some measure upon what we think about his beginnings. The Christian doctrines taking form before the age of science, and written by churchmen profoundly ignorant of their world, present a mistaken notion of man's basic nature. According to these doctrines man was created perfect, but fell from grace through Adam's misbehavior. As the New England Primer put it, "In Adam's fall, we sinned all." The consequence of belief in this doctrine is a low estimate of mankind. It looks backward, stressing the good in the past rather than improvement in the future. Indeed, it offers little prospect of improvement on earth, but only in some state of sinlessness beyond this life.

The non-fiction story is quite different. Man is the product of the natural forces of his world. He was not deposited upon the world, but grew from within it. He was not set down on this planet in the midst of the other objects of creation, but emerged out of the total earth process. Here he is subject to the conditions of his surroundings. The natural laws act upon him as they act upon all other creatures. He has to make his adjustments in order to survive, even as the other creatures. Through the growth of consciousness and intelligence he is able to control many of the natural forces and thus cause them to contribute to his well-being. Man is a part of his universe—chemically, biologically, and spiritually sharing its living reality. To remember this is to avoid many of the pitfalls of primitive notions incorporated into mediaeval theologies. We have kinship with the earth. We are of the stuff of animals and trees and flowers and stars. Our rise to the state of manhood has been honorable. Our kind has won its way to the status of humanity.

But man is something more than animal, and that something more is of very great consequence. He has been something more for at least fifty thousand years. Within this period he has developed not only the capacity for self-consciousness but certain kinds of brain activity which make him unique. His use of speech creating words for objects, his use of tools, his power of reason, his ability to look both backward and forward,—all these qualities and others add up to the fact that man is more than an animal walking on two legs.

His worth is to be estimated not alone by his history, but by his possibilities. Within his mysterious nature is the faculty for conceiving ideals of compelling majesty, and the planned endeavor to build these ideals into reality. Probably he is the only creature possessing that inner quality which makes him critical of himself and remorseful over his failures. He is probably the only creature that appraises himself and makes use of means to change himself to become what he thinks he should be. This is the spiritual quality of man, mysterious above all other mysteries. To name it by calling it "soul" or to explain it by saying it is "the life of God in the soul of man" explains nothing. The important fact is that this is a quality of man and a quality of all men. To recognize this quality not only in ourselves but in all other human beings, however different they may be in other respects, is close to the heart of the Universalist religion.

.   .   .

Confidence in the spiritual leadership of Jesus has been from the beginning a foundation of Universalism. Frequently non-Universalists have said of us that we do not accept

Jesus. What they mean is that we do not accept the traditional notions about Jesus. Orthodox Christianity teaches certain ideas regarding the nature and the mission of Jesus that to Universalists and to other religious liberals are altogether unsatisfactory because they have no basis either in his estimate of himself or in his ethical teachings.

All that is known of Jesus is found in the books of the New Testament, written many years after his death. Some of these writings appeared only after the theologians had already taken over doctrines of the pagan religions and were attempting to make Jesus fit into magical patterns. Yet the effort to make him a magical figure has not been altogether successful. His natural human character has never been completely overshadowed by the manipulators of records, or by the work of the creedmakers. The doctrine of his birth from a virgin was borrowed from other and older religions. Magic and miracles were common to the pagan religions. Even Christmas, so universally celebrated by Christians, was borrowed from the pagan ceremonies of the winter solstice season.

It is true that Universalists do not believe in the Christ of the creeds—in Jesus as a god, or as a magical savior. These theories constitute beliefs about Jesus. When Universalists avow their faith in the leadership of Jesus, they mean faith not in a religion about Jesus, but in the religion of Jesus, as has been so often pointed out.

When we look beyond and beneath the distortions and the perversions of the gospels, we discover a human Jesus who bears very little likeness to the Christ of the dogmas. Dogma claims that all members of the human race are born evil because of an error that Adam made in the garden of Eden. It is asserted that man by himself is helpless and lost until he accepts the interpretation which some church places upon the redemptive power of a crucified savior. There is the dogma that only through blood atonement, and not by means of character or good works, can a man do anything effective for the welfare or salvation of his soul. Equally unfounded is the claim that Jesus appointed a special class of professionally religious men to rule the churches. Concerning none of these dogmas did Jesus utter one word.

They are purely the fabrication of men, a distortion of Jesus' teachings, and an offense against his simple, beautiful life. Such beliefs, moreover, have little virtue. One may hold them all, and others equally fantastic, without in any way becoming the better, the wiser, or the happier because of them.

When we turn to the moral leadership of Jesus, however, we find one of the great teachers of men. He was not a lawgiver, he founded no church, he was not even a Christian, because in his time there were no Christians. He remained loyal to his Jewish faith to the end. But he left to mankind a free and simple way of living, an example of glorious leadership, and the memory of an heroic death.

It is no accident that he is called the Prince of Peace, because he not only taught non-violent action, but he practiced this principle even to the extremity that brought him to his crucifixion.

There have been other men who have taught a gospel of returning good for evil, but no man in history has impressed this teaching upon the world by precept and by example as Jesus did.[8]

, ,

In the 1830's and 40's as Emerson prepared to abandon the pulpit he complained that a corpse-cold Unitarianism pervaded the churches. The introduction of humanism one hundred years later brought with it the same danger in the worship of the liberal churches. Some humanist ministers eschewed emotion in their services and sermons in the apparent conviction that feeling could be associated only with theism. Professor Alfred Storer Cole, long an associate of Clarence Skinner at Tufts, brought to his teaching of homiletics the same passion that Skinner brought to his courses in applied Christianity. Cole fought an uphill battle to persuade a generation of young preachers that poetry and emotion are central to the worship experience. In his "Touch Not My Lips with the White Fire," one of the finest examples of humanist sentiment, he did not hesitate to use the ancient symbol of God to help convey his conviction of man's unity with nature.

‘ ‘

Touch not my lips with the white fire
From the glowing altar of some peaceful shrine.
Thrust not into my hands the scroll of wisdom
Gleaned through the patient toil of the centuries;
Give me no finished chart that I may follow
Without effort or the bitter taste of tears.
I do not crave the comfort of the ancient creeds,
Nor the sheltered harbor where the great winds cease to
    blow;
But winnow my heart, O God; torture my mind
With doubt. Let me feel the clean gales of the open sea,
Until Thy creative life is my life and my joy;
One with the miracle of Spring and the blowing grain,
The yearning of my fellowmen and the endless reach of
    stars.[9]

, ,

Chapter Nine

The Larger Faith

> Universalism cannot be limited to Protestantism or to Christianity, not without denying its very name. Ours is a world fellowship, not just a Christian sect. For so long as Universalism is universalism and not partialism, the fellowship bearing its name must succeed in making it unmistakably clear that all are welcome: theist and humanist, unitarian and trinitarian, colored and color-less. A circumscribed Universalism is unthinkable.[1]
>
> Robert Cummins

At the close of World War II, as many others, Universalists were taking stock. The debate over humanism within the denomination continued in a somewhat lower key. The choice seemed to be either to blend into the mainline Protestant religious scene or to venture into new avenues of development. The former became less palatable when the Federal Council of Churches (forerunner of the National Council) rejected the application of the Universalist Church of America for membership in 1942. Although membership was sought by officials of the denomination in order to promote unity and cooperation in wartime, and rejection came as a heavy blow, it probably facilitated the rebirth of a distinctive spirit among Universalists that was noticeable following the war. There was now a tendency to challenge the presupposition that Universalism was just one of a number of Protestant denominations and a growing tendency to look on it as a movement whose roots were in Christendom but whose future lay beyond Christianity.

Dean Clarence R. Skinner stressed the need for a radical religion, that is, one rooted in the common experiences of mankind, in *A Religion for Greatness* (1945).

Beneath all curious customs and beliefs, deeper than ecclesiastical creeds, more vital and basic than priestly rites, stands out one impressive fact—namely, man touches infinity; his home is in immensity; he lives, moves, and has his being in an eternity. This magnificent assertion is man's greatest affirmation. Nothing else surpasses it in sweep of imagination or depth of understanding. It is a truth proclaimed by all that we know of modern science, and it stands the test of experience as the enduring reality.

It is man's effective protest against all that lessens and divides. It is his emphatic denial of any attempt to separate him from his home and heritage. It expresses his uncompromising unwillingness to be reduced to insignificance and utter isolation. This radical interpretation would rescue religion from its fringes and accretions. It would scrape the barnacles off the elemental truth and reveal the basic reality in its purity and power. So many superficial impedimenta have been heaped upon religion by its devotees that it is frequently impossible to recognize the genuine from the spurious. But by rethinking religion and by performing a major surgical operation upon it, we can discover the vital organs. The radical interpretation refuses to be led aside by the extraneous. It insists upon returning to what is the essential core of religious experience; namely, the seeking after and finding man's relation to the unities and universals. . . .

Insight. The dictionary gives us the following: "A perception of the inner nature of a thing." In our view this ability may be purely intellectual, or it may be due to some causal factor which works in conjunction with intelligence. It may be close to intuition. Perhaps even some mystical quality may inhere in this ability to grasp the inner nature of some form of reality. Whatever the cause or character of the insight, we shall assume its validity when, like any other form of knowledge, we test it by empirical methods.

Unity. Again, the dictionary says, "The state of being indivisibly one; harmony, concord." This unity may be purely physical, as the unity of the human body; it may be intellectual, as the unity of a scheme or plan; it may be used as a metaphysical term, implying a fundamental unity underlying all aspects of reality. It may be used with all these meanings in this volume, but always it will mean the coherence of what may seem to be separate, into a oneness. Unity means an operative harmony, a functional relationship which belongs to all the parts of a whole.

Universal. Funk and Wagnalls says: "Relating to the entire universe; unlimited; general. Regarded as existing as a whole; entire. Including all of a logical class. A universal concept; that which may be predicated of many particular things or persons." We shall give all these connotations to the word. The universal will mean the all-inclusive as far as we can imagine it—the entire cosmos with all it contains. Again it will mean all of a class, as, a universal religion or a universal language. Finally, we shall mean by the term that which is the antithesis of the limited, or fragmentary. It is the opposite of the partial. When we speak of universalism we shall mean a philosophy of life or system of values which stresses the largest possible *Weltanschauung*, or world outlook, in contrast to the narrow view which is herein denominated partialism. . . .

Taoism, in its sacred scripture, the Tao-teh-King, gives a remarkable example of this insight: "Man takes his norm from earth; earth from heaven; heaven from Tao; the Tao from itself." Without going into an extended and unnecessary discussion of the meaning of the terms used by Lao-tse, the founder of the movement, we see at once the kind of philosophy, or mysticism, which religion gives to a noble mind. Man is surrounded by earth and all its forces. To put it scientifically, we are geocentric. We are related to soil, climate, flora, fauna, and all the chemical and physical laws which operate on the earth. This planet, however, is by no means an isolated fact. It swings in a vast cosmos, and so, as man takes his norm from earth, so the earth takes its norm from heaven. Needless to say, heaven did not mean to the Chinese twenty-five hundred years ago what it means today. The significant thing about the statement is not its astronomy, but its early insight into the fact of orderliness and interrelatedness. If heaven meant to Lao-tse something in the nature of a moral as well as physical order, so much the better for our argument. It simply extends the sweep and scope of the author's insight into the unity of all phases of the universe, whether moral or physical. Heaven, however, is not an ultimate and final fact, but it, too, is dependent on something more elemental and self-sustaining. The Tao is the uncaused cause, the prime mover, the *Ding an sich* which all philosophers must assume as the ultimate reality. It gives measure, shape and meaning to all else, including the wide expanse of the cosmos, this planet, and even man, small as he may seem in the universal order of things.

It would be difficult indeed to find a more complete and satisfying statement of radical religion than this logical and penetrating summary by the sage Lao-tse.[2]

, ,

An explicit rejection of Universalism as a branch of Christianity was voiced by Brainard F. Gibbons, minister of the Universalist Church of Wausau, Wisconsin, when he addressed the Universalist General Assembly meeting in Rochester, New York, in 1949. His controversial sermon did not stand in the way of his election as president of the Universalist Church of America in 1951 and as General Superintendent of the U.C.A. in 1953.

‘ ‘

While fully aware of its Christian heritage, many equally sincere Universalists maintain that an inherent spirit of inquiry has carried Universalism beyond Christianity. A new type of Universalism is proclaimed which shifts the emphasis on universal from salvation to religion and describes Universalism as boundless in scope, as broad as humanity, and as infinite as the universe. Is this Universalism's answer: a religion, not exclusively Christian or any other named brand, but a synthesis of all religious knowledge which passes the test of human intelligence, a truly universal religion?

Every Universalist realizes that Universalism has changed considerably since the days of its New England forebears and many Christian dogmas have been gradually supplanted. Even the sketchiest summary reveals the vast differences between then and now. Divine revelation has been replaced by human investigation, ignorance by knowledge, superstition by reason, the closed mind by the open, stagnation by progress, celestial nonsense by common sense. Hence, Universalists today consider all religions, including Christianity, expressions of human spiritual aspirations, not God-founded institutions; the Bible a marvelous work of man, not the miraculous handiwork of God; Jesus a Spiritual Leader, not a Divine Savior; man's fate in human hands, not superhuman clutches; faith the projection of known facts into the unknown, not blind creedal acceptance; the supernatural merely the natural beyond man's present understanding, not a violation of nature's laws.

Indeed, Universalism has disavowed many essential Christian doctrines. What remains that is uniquely Christian? God is not a Christian invention nor monopoly, and Universalists find God more fully and truly revealed in the universe and man than in the Bible. Brotherhood is more reliably demonstrated by biology than the Bible and is common to several world religions. The supreme value Universalism places upon every human personality, here and hereafter, is actually more than Christian and is part of philosophic speculation entirely divorced from Christianity. Universalism does not insist that man must swallow some Christian capsule of creedal beliefs that is, of supreme value, to be "saved." The avowal of faith in Jesus as Spiritual Leader implies denial of him as God and, hence, of Christianity. The very name, Christian, is derived from the title of Christ given Jesus, a title signifying the supernatural nature imputed to Jesus and, accordingly, to Christianity. However much Universalists may revere Jesus as a man and strive to follow in his footsteps, that alone does not make Universalism Christian. At most, Universalists are nominal Christians, and that solely by virtue of their own definition—a definition not acceptable to the great body of Christianity!

For a long time, though formally acknowledging it but recently, Universalists have been reaching beyond the narrow bounds of Christianity to pluck their grapes of knowledge from vines growing in the boundless vineyards of truth, and the religious wine pressed from them cannot be contained in the old Christian bottles. Only historical and emotional ties to Christianity have prevented Universalists generally from realizing sooner the dynamic effects of the truth deliberately sought and in which they now avow faith. Only fear of bigoted opinion will prevent an enlightened Universalism from declaring to the world what fidelity to truth has made it, a unifying universal religion.[3]

, ,

The most energetic advocate of a world Universalism was Kenneth L. Patton, who became minister of the Charles Street Meeting House in Boston in 1949 and with the congregation set about the task of creating worship materials, hymns, and an architectural setting for a new, syncretistic Universalism. Patton's convictions in religion grew out of his study of anthropology and his belief that all men share a common humanity.

‘ ‘

Beginning on the Persian plateau, in Mesopotamia and Egypt, about 3500 B.C., possibly coming to its first efflorescence in Sumeria, civilization as we know it spread out in all directions. It is here that we must look for the beginnings of developed religion and the migration of symbols. Somewhere in the third millennium B.C., civilization moved east into the Indus River valley and into China. Later China and India themselves became sources of this migration as it moved into southwest Asia, Indonesia, and the islands of Oceania, all the way to New Zealand, Easter Island, and the Hawaiians. The Negro people came into Africa from the East, forcing back the native Bushmen. The American Indians, in migrations that proceeded for thousands of years, trekked across the Bering Straits from the great cradle of Asia.

Anthropologists believe that many of the so-called tribal cultures, rather than being really "primitive," are the result of a disintegration of higher cultures in the past. Of one thing we can be sure: this movement and mixture of the people of the human race, which the anthropologists call "diffusion," was an immensely long and involved process. We have only begun to trace it. Without in any way minimizing the cultural differences of humanity, we may say that the outcome of this diffusion has been a universal sharing of basic cultural inventions which justifies our assertion that there is only one human culture. The differences are only variations within an impressive unity. It is because of this inherent unity of the human community that a people can move in one generation from an untouched tribal condition to an awareness of the need to live in the world community, as Margaret Mead's description of the Manus Islanders in her brilliant book *New Lives for Old* reveals. It is for this reason that the grandson of a cannibalistic Melanesian chieftain can win a Ph.D. in a great university. The differences between our cultures may seem to be vast, but the fact that the basis of all these variations is fundamentally the same allows movement from one cultural style to another within a generation or two.[4]

.   .   .

The Meeting House has one basic and simple idea: to find a religious setting for a religion of one humanity and one world. It is the United Nations idea, especially as it is embodied in Unesco, applied to religion. Our unofficial motto comes from Terence: "I am a man, and nothing that is human can be alien to me." We are a completely free-mind fellowship, with no creed or confession of faith. We look for insight and wisdom to all of humanity, for truth and goodness have never been the monopoly of any one people or religion. For this reason we do not call ourselves Christian or Jewish or Buddhist, although these traditions are greatly cherished along with the others. We include all and exclude none, for only thus can we be positive and non-exclusive in our approach.

This, however, does not mean that we are uncritical; quite the opposite. The criteria of evidence, reasonableness and consistency are applied to all. The scientific method and attitude, with the findings of the various branches of science, are allied to the arts, to philosophy and to "naturalistic mysticism," to give us a religious approach that is at once hard-headed, tough-minded, and appreciative and warm-hearted. Belief is allied with

doubt, affirmation with criticism. We reject all creeds and dogmas on principle, for only the open mind is free to probe and
discover. But we can accept the other person's faith as part of
the human scene, *and appreciate it*, without accepting it as adequate for our own use. To criticize is not to reject. This point
must be emphasized, for it is the dividing line between the free
mind and fanaticism. It is the doorway to a universal religion
that rigorously seeks the truth, and yet is also inclusive and wel-
coming to all.

What are the fundamental symbols for such a universal
religion? The United Nations found its symbol in the world
encircled with the olive wreath of peace. The symbols which we
have chosen and created are of several kinds. What are the core
realities of the human situation? How can they be symbolized?

First is the universe itself, from which our name "universal" is taken. The universe is symbolized in two ways: in a "stel-
lar globe" which gives the constellations of both the northern
and southern hemispheres, and makes an attractive luminous
sphere when lighted at night. At the front of the auditorium in
an arch which is fifteen feet wide and twenty-five feet high, we
have reproduced the Great Nebula in Andromeda from astro-
nomical photographs. This nebula is our next-door neighbor in
space, practically a twin of the Milky Way Nebula of which our
solar system is a part. It gives us a "window into the universe,"
and provides us with the key for our cosmic orientation, since
this nebula is seen through a screen of stars in our own galaxy.
We call it a "symbol of the fact." It is a photographic reproduc-
tion. Each person is left to make his own interpretation of this
reality. He can say: "The heavens declare the glory of God," or
"The heavens declare the glory," or he can just say, "My
heavens!" Another astronomic scene, the Horse's Head Nebula
in the constellation of Orion, a portion of our own galaxy, is
painted on one of the walls downstairs.

The earth is symbolized by a large polar-projection map
of the earth inlaid in linoleum in the very center of the auditorium. All national boundaries are eliminated, giving the one land
mass, the one earth. Around this is a golden circle, which we
have chosen as the master-symbolism of Universalism. The circle

is found in all cultures, and has variously symbolized the universe, the sun, the moon, the earth, unity, perfection, holiness, peace. The earth within the circle is repeated downstairs, with the symbols of the world religions inscribed upon it at the point of their origin.

The pews have been rearranged to face in four banks toward the center, coming in from the four corners of the room. Thus the people, being seated in a circle, symbolize unity and one world in their very arrangement. "Religion in the round" is also a symbol of democracy, since the people face one another, and not the altar. The minister and the choir sit in the pews with the congregation, and the preaching is done from the edge of the map in the inner circle.

Hanging from the ceiling opposite the mural is a "construction" which is an allegorical symbol of the microcosm, the atom, the cell, the seed. This is the work of Jack Burnham, a young Boston artist, who designed and executed it and gave it to the Meeting House as his contribution to the project. The center of it is lighted, and the mural of the nebula is painted in "black light," and gives a very close representation of the night sky. When the construction and the mural, microcosm and macrocosm, are lighted in an otherwise darkened room, the position of man, who in size and complexity is about halfway between the two, is effectively symbolized.

In time we plan to have a large bas-relief sculpture in the arch opposite the mural of the nebula, symbolizing humanity. This might be a single figure, or a family scene. Man is otherwise symbolized in art, in photographs, paintings, sculpture and etchings. But the large symbol of man is still for the future.

On the platform at the front is a large bookcase which houses the major writings of all the world cultures and religions. Whereas dogmatic religions sometimes put "the one book" front center, we put the many great books of mankind together as a symbol of our acceptance of all human wisdom and poetry and literature as ours. A smaller bookcase beside it houses the Torah, the Megillot, Buddhist texts inscribed on leaves made from palm. We will add an original Koran and other books in their native languages and styles of publication.

On the bookcase is a lamp made from Greek and Roman design, which is a symbol of light, life, wisdom, the hearth, the home, and aspiration. The lamp is lighted at the beginning of the service and snuffed at the close.

The use of the high-fidelity sound system is another symbol, for we have a collection of the music of the world cultures, which is used as a background for readings from the various cultures.

Alongside these core symbols is the symbol project itself. As a whole, it too is a core symbol, since it is made up of some sixty-five symbols taken from the world religions, ancient and modern, and symbols of the "universals," of the common ideals, goals, and occupations of humanity. These symbols adorn the panels on the facing of the balconies, and two panels to either side of the mural of Andromeda. The designing, research and execution of these symbols took five years. They are made of brass, copper and silver, and the metal work was done by a brother and sister, Charlotte and Ralph Edlund.

The whole of the auditorium of the Meeting House has been made into one integrated symbol. The map of the earth in the center is the key. If you draw a line from the North Pole at the center outwards, it will lead you, say, across Japan, then to the symbols of Japan on the balcony, and behind them to a space between the windows on the outer wall where the art of Japan is located. Thus "centers" of the art of the world religions form the outer ring, within which the people meet. Beginning at the front to the right, the "centers" in order are Oceania, Japan, China, Tibet, India, Buddhism, Oriental Universalism, Egypt, Africa, Islam, Judaism, Christianity, Aztec, American Indian cultures. There will be another ring of centers in the balcony for some of the auxiliary cultures, such as Greece, Rome, Babylonia, Parsees, Stone Age, Confucianism, Taoism. Large wall hangings are planned for the four corners. Already we have a large Tree of Life Persian rug, on loan from the Universalist Church of America, and in time hangings from India, China and Mexico will be added.

The collection of the art of the world religions has been our major occupation of the last year and a half, and has progressed far beyond our expectations. Some major gifts have been received, and great personal sacrifice on the part of various members of the Meeting House has made other purchases possible. Excellent cooperation has been forthcoming from art dealers and collectors, and we have only begun to explore the possibilities.

The arts are the voices of humanity. Through sculpture, painting, music, literature, the dance, drama and architecture, men communicate their most profound thoughts and emotions to one another. The arts always have been, and always will be, peculiarly the language of religion. Through the use of these communications from the many branches of humanity, past and present, we hope to assemble a truly universal setting or "frame of reverence" for our universalist celebrations. It is our hope that the composers, painters, sculptors, dancers, dramatists, musicians of Boston will join us to find, through the expressions of the arts, a religious voice for our age.[5]

, , , , , , , , , , , , , , , ; , , , , , , , , , ,

Notes on the Documents

Chapter II. Forerunners and Founders

1. *The Life and Trance of George De Benneville*, ed. Ernest Cassara, *Journal of the Universalist Historical Society* II (Boston, 1960–61) 74–76, 78–80, 81–82, 87.
2. *Records of the Life of the Rev. John Murray . . . written by Himself . . . to which is added a Brief Continuation . . . by a Friend* [Mrs. John Murray] (Boston, 1816) 91–97, 130–34, 143–46.
3. James Relly, *Union: or a Treatise of the Consanguinity and Affinity between Christ and his Church* (Philadelphia, 1843) 22–23.
4. John Murray, *Letters and Sketches of Sermons* (3 vols.; Boston, 1812–13) I, 326–29.
5. Jonathan Mayhew, *Two Sermons on the Nature, Extent, and Perfection of the Divine Goodness* (Boston, 1763), in Richard Eddy, *Universalism in America. A History* (2 vols.; Boston, 1884–86) I, 93–95.
6. Charles Chauncy, *The Mystery Hid from Ages and Generations . . . or, the Salvation of All Men* (London, 1784) 260–64, 319–22.
7. Elhanan Winchester, *The Universal Restoration: exhibited in Four Dialogues* (Philadelphia, 1843) 33–34, 41.
8. Joseph Priestley, *Unitarianism Explained and Defended* (Philadelphia, 1796), in Eddy, op. cit., I, 474–76.
9. *Proceedings of the Massachusetts Historical Society* XVII (Boston, 1903) 368–69.
10. Edwin Martin Stone, *Biography of Elhanan Winchester* (Boston, 1836) 195–97.
11. Benjamin Rush, *Letters*, ed. L. H. Butterfield. (2 vols.; Princeton, 1951) I, 583–84.
12. *Articles of Faith and Plan of Church Government, composed and adopted by the Churches believing in the Salvation of All Men* (Philadelphia, 1818) 6–7.

Chapter III. Universalism of the Enlightenment

1. Hosea Ballou, *A Treatise on Atonement* (Boston, 1882) 44–45, 62–64, 71–75, 87–89, 108–12, 146–47.

2. Walter Ferriss, "Book of Sketches, Records, &c. collected, some from Memory and some from Old Papers, etc."; 96, 99–100; a manuscript book, 1804–06, in possession of the Universalist Historical Society Library. An excerpt from this manuscript was published by Eddy, *op. cit.*, II, 57–58. It was given him by a descendant of Ferriss. Eddy correctly surmised that it had come loose from a journal kept by Ferriss. Only in recent years, however, has the rest of the manuscript been rediscovered.
3. Nathaniel Stacy, *Memoirs* (Columbus, Pa., 1850) 94–96.
4. Clinton Lee Scott, *The Universalist Church of America: A Short History* (Boston, 1957) 40n.

Chapter IV. Universalism on the Frontier

1. Walter Ferriss, *op. cit.*, 35–40.
2. Nathaniel Stacy, *op. cit.*, 70–73, 81–83, 223–27.
3. S. R. Smith, *Historical Sketches and Incidents, illustrative of the Establishment and Progress of Universalism in the State of New York* (2 vols.; Buffalo, 1843–48) I, 91–93, 130–35.
4. *Star in the West* X (February 15, 1840) 349.
5. *Ibid.* XIV (November 11, 1843) 247.
6. Thomas Whittemore, *The Plain Guide to Universalism* (Boston, 1840) 260–62, 274–77.
7. Thomas Baldwin Thayer, *The Origin and History of the Doctrine of Endless Punishment* (Boston, 1855) 44–48.
8. Thomas Baldwin Thayer, *Theology of Universalism* (Boston, 1866) 295–98.
9. E. E. Guild, *The Universalist's Book of Reference* (Boston, 1859) 376–77.

Chapter V. Divisions Within

1. Hosea Ballou, *An Examination of the Doctrine of Future Retribution* (Boston, 1834) 16–20, 23–24, 28–29, 35–36.
2. Charles Hudson, *A Series of Letters addressed to Rev. Hosea Ballou . . . being a Vindication of the Doctrine of a Future Retribution* (Woodstock, Vermont, 1827) 91–93, 106–08, 288–89, 290–92.
3. Walter Balfour, *Three Essays on the Intermediate State of the Dead . . . with Remarks on Mr. Hudson's Letters . . . to Mr. Ballou* (Charlestown, Mass., 1828) 355–59.
4. Abner Kneeland, *An Introduction to the Defence of Abner Kneeland, charged with Blasphemy* (Boston, 1834) 37–39.
5. *The Trumpet and Universalist Magazine* XX (December 11, 1847) 102.

Chapter VI. The Conscience of Universalism

1. Elhanan Winchester, *The Reigning Abominations, especially the Slave Trade, considered as Causes of Lamentation; being the Substance of a*

Discourse delivered in Fairfax, Virginia, December 30, 1774, and now published with several additions (London, 1788), 15, 17–19, 21.
2. Benjamin Rush, *Selected Writings*, ed. Dagobert D. Runes (New York, 1947) 3–5, 41–42, 19–22.
3. *Articles of Faith and Plan of Church Government, composed and adopted by the Churches believing in the Salvation of All Men* (Philadelphia, 1818) 12–14.
4. Sylvanus Cobb, *Autobiography of the First Forty-one Years . . . to which is added a Memoir, by his Eldest Son, Sylvanus Cobb, Jr.* (Boston, 1867) 250–52, 315–18, 320–21.
5. *The Trumpet and Universalist Magazine* XVI (October 7, 1843) 62.
6. Sylvanus Cobb, op. cit., 418–20.
7. Adin Ballou, *Autobiography* (Lowell, 1896) 319–24, 326–28.
8. Adin Ballou, *History of the Hopedale Community* (Lowell, 1897) 348–53.
9. Abel C. Thomas, *Autobiography* (Boston, 1852) 266–67.
10. E. H. Chapin, *Moral Aspects of City Life* (New York, 1853) 145–47, 156–57, 160–62.
11. *The Trumpet and Universalist Magazine* XX (October 2, 1847) 62.
12. Olympia Brown, "The Higher Education of Women," *The Repository* LI (February 1874) 85.
13. Augusta J. Chapin, "Women in the Ministry," *The Repository* LI (February 1874) 128–29.
14. Horace Greeley, *Recollections of a Busy Life* (New York, 1868) 70–74.

Chapter VII. The Challenge of Modernism

1. Orello Cone, *Gospel-Criticism and Historical Christianity* (New York, 1891) 337–38, 343–46.
2. Orello Cone, *Rich and Poor in the New Testament* (New York, 1902) 210–18.
3. Marion D. Shutter, *Applied Evolution* (Boston, 1900) 3–10, 27–31, 44–46, 66–67, 218–220.
4. Henry Blanchard, "The Study of the Scriptures in Our Colleges," *The Universalist Quarterly and General Review* XLVI (April 1889) 190–91.
5. L. B. Fisher, *A Brief History of the Universalist Church for Young People* (n.p., n.d.) 108–109.

Chapter VIII. The Old and the New Universalism

1. Phineas T. Barnum, *Why I am a Universalist* (Boston, n.d.) 4–6.
2. Clarence R. Skinner, *The Social Implications of Universalism* (Boston, 1915); reprinted in *Journal of the Universalist Historical Society* V (1964–65) 94–97.
3. A Social Program, Report of the National Commission of the Universalist

Church, Universalist General Convention, October 17–21, 1917; in Emerson H. Lalone, *And Thy Neighbor as Thyself* (Boston, 1939) 111–12.

4. Lewis B. Fisher, *Which Way? A Study of Universalists and Universalism* (Boston, 1921) 9–11.

5. John van Schaik, Jr., *Universalists of Today. Who They Are and What They Believe* (Boston, n.d.) 3–7.

6. *Universalist Year Book for 1936* (Boston, 1936) 4.

7. "A Humanist Manifesto," *The Christian Leader* XXXVI (May 13, 1933) 592–93.

8. Clinton Lee Scott, *Religion Can Make Sense* (Boston, 1949) 1–3, 34–35, 62–63.

9. Alfred S. Cole, "Touch Not My Lips with the White Fire," *The Crane Review* I (Winter 1959) 65.

Chapter IX. The Larger Faith

1. Statement of Robert Cummins to the General Assembly of the Universalist Church of America, New York, October 1943, quoted in his *Excluded. The Story of the Council of Churches and the Universalists* (Boston, 1966) v.

2. Clarence R. Skinner, *A Religion for Greatness* (Boston, 1945) 13–15.

3. Brainard F. Gibbons, "New Wine and Old Bottles!," *The Christian Leader* CXXXI (November 1949) 403–04.

4. Kenneth L. Patton, *A Religion for One World* (Boston, 1964) 72–73.

5. Kenneth L. Patton, *Art and Symbols for a Universal Religion* (pamphlet reprint of an article in *The Universalist Leader*, October, 1956) 2–6.

Index